Traveling through the Boondocks

Traveling through the Boondocks

In and Out of Academic Hierarchy

Terry Caesar

STATE UNIVERSITY OF NEW YORK PRESS

Published by
State University of New York Press, Albany

Chapter Two appeared in *Journal X* 1.2 (Spring 1997): 175–88.

A version of Chapter Four appeared in *Writing on the Edge* 4.2 (Spring 1993): 47–61.

A version of Chapter Seven appeared in the *Yale Journal of Criticism* 6.2 (Fall 1993): 221–35.

A portion of Chapter Eight appeared in *Pennsylvania English* 15.2 (Spring/Summer 1991): 31–9.

For information, address State University of New York Press
State University Plaza, Albany, N.Y. 12246

Production by Diane Ganeles
Marketing by Dana Yanulavich

Library of Congress-in-Publication Data

Caesar, Terry.
  Traveling through the boondocks : in and out of academic hierarchy / Terry Caesar.
    p. cm.
  Includes bibliographical references (p.   ).
  ISBN 0-7914-4659-X (hc : alk. paper) — ISBN 0-7914-4660-3 (pb : alk. paper)
    1. Education, Higher—Political aspects—United States—Case studies.   2. College
teaching—Political aspects—United States—Case studies.   3. College teachers—Selection
and appointment—United States—Case studies.   4. Universities and colleges—United
States—Departments—Case studies.   5. Clarion University of Pennsylvania.   I. Title.

LC173.V34   2000
378.1'22—dc21
                                                          99-053741

10   9   8   7   6   5   4   3   2   1

Contents

Acknowledgments

Acknowledgments are nothing if not an exercise in hierarchy. So let me go straight to the top and record my debt to the National Humanities Center. I'll never forget just the feel of those plush carpets, upon which I was blessed to trod just at the right time in my career, between post-tenure review and retirement. But there is more, much more. Given the wide, not to say global, variety of contexts in which this book has labored to be born, there are naturally more people than I can possible name. Let me merely gesture at various hosts and audiences at Columbia, Duke, Harvard, and Yale (to mention these only) in gratitude for their astute questions, fine wine, and comfortable quarters, right on campus. From Gayatri and Stanley to that custodian who used to be an adjunct, I love you all.

Back home, I am virtually embarrassed with a wide circle of friends who have commented on various chapters, sponsored the presentations of different sections, provided stimulating discussion for many issues, and collectively comprised an intellectual community so congenial that some mornings I still wake up and lie in bed stunned. My administration I would of course shower with praise, especially my dean—the last one, not the present one—who came through for that special faculty leave that enabled me to write the last few notes for my final chapter in a tropical setting, where they, if not I, belonged. I'm sure I would even thank my students, if I could have dreamed up a grad course to accommodate one of the subjects of this book.

Just kidding.

No one writes a book such as this while feeling flush with a greater professional context in which the words have been shaped or grateful for the more local society in which the experience has abided. Indeed, this book constitutes a kind of intricate disacknowledgement of the conditions of its own production, ranging from sundry ephemera down the hall to social and political circumstances across the nation. If this were not so, the title— including the double sense of "through" and the play on "ins and outs"—would have no real basis, and the boondocks would have neither the peculiar pathos nor the elusive authority that I try to represent.

So let me be content to name just two people: one is my former agent, Tom D'Evelyn, who believed in this book as only someone could who is at once intimate with its peculiar life and yet removed from it, by choice. "If you think you're an academic," Tom said to me, very memorably, once, "you're really fucked up." After such knowledge, what forgiveness, for I fear I really am an academic?

The other person is my wife, Eva Bueno, whose own personal boonbocks have provoked me to understand mine better. Despite the fact that she's neither an academic nor fucked up, she has supported me in every syllable of my experience, and her care has extended right down to tedious hours at the computer trying to establish the right program for a complete print-out of this manuscript, with notes in the back, where they belong.

Introduction:
Representing Exclusion,
Writing Personal Narrative,
and Selling Influence

This is a book about certain topics in academic life. They do not have directly to do with public policy issues. Indeed, if only because the experience throughout the following pages is emphasized as mine, everything about it is more commonly the sort of thing that appears in fiction. In Michael Malone's recent academic novel, *Foolscap*, for example, there is a moment early on where the old chair, Dr. Bridges, speaks to the young hero, Theo. Theo is respectable. (He has published a book.) Theo is reasonable. At a time when one possible candidate for a prestigious chair is ridiculed for being "hopelessly concrete" while another stands accused of "spreading herpes along the Northeast corridor," Theo's quiet virtues especially matter. Alas, however, there is one problem: Theo is not ambitious.

"The way academia is today," declaims the old professor, "only the *very* ambitious make it to the top. And the top is all there is now. Even for those who aren't in it. In my time, you could live a happy, productive life in the middle. Now the middle is simply not the top. You could be the top, if you'd only try" (28). One way I can describe this volume would be to say that it features a series of chapters about life in the middle. What is it like? How different is it than that commonly presumed in discourse about academic matters? And, most important, how is life in the middle shaped by "the top?" If the time for a happy, productive life farther down is over, as the old professor states, then precisely what sort of life can now be realized there, especially if you still want to be ambitious?

Another way I could characterize this volume follows more bluntly: it would not have been written if I had enjoyed a career at the top. The question of how to *locate* ambition is everywhere here written, sometimes as a political one, sometimes as a more formalist one, and always in personal terms. Alas, though, my location of ambition is seldom comic. This is one reason this book is not fiction. Malone's novel demonstrates the sort of assumption academic fiction customarily makes: life at the top is funnier because its ambition can be realized, and therefore we enjoy a secure position from which to laugh at the folly. Life in the middle, on the other hand, is much less consistent and normative, and we regard it, if at all, without a very firm sense of how it fits into the social order (much less the secret life) of things.

I want to test the fit. What would a nonfictional representation of personal experience in American higher education look like that does not offer itself as immediately convertible into larger political or social issues? Paul Lauter, for example, introduces his recent admirable collection of essays, *Canons and Context*, thus: "Poverty and homelessness, industrial stagnation and meaningless work, racial and sexual discrimination, drugs, violence, pollution and crime—what relationship has education to such social issues" (1)? Compared to Lauter's, my view of higher education explores no relation to any of these things.

Lauter ultimately conceives of his own experience differently than I do. Early in the very first essay, "Society and the Profession, 1958–83," he indicates something of the history of his own political activity and then states as follows: "I speak of my life because it reflected, in a sense became a vehicle of, the force for social change I am to write about here" (4).[1] I'm not sure what my own professional life has been a vehicle of. (Compare, for example, another writing of academic life, Steven's Carter's *Reflections of an Affirmative Action Baby*. Carter can be so confident about his subject because, even as he protests on virtually every page, his identity as a black man ceaselessly gives his professional life the automatic status of a Problem.) But it has not been a vehicle for social change. Indeed, one way these chapters may be read is as a record of a peculiar species of academic stagnation, utterly closed off from the energies of the larger society.[2]

Later in this same initial essay, Lauter remarks that one consequence of the rapid growth of American higher education in the

1960s was that professional hierarchy was at least "becoming permeable." While some of us, he continues, got "a two-course load and a $75,000 contract" at Yale or Berkeley, far more "settled into what were formerly teachers' and technical schools or branch campuses newly expanded into liberal arts colleges and giant graduate institutions" (9).[3] These latter institutions mark the limit of Lauter's view. Of course it makes a difference (to cite one of his subsequent examples) how much you get paid to teach theory at Texas or freshman English at San Jose State. My own view is that it makes just as much difference if you're not at either one, and instead at the sort of teacher's college that never expanded very much at all. The relation to professional hierarchy possible at a Clarion University is the remorseless subject of my own considerations.

What difference *does* it make? If I can't claim it's an issue of great social moment, I can claim that the way to stifle some articulation is to insist that it must be. The difference my peculiar experience makes involves more abstract, less politically governed questions of exclusion, power, and representation. These things cohere for me around the issue of academic hierarchies. Of course the reason theory at Texas merits a higher salary than composition at San Jose, for example, is because of one such hierarchy: the superior position of research to teaching. (I will have something to say about this particular issue in a moment.) Overall, I'm far more concerned with another: institutional reputation. Crudely put, Clarion University is in the boondocks.

One of fourteen universities in the Pennsylvania State System of Higher Education (SSHE), Clarion would seem to make very little difference within the economic and social interests of American higher education. To a town of some six thousand, with only one major industry (a glass plant), the urgent social issues that Lauter mentions appear positively sexy. To a campus community including another six thousand students, the cultural changes of race and class he says became evident in the 1970s are not fully manifest at Clarion in the 1990s. The majority of Clarion students still come from the same region (western Pennsylvania), share the same racial and class backgrounds (white, middle class), and have the same SAT scores (upwards of 450 Verbal). So if you teach a novel about life in India, most of the students will not be enlightened if you tell them that "the Mahatma" refers to Gandhi. They won't know who Gandhi was. They won't have gone to school with Indians. They will by now have heard various educational pieties concerning the necessity of "diversity" in education. But very many can't be expected to lament the absence of minorities, and maybe not even novels, in their own lives.

The reasons why institutions such as Clarion are ignored are not difficult to understand. Clarion produces workers, not leaders. If an alumni is a dean somewhere, it's likely to be at a community college. For every Clarion graduate who becomes a CEO, a hundred abide as clerks, secretaries, or mid-level managers. Or should this be a thousand? Five thousand? Who cares? As Russell Jacoby—standing in the parking lot of West Los Angeles College—writes: "It's neither new nor specifically American, but most people prefer to hear (or read) about the rich rather than the poor, the successful rather than the unsuccessful."[4] So to be in the boondocks is probably to have to resign oneself to being lost in more visible configurations, whereby centers of various kinds are always more compelling than provinces of any kind. Nobody is going to write a book about Clarion as the very model of anything, as in *Alma Mater* P.F. Kluge offers secluded, precious Kenyon College on the inescapable model of the elite liberal arts college. Give it as much specificity as one cares to (including the odd student from India, who is likely to be more sophisticated and motivated than most from nearby Brookville), the fact may as well be admitted: Clarion is just too small, too obscure. It's even too far away from Pittsburgh.

And yet Clarion University does turn out to stand for what I take to be the immense power of a single question: how to suffer exclusion? Of course you don't have to suffer it. Many—faculty and students both—don't. Some even enjoy it. But you do have to acknowledge the question. To me, how much you acknowledge exclusion depends upon how ambitious you are. And how ambitious you are may well depend, in turn, upon how what sort of relation you can afford to acknowledge to the top. One thing for sure: the relation will be mediated through the one the institution has already rationalized. Moreover, no matter how carefully and systematically deployed, this relation will ultimately be a disingenuous one. Academic hierarchy guarantees it.

If first-rate institutions require the category of second-rate ones in order to maintain a superior identity, second-rate institutions— lest they be thought second-rate—must strive to recreate the same superiority in their own ways. No issue is more crucial in this respect than teaching. First-rate institutions can afford to disdain it. Second-rate ones can't. I don't say much about teaching in the following pages. One reason is that Clarion's "mission" as a teaching institution isn't as noble and coherent as, say, that of a liberal arts college, so I wouldn't concur with one of the professors Kluge quotes, after a couple of pages on how the campus is "Yugoslavia plus": "Thank God I love teaching. And I love the kids. Otherwise it would be a fucking zoo" (80). But before going any further I need to say more about teaching.

1.

Once a colleague of mine met one of his professors from graduate school at a conference. "What are you working on?" the professor asked. My colleague hedged. He really wasn't "working on" anything. He wasn't expected to be. He was expected to teach. How to explain to the professor that most American colleges and universities simply don't share the agendas of the major research institutions? Eventually, though, the man seemed to have intuited that his question was inappropriate. "How do you like it there?" he finally asked.

This book is not about teaching, because it's about how teaching, along with anything else, is subject to the imperatives of academic hierarchy. Therefore, even at Clarion, the important thing I want to emphasize about teaching is how it's embedded in a narrative of research. Even after the curriculum committee has made its report at the last department meeting; after a vote has been taken for the latest changes on the checksheet concerning optional and required courses for majors; after the chair has reminded everyone of the date when textbook orders are due; after all this and more, the peculiar questions posed exclusively by research won't go away.

A recent document entitled *Priorities*, put out by the Planning Commission of the Pennsylvania State System of Higher Education (SSHE) demonstrates the problem with unusual clarity—to a point. After that point, the venerable hierarchy between teaching and research is confounded in a manner that's probably not unusual in other state systems or individual institutions, all lacking the funds to recognize the division in the first place. The solution? Teaching is upgraded, and any hierarchical opposition with respect to research is only recognized in order to be overturned.

A section of the report, "Broadening the Definition of Scholarship," establishes for the fourteen state universities "legitimate forms of scholarly activity congruent with their mission." Pennsylvania youth, it seems, will not be served by "illegimate" forms. These are the kind practiced in doctoral programs at research universities, whose purpose is, according to the report, "to contribute to the national reputation and grant coffers of the institution." SSHE universities, in contrast, stand foursquare for service rather than self-promotion.

Yet system faculty are not to think of themselves as merely bending their noses to the grindstone. In fact, for scholarly production in the 90s it turns out that they are sharpening the cutting edge. "Prominent scholars and leaders in American higher education," *Priorities* assures us, "have challenged the traditional view of academic prestige, suggesting that its overemphasis on published research and concomitant devaluation of teaching have served neither faculty or students well." The document forebears consideration of such questions as where these leaders teach themselves, why they got to be so prominent, and how the very people who must be cited to make the statewide case attest to a national scale of evaluation whose "emphasis" might be at variance with the argument being conducted here.

Much of American education often appears to boil down to the difference between those who hold forth about the wonders of teaching (faculty development programs, interdisciplinary projects, outreach this and computerized that) and those who actually teach. I once knew an assistant professor at Stanford. His teaching load was nine credit hours per year. He complained it was too much. He didn't have time for research. I know another woman who teaches at a community college. Her teaching load is thirty credit hours per year. I don't believe she dreams that one day she won't have to teach so much. She likes to teach, she says.

But she doesn't write about it, and she doesn't have any particular authority beyond her classroom. Few teachers do. That the division between teaching and research is a perennial one in higher education doesn't mean it cuts any less deeply at present. Indeed, it might cut more deeply in the downsized 90s, when official, deficit-ridden discourse in many locations throughout the country has grown fond of citing prominent scholars saying the old division should be retired at last. People who teach a lot, of course—the standard SSHE load is twelve hours per semester—have little choice but to attend to this discourse, and it's important that their attention be undivided.

In urging SSHE faculty to invest all their time in teaching, *Priorities* not only accomplishes a fatefully "concomitant" devaluation of research that reproduces the original division. It also illustrates why this division continues to be a structural feature of American universities; as Burton Clark states, "The reward system of promoting academics on the grounds of research and published scholarship has become more deeply rooted in the universities (and would-be universities and leading four-year colleges) with almost every passing decade" (25). Higher education is scarcely conceivable apart from hierarchy, and the whole disposition of academic work designed to implement it. What goes on in the doctoral programs of research institutions merits the most prestige, commands the field, and sets the terms through which other institutions negotiate their various identities, as they can.

Central to the SSHE "mission" is that the whole division between teaching and research is inadmissible—lest it be disclosed as an opposition, and stand revealed to be a hierarchical one. So, for example, there is the following contention in the report: "Recent research on faculty work shows that most American professors devote most of their time and scholarly endeavors to teaching and would prefer to be recognized and rewarded as teacher-scholars, rather than as pioneers on the frontiers of disciplinary knowledge." This may well be so. But research must be invoked in order to create a space for the teacher-scholar.

I've never met one. Even people who take life back home in the classroom to be capable of just as much adventure as the frontier recognize that there's a difference nonetheless between a settler and a pioneer. Awhile ago I visited a friend who was once a top scientific researcher in his own country. Now he's an exile, lucky to have a position as an assistant professor at a tiny liberal arts school. But he was gloomy anyway: none of his colleagues read anything, he said, and why should they, since all anybody is asked to do is teach. I don't think he would have been consoled had I invited him into the Pennsylvania state system, where he would be reborn, along with everybody else, as a scholar-teacher.

To the teacher, what's at stake in teaching, beyond whether or not students learn something? Not, or not only, highly specific and acutely localized pleasures of the classroom—all stuff of so many sentimental clichés that one hesitates to speak of the times when a thing so simple as who Gandhi was comes vividly alive, important, and exciting. Let me try to characterize the stakes by way of a moment in James Phelan. At one point in his journal, Phelan observes (informally) a class of his colleague, Mac. What strikes Phelan is the difference in their teaching styles: "For Mac the text is a launch pad, while for me it's a diving pool." This day, he

concludes, Mac performed "a successful takeoff" (161).[5] Phelan tries
not to sound defensive; with characteristic fairmindedness, he sums
up that students benefit from both kinds of training—either to be
astronauts or aquanauts. This strikes me as lovely distinction for
the significance of teaching: is its purpose to transcend its circumstances or to immerse oneself in them?

The question is to some extent blunted if the reply is, it depends, not only upon your students but upon where you teach. Of
course it *does*, especially if where you teach asks you to do nothing
more than teach (whether or not it asks, in addition, that you think
of doing this like research).[6] Nevertheless, there is in any life its
higher aspirations, its transcendent circumstances, its "beyond"—
no matter how open or closed in relation to its middle range, or
even its lower reaches. Phelan's own notion of "beyond" is con-
nected to astronauts and space; earlier he mentions how effected
he was at the jaunty egotism of Gordo Cooper, in the movie version
of *The Right Stuff*, when asked about whom he thinks is the best
test pilot. Furthermore, there is a compelling analogy in this whole
equation of the educational enterprise to the space program: the
one has not enjoyed, alas, the rare public support of the other.

Hence, there's an additional thrust to to this analogy: teaching
will ultimately be valued in terms of its vertical direction—upwards and outwards, into the unknown. We may grant that all
sorts of academic experience, both within and without the classroom, partakes of sheer *immersion*; indeed, water may be its basic,
or even only, element. Nevertheless, the whole rhetoric of risk,
acclaim, and wonderment lies elsewhere. Therefore, if it's not necessarily better to train students to be astronauts, it's better—more
glamorous, more irresistably vain—to be an astronaut oneself.
Astronauts are the luminaries in terms of which any discipline (not
to say any society) organizes itself. (See Shumway and O'Dair on
the star system.) This is why, for example, well-funded programs at
select universities to send at least some pioneers aloft exist at all.

Conversely, this is also why you only get to be at best an
aquanaut if you spend too much time in the classroom. Finally, and
more to my explicit theme throughout this book, the significance of
transcendence—in teaching no less than in any other endeavor—
explains why even the best teacher can feel, as we say, "down"
when he has to admit he's not "working on" something. It explains
why Perry Lentz, the celebrated, consummate Kenyon teacher in
Kluge's account, has to position his belefs in terms of the ephemeral (to him) vicissitudes of current scholarship.[7] And the sheer

power of transcendence certainly explains why a well-intentioned state system would want to urge all of its faculty to forget about the difference between a launch pad and a diving pool.

2.

It's one thing to speak of hierarchy. It's another thing to speak of class. And it's a third thing to try to speak of each of these things in quite personal terms from within the peculiar context of academic life, where the first is widely taken for granted, while the second is largely suppressed. If you're going to try to speak of hierarchy and class in this way, and thereby appear transgressive, you had better begin by acknowledging how the very subjects you would disturb (if not dismantle) are the same ones that enable you to speak at all.

Much of this book arose during a particular moment in my career when I realized I had one—in deciding to write about why I didn't. It's no accident that I begin in the following pages with an account of the reception of a rather infamous publication. I wrote the article during a sabbatical. It was subsequently included in my first book. A book! This meant to me that I was no longer only, or rather merely, a teacher. It was as if I had been liberated from some vast, imperious, and intricately conceived system of subjection. If I remained at the same university, it felt as if I had at least risen in—what else to call it?—class.

The estimilable Lauter, for one, understands the academic world precisely along the lines of class. He observes, for example, that the economic conception of the labor force as divided between "primary" and "secondary" sectors fits higher education pretty well. There is, however, the following qualification: "The vast majority of us are not, of course, at the core or at the periphery but in the great middle class of our profession" (12).[8] I think this qualification is more telling than he does; in effect, what Lauter discloses is how the very idea of a middle actually functions as a compensatory construction in the face of a static, implacable condition of hierarchy—the sort of fact suggested by Jane Tompkins when, for example, she registers the difficulty of commuting between Johns Hopkins and Temple, the one "at the center of the universe," the other "beyond the edge of the known world" (105).

It is on the basis of such convictions that the old chair in Malone's novel, *Foolscap*, declares that the upper class is now all there is. He is of course speaking of relations among institutions. In this book I propose certain consequences as a result of how these relations are fixed and maintained by professional elites; one is that if you publish a book you feel closer to them, no matter where you are. On the other hand, though, relations within any one institution—and within a department—are more loose and negotiable. It is upon the basis of intra-institutional arrangements that a model of class can be more accurately derived. And so I think one can speak, for instance, of how the most marginal teaching within a discipline effectively results in a "proletarianization" of work.[9]

But class doesn't map so neatly onto institutional hierarchy. Hence, while discussing the 1995–96 Yale strikes, Crystal Bertolovich pronounces "the question of how to deal with the relatively elite status of Yale graduate students in relation to other graduate students" a "thorny" one. She is pleased instead to resort to the smoother intra-institutional or departmental framework: "One thing that is clear, however, is that no matter how privileged they may be in relation to graduate students in other sites, they are not privileged in relation to the senior faculty in their departments" (232). Indeed, my feeling is that an insistent application of a class model to the comprehension of academic life only conceals the more underlying, unchanging *fact* of hierarchy at the institutional level.

"The gulf is widening," Zelda Gamson writes, "between a small number of affluent and highly selective institutions—where competition is fierce and mostly privileges the wealthy—and hard-pressed public and private institutions. Low-income students increasingly are concentrated in the community colleges. This divide mirrors the growing income inequality of society as a whole" (73). However, within the confines of your own particular university there remains conflict aplenty, albeit of the same old narrow sort, because there vertical movement is possible. (Assuming of course that you're tenure track; everyone agrees that part-timers are a *lumpen* class without revolutionary potential.) You can move up. You can serve on the right department committees, campus-wide committees, or union committees. You can win release time from teaching the most slavish courses, or even from teaching anything. You can even become a dean.

What you can't do if you're in the boondocks, however, is move up by moving out, and into a position at a first-rate institution. No wonder Emily Toth's Ms. Mentor advises her earnest grad student inquisitor thus: "Without publication, Ms. Mentor guarantees that your career will truly perish" (19). She means not only that you won't be able to get a tenure-track position, but that at best you'll get only one—at the sort of place Michael Bèrubè advises *his* graduate student she can only "escape" through publications, after finding she is "seriously mismatched" (105). But successes are few, and only prove the rule. The fact of institutional hierarchy fixes your professional horizons as wholly as if you were located in a caste system. Awhile ago a friend of mine who teaches at a branch campus of a large state university received a paper from a friend of hers who teaches at another branch campus. She said it was a brilliant paper, but her friend had no idea where to submit it. She could only think of a couple of possibilities herself. Having ambition—not to say the full measure of a career—consists of such knowledge, which you won't get unless you're already in position to have it, in which case the knowledge often seems so obvious it's difficult to imagine what it would be like for anyone not to have it.[10]

The decisive moves in professional life may depend upon *whom* you know. But the crucial factor is *where* you know. "Bluntly," Jeffrey Williams writes, "you don't usually hear of someone from Southwest Missouri Central College being called to serve as assistant secretary of defense or education or as a consultant for NBC News" ("Life of the Mind," 139). Just so, you don't usually hear of someone from Southwest Missouri Central publishing a book from Routledge or Duke on some trendy subject such as sodomy and Shelley or slasher films and eighteenth century satire—not to mention a book on Southwest Missouri Central itself. More commonly, someone from the Southwest Missouri Centrals of the nation doesn't publish much of anything. As Stanley Aronowitz and William DiFazio write, "The typical response of a faculty that experiences its work as a degradation from the expectations many had in graduate school is to focus its energy on making more money, devising ways to reduce the actual teaching requirements by duplicating sections of the same course . . . and, for a minority, to leave teaching and join the ranks of the administration" (253).

Sharon O'Dair's institutional fiction is exemplified by West Jesus State, where at "a certain moment" the young professor there concludes, "Especially once she is tenured, [that] she is never going anywhere else, no matter how often and how well she publishes. Never. Going. Anywhere. Else" (623). If we ask exactly why this is so, my contention is that class alone will not explain such lack of mobility. In terms of hierarchy, class—contrary to the notion advanced by Aronowitz and DiFazio—simply ceases to have "an active relation to the labor process" and instead becomes a stagnant category (273). The individual can indeed become conscious of herself in some fundamental political sense. But at Southwest Missouri Central or West Jesus such consciousness has nowhere to go and no goal (especially a collective one) to pursue, except to restore itself to the available labor processes on campus, in or out of the department.

Class simply drops away as an explanatory concept in academic life away from home, not because no agency is possible but because no class position of inequality can be productively admitted, either on the part of individuals or of institutions. Instead, such an admission invariably assumes the function of failure—of career, of "mission," of something. Failure, in turn, takes on the character of confession. We can see this fateful process most clearly with respect to the category of the personal in academic discourse at the present time. If you want to try to represent your experience at Southwest Missouri Central, West Jesus, or Clarion, you have to be personal; there's no institutional authority behind your experience. And yet in order to be personal you have to begin by acknowledging that, if the effort is not going to sound exactly vulgar, it might well seem beside the point. Considered as a politics—and granting the difference between Temple and Clarion (which doesn't matter much to Hopkins)—institutional relations have already foreclosed labor relations.

3.

How to represent exclusion *as* exclusion—and not seek to have it ultimately comprehended as merely the latest provocation to an inclusion that has already taken place? I see no other way to begin than by taking inclusion personally, and reestablishing it in personal terms. At the outset of *Token Professionals and Master Critics*, James Sosnoski relates a brief story to the effect that his work can be interpreted as just griping. The ancedote, he continues, "trivalize[s] the issues and obscure[s] the general implications. I have chosen to employ a different rhetorical mode in this book" (xxix). So be it. I can only confess that it seems to me a more radical intervention is necessary in the public discussion of such matters as academic departments, hiring, and sabbaticals. Academic hierarchy has usurped any power the category of "the trivial" might have, while "general implications" have resulted in a thinning out of the base.

Already just writing personally—about literature, but really about anything—turns out to possess so much unsettling potential in an academic context that the writing (if not the unsettling) has become an extremely intricate theoretical issue.[11] Why should this be so? Is it merely because the time to be interested in excluded experience is when jobs are infamously tight, professional mobility notoriously constricted, the idea of professionalism regnant as a god-term, and a soverign critical agenda on the lookout for fresh stimulations?

At present the academic climate for personal writing ought at least to be full of provocative, invigorating examples. Instead, one only finds acceptable ones. Let me take the example of Nancy Miller's recent book on the autobiographical presence in critical performance. When we consider the best of "the autobiographical act in criticism," she writes, "the personal in these texts is at odds with the hierarchies of the positional—working more like a relay *between* positions to create critical fluency. Constituted finally in a social performance, these autobiographical acts may produce a new repertory for an enlivening cultural criticism" (25).[12] This seems to me to get it all wrong, albeit in interesting ways.

Miller blithely refuses to consider any unsettling potential in the autobiographical. Instead, once again, personal terms of any sort must be translatable into social terms. More interesting is her argument that personal acts *preserve* hierarchies, albeit "oddly." What does Miller appear to think a hierarchy is? Two things: first, a plural notion (a hierarchy is implicated in others), and, second, a "positional" one (there is no hierarchy of hierarchies). Yet what does she think an example of the personal is? Something inextricable from the hierarchical. Therefore, while ostensibly in opposition to the category of the hierarchical, the category of the personal actually permits hierarchy to negotiate between or among levels. It doesn't matter how this negotiation occurs. Miller's point is that autobiography is now an *available* category for her theoretical project. Autobiography is a "field"—for gender, identity, self-representation, cultural production, you name it.

If to Miller, we might say, autobiography stands alone, its whole "fluency" lies in how it can be comprehended as standing for any number of other issues. Just so, in academic terms, we might continue, nothing ultimately stands alone. Everything fits. (My conviction of the academic way of life as a *total* one explains one reason a friend would commend to me Andrei Sinyavsky's chapter on "The Soviet Way of Life" in *Soviet Civilization*.) Of course the provocation of anything personal or autobiographical is that it might not fit. What to conclude when it doesn't? What to do, for example, with the times when an academic subject is, so to speak, *left* with his or her personal opinion, and there is no possibility of what Miller would term a "relay?" Her understanding of the autobiographical act appears to be that this sort of thing doesn't happen—and so Sosnoski, above, for example, should not have been so concerned about rhetorical modes.

My understanding is that such relays fail to happen all the time. (For a fine consideration of the present rhetoric of "ethnicity" in autobiographical writing, see Kwasny.) Indeed, to fail to consider the whole notion of the autobiographical as something that *fails*— either to move among levels or to occupy a clear position—is effectively to banish arguably the most vital and powerful thing about it. Sosnoski himself writes elsewhere: "In the humanities, theorizing leads inescapably to inquiries into subjectivity (because the subject of its study is subjects) and has to be villainized. To theorize is to encourage the Hyde in us to come forth" (141). With Miller, on the contrary, to theorize is to discourage the Hyde, by making subjectivity strictly the stuff of an enriched social repertory. What about when it fails? What might it mean to claim that some idea of hierarchy—either of form or institution—is thereby disturbed?

One day an old colleague recalled how a former one of ours (happily gone) was once reviewed by an evaluation committee. The committee went through all the requisite procedures. Teaching observations were filed. Student evaluations were summarized. All appeared in order. Then there was a moment of silence. My colleague said he looked up and mused, "You know, come to think of it, B. is really an asshole." One of the reasons I love this anecdote is because it's not exactly what Miller might term a "social performance." It's too, well, "autobiographical." Most acts are. The peculiar fixation academics have to *form* (quite apart from whatever matter is to be subject to it) is often rebuked by the ancedotal or the personal, each too provisional and fugitive to count as material for hierarchial construction. But another reason I love this anecdote is because it illustrates how sometimes form has nothing whatever to do with its object; in this case, the very person who provided the occasion for the formal process was precisely the one who finally got excluded from its result, because the process worked so well.

A certain *space* for the personal is consigned to academic decision-making. But the decision itself is finally almost impossible to rationalize or justify, no matter how many formal determinants are installed to lead up to it. Anything to do with hiring expresses such impossibility in especially precious ways, and this is one reason I have a chapter on the subject. It may be too simple to go on to claim that the space for the personal is an utterly compromised one. I would only insist that the personal be comprehended as in some unrecuperable and decisive way opposed to what proceeds from it. What we would have, then, is the sort of dilemma I like to examine: the more empowered you are, the more personal you get to be—as if to flaunt the very system that gave you the power in the first place. Witness the following summary aphorism about the academy delivered by the eminent Stanley Fish: "Academics like to eat shit and in a pinch, they don't care whose shit they eat" (*No Such Thing*, 278). (For additional comments on these words, see Caesar, *Writing*, 153, 166). His occasion was the prestigious English Institute that convenes annually at Harvard. You can't get much more empowered and more personal than this.

In the following pages, institutional hierarchy is the name of what ultimately *authorizes*. It doesn't authorize every single thing. It didn't authorize, for example, my colleague's comment, and no matter that there were careful gradations to be made among what sorts of things counted for evaluation purposes. If hierarchy authorized everything, academic life would be grimmer than even I make it out to be. (Or Sinyavsky Soviet life.) Nonetheless, let me contrast another ancedote where hierarchy of a more specifically institutionalized sort is more apparent. William Schaefer (a past president the the Modern Language Association, no less) tells the following story from his recent book on higher education in a chapter about how the profession is perishing by publishing: "We in the humanities," he maintains, "have created a faculty so narrow in their specializations that they can't even teach undergraduate courses." It is of course a familiar complaint, and familiar because, once again, it emanates from a major research institution whose faculty is defined by the research, not the teaching, it's expected to do.

Schaefer's anecdote has one of his new assistant professors at UCLA in the late 1960s simply refuse to teach a sophomore level survey because he declares he has never read Spenser or Milton. Schaefer is careful to mention that the man was "proud possessor of an Ivy League Ph.D" (108). Why mention the Ivy League? Presumably to certify the fact of specialization. But would the man have refused his assignment if he hadn't had an Ivy League degree? Is he suggesting by his refusal that he really doesn't belong at UCLA? One wonders. Schaefer doesn't. Perhaps it's an open question how pluralized the very notion of hierarchy might be in this incident or how at odds the man's refusal is with departmental definitions because he can assert the superior claims of the very top. Less open, I think, is the question of how pervasively institutional hierarchy itself functions even within institutions or departments.

Usually it's not easy to see how it does in books about American higher education. They're all about UCLA; another thing Schaefer's account guarantees, right down to the anecdotal level, is a portrait of higher education that does not include lower, second-rate, comprehensive universities, whose teaching is almost exclusively undergraduate. His man's refusal would be, for example, inconceivable at Clarion; my own first years were spent teaching a world literature course featuring authors I'd never read who originally wrote in languages I couldn't read. English departments at most universities in the U.S. still routinely expect their faculties to teach such surveys, whether anybody has read Spenser (or Dostoevsky) before or not. Now, however, in our professionalized, multicultural times, the particular survey I once taught has been reconceived and reintroduced as a subject for which the department needs a specialist. (The subject, in fact, of the specific job search treated in my second chapter on departments.) What hasn't changed is how the most politicized agendas of the boondocks trail along after those of elite ones, while other agendas grow further apart; Clarion still has a sophomore survey designed to "cover" Spenser and Milton, although the days when someone could be hired on the basis of being a specialist in either one are as gone as the days of the quest romance or epic poetry.

Of course we can always pose the question once more: what sort of hierarchies are in position here? Class, with respect to students? Cultural, with respect to the knowledge that needs to be taught? Disciplinary, with respect to what subjects have more theoretical clout? Institutional, with respect to who commands the resources to teach what? Furthermore, how distinct are these? In this book I try not to pursue what may well be an undecidable moment in which these differences cannot be disentangled or else there is only the most opaque profit in trying to do so. What impels me most of all in the following chapters, whether attending conferences, applying for grants, or going on sabbaticals, is how the whole matter of hierarchy itself gets muffled, elided, and excluded—and, along with it, both my own institution and the story of my own experience in it.

4.

Thomas Newkirk has a nice comment at the end of an essay on "The Politics of Writing Research" that deserves to have a much wider application. He is speaking of the source of the authority teachers have: "It does not come through deference to expert opinion or through suppressing intuitive resources in favor of more distanced—and more academic respectable—means of observation. The opportunity will be lost if teachers fail to recognize the source of their strength and instead adopt the values of the hierarchical systems that have silenced them in the past" (133).[13] These are stirring words. I believe them. The discourse about American education badly needs not so much more voices as voices from different institutional positions.

And yet, there is a final problem, and I want to address it in these introductory pages: what should these voices speak about, if they could, other than their own exclusion? Not only does my own text suggest that even the most personal source of one's own strength is inextricable from professional constraints. Moreover, not only does this same text dramatize—in the words of Michel Foucault's well-known stricture—"where there is power, there is resistance, and yet, or rather consequently, this resistance is never in a position of exteriority in relation to power" (95). (For a more anti-Foucaldian discussion of possible resistance, see Scott.) The problem of exteriority is the problem of narrativity. Worst of all, hierarchy may flatten any personal story (mine or any other) that can be told about being interior to it. Exclusion from research positions, conference occasions, grant opportunities, and job mobility? No small part of any power is being able to reply very simply: "We've heard it all before."

This book has many stories. I wish there were more. Most of all, I wish the *one* story that is mine possessed one thing in particular: a clean plot line. If it had, it would be one of travel. As it is, though, it's only really possible to take off at the top. Throughout *Foolscap*, for example, there abides, or rather flies, one Jane Nash-Ganz, holder of a Ludd Chair, radical feminist extraordinaire, only thirty-nine. At one point she's off to Barcelona to lecture ("The Anorexic Text: Minimalism as Sexual Politics"), if she can just get "the damn thing" written on the plane. She hardly has time to talk to Theo. Her secretary tugs her arm. "You know what success is, Theo? Success is exhaustion" (106). What if, very much on the contrary, your exhaustion as an academic is not based on the rigors

of giving lectures at international conferences? Your book will be
very much interested in travel, and on why it is assumed to be
equivalent to academic success. But it won't be able to offer a
record of conferences. "I have lost count of the foreign countries in
which I have attended conferences," allows Henry Rosovsky,
Harvard's famous dean, whose book on the university makes no
apologies for its view from the top. He jokes that some of his friends
have been referred to as "Pan-American Airways Professor of Biol-
ogy" or "the Swissair Professor of Physics" (166). I wish the experience contained here had such comedy. Instead, there is a concluding
chapter on sabbaticals because sabbaticals represent the only usual
way *out* of business as usual that I know.

It's one thing to get out, and another thing to stay out. Few
will read my chapter on writing teaching observation reports and
wonder if I'll be fired as the result of filing an especially outrageous
one. From a purely narrative point of view, getting fired, or quit-
ting, would read, I believe, as an easy out. Once you catch a ride
on the tenure track, it's not so difficult to remain inside academic
structures; the fact that most of them are stifling constitutes, in a
sense, much of their point, which is to promote comfort and security. (See the last chapter on resignation in Caesar, *Writing*.) Hence,
the academy is popularly understood as enabling so little outward
event that, when something unusual does happen, from the inside
it appears to be possibly more bemusing than amazing. Something
of this response is evident, I must trust, in my first chapter, about
a brief, wildly exceptional moment of local infamy.

The infamy itself amounted to no more narrative resource than
a chapter could use. In the rest, there is outwardly even less on
which to center. In narrative terms, what *does* follow, not only if
one wants to write of insulting one's university but also voting in
one's department; hoping to deliver a paper at a major convention;
trying to get a major grant; writing up observation reports on one's
colleagues; suffering the absence of professional mobility; teaching
in the boondocks; and going on sabbatical? Two things. First, the
absence of one comprehensive story. Second, the presence of lots of
other stories. Two of the following chapters are structured around
specific narratives, while two more chapters are, respectively,
grounded in a single event and overcome by too many narratives.
If there's no one plot, there's no lack of plotting.

Correspondingly, this book has two aims. The first is to try to
outwit the narrative of exclusion. Already simultaneously mine and
not mine, this narrative might appear too monotonous or oppres-

sive. Yet does this mean it cannot be lively? My wager is that it can be. There's no small inspiration to be derived from all sorts of disparate people, such as, for example, James Kincaid's disruptively self-conscious practice where "the challenge is to find bad stories to tell so badly they defamiliarize the conventions of approved narratives" (8). Indeed, at least half the spirit in subsequent pages bids to be found in the defamiliarization or the disruption itself; in an essay on the essay Philip Lopate cites Adorno to the effect that the "law of the innermost form of the essay" is heresy: "By transgressing the orthodoxy of thought, something becomes visible in the object which it is orthodoxy's secret purpose to keep invisible" (84).

A second aim of this book might not be so apparent: to seek out what of my own professional experience is representative in nature. But how to do so on the basis of a way of life where it is customary for personal agency, as Charles Altieri suggests, "[to] become manifest in a variety of forms that extend beyond autobiographical contexts into modes of self-reflection defined by the social practices they are imbedded within" (59)? On this basis, the burden for the individual would seem to be to get beyond narrative. Alas, it appears I never do. What to reply but that the reasons why I never do constitute the logic for whatever representativeness my experience could claim in the first place? Kluge in *Alma Mater*, by contrast, doesn't have to worry about being excluded for the same reason he doesn't have to worry about being representative: he's happy to be a temporary, part-time teacher only. I'm not.

What follows from this, besides plenty of stories? One very emphatic thing, which I would have my like-minded, similarly excluded, solitary reader discover as if for the first time: absence of society. Indeed, although the life in this book is the product of being among people and being defined by their formal occasions (meetings and conferences as well as classes), there is very little society. Citing fiction is one way to compensate. However, doing so only discloses, in part, how unsuitable, finally, fiction is for academic life. "The novel tends to be extroverted and personal," writes Northrop Frye, "its chief interest is human character as it manifests itself in society" (308). Academic life, much to the contrary, tends to be introverted and impersonal. Is this why its fiction all runs to farce and burlesque?

It's very telling that one of the following chapters features a man I never meet, whose name I don't learn. Another chapter is focused around a person who never appears, and who must remain absent. No matter how I try to keep naming names, the contrast with fiction could not be more striking: the fictional characters cited not only all have names but identities and histories. Insofar as it's introverted, romance may well be a far more suitable mode for academic life. So, for example, I construct much of my last chapter (in the middle of which sits a self-interview) on the basis of David Lodge's novel, *Small World*, an excellent, very self-conscious example of romance. Of course, everywhere in the following pages are lots more books than people. One could well wonder if our narrator prefers the one to the other. In fact, could it ultimately be so simple as to conclude there's no basic plot in this book because there's really no society at all?

I don't think so myself. Admittedly, the whole notion of plot here—not to say its wider resonances—is an abstract one. I once recommended Stephen Carter's book to a friend. "Does he get laid in grad school?" he asked. I had to assure him that it was not *that* sort of book. Mine isn't either. Thinking about it, I've come to realize how I forbear examining erotic undercurrents directly, as if (after Altieri) to make them available for wider, more discursive possibilities. Academic novels, I believe, work the opposite way. They're love stories. The main character is either a husband or wants to be. (See Lodge.) Husbands are the sort of people who merit respect. Husbands live comfortably within the social order. For better and probably worse, though, the main character of *Traveling through the Boondocks* doesn't know if he wants to be a husband or a lover. To me, this provides the plot.

To summarize briefly in these terms: complications ensue immediately with a scandalous infidelity. All appears clear. Then everything gets quickly confused by the crucial matter of to whom exactly is he married; it may be too superficial to presume it's to his institution. The discipline, then? But precisely how is this different from the profession? And isn't the hero in reality married to his department? However, as it develops, can't the very act of writing about the department be interpreted as another betrayal? Such worries continue. They plague the hero himself—at times perversely, perhaps, and at other times in vain. Some sort of affair does seem to be going on. Although the name of whom he loves instead isn't very certain, our hero does appear much too disingenuous when he suggests that there really isn't anyone else. We will grant, however, that he may just be confused and self-absorbed, as lovers always are. And we will try to understand when he protests: so much of what he does only acts out a pale copy of bolder, more powerful romances, where we always know who the hero is, and why.

Some readers will undoubtedly find this sort of story more compelling than others. Most will admit that, rather than being an imitation of an action in the Aristotelian sense, the plot is fundamentally static, representing a state in itself. Is the stasis comic? Sometimes, perhaps in Frye's venerable sense, complete with a tyrannical old order, blocking characters, and so on. But most often, no—for the following reason: there's no reconciliation. Indeed, except for love, the hero lacks illusions, as if in response to the whole social order, itself swollen with illusions—called convictions and rules—of every sort. Just as crucial, there's no green world. How could a story of academic life make so little concession to its wider cultural placement as the very image (capped by ivory towers) of such a world?

We return, then, to the question of travel and the trip not taken. Even if here not much specific imagination is invested in anywhere else (and it remains most unclear to the end who, if anyone, would either accompany our narrator or welcome him), this particular book, like any travel book, is written for people back home. They might never leave, or even want to. They are probably comfortable where they are. But this doesn't mean the folks back home haven't variously felt excluded from grander visions or greater heights. The fact that they never leave doesn't mean that they aren't subject to a whole spectrum of emotions (ranging from admiration to contempt) about privileged others who get to go anywhere, first class, all the time. These people might not have more education. But they have access to undreamed-of levels of power and influence.

Enough of travel. About the question of access, let me conclude this introduction with a final story, told by Andrei Sinyavsky. In his accounting, the more total the rule of a socio-political system, the more devious the forms of plot designed to counter or contend with it. Some plots are so devious they're almost inseparable from those sponsored by the system, especially with respect to such categories as those of the permanent and the uncertain, or the official and the criminal, each horrifically confounded by the communal apartments or the long queues of Soviet life. At one point, he gives the story of the invalid who used to sell trinkets at a Moscow market.

The man had a sideline. He promised to get anybody into any university or institute. Lots of parents paid. He promised a refund if he failed. Nobody ever asked for one. How did he do it? Sinyavsky asks. "Very simple. He didn't! He didn't go anywhere, didn't do anything, and generally had no connections whatsoever." What the invalid did instead was reason that parents were probably bribing everybody in sight. One might succeed; they would never know who. "Finally, there was always the chance that the actual applicant might be diligent and succeed on his or her own merits" (182).

I like this story for a couple of reasons. First, although it *contains* plenty of plot, it has no plot itself—except to function as a nodal point where related narratives converge. Of course all have to do with education, defined in terms of aspiration, privilege, and hierarchy. None of these things will be important to you if you don't want them in some way; if you want education, you have to want them in some way. Hence, a second reason for citing the above story: no plot of any kind about even the most rigid structures is going to be a very good one if it doesn't allow for individual initiative. What the invalid knows about the system or students he demonstrates by the example of his own person: despite the imperative to have a respectable position, one can still set up shop pretty much anywhere if one is resourceful enough, and proceed to sell avowals of influence on the basis of a structural condition of more or less complete divorce.

❦

CHAPTER ONE

A Credit to the University

"Tell us you didn't want to stir up debate. Tell us you didn't want controversy," wailed one of my colleagues to me some years ago in the form of an open letter to the department. Her occasion was my own open letter to the department head protesting his sudden distribution to the department of copies of my article, "On Teaching at a Second-Rate University," originally published in the *South Atlantic Quarterly*.[1] "You don't care who gets hurt by the analogies you make public," she continued, "and you hide behind the curtain of a larger idea, a larger premise." Perhaps the first thing to say about a second-rate university (other than the fact that you sure as hell better not write anything so designating yours) is that it largely comprises its own audience.

It wasn't so much what I had said about Clarion. It was more that I had structurally situated its sheer obscurity and provinciality, and offered some personal anecdotes about the comedy of being somewhere that had no institutional power to command any larger vision of itself. What I wrote can be explained by way of contrast. At one point in his memoir of a year teaching at Kenyon College, P.F. Kluge quotes a colleague in the English department as follows: "At Kenyon, elitism is moderated by a sense•of fundamental second-ratedness. Who else do you think's going to come here and pay twenty thousand dollars for something that, in principle, is of no immediate practical use? We know we're not Williams, and that's part of our identity. We're the best imitation of Williams west of the Alleghenies. There's always a market for the second-best Italian restaurant in town" (180).

"Second-ratedness" here means something like happy amateurism. Kenyon can afford to think of itself in this way because it can maneuver itself while remaining secure at the top of a hierarchical structure. Clarion, however, simply can't afford to think of itself at all in terms of this same structure. Its students don't even pay a fifth of what Kenyon students pay, and many can barely pay that. Its degrees have no other source of appeal than practical use. Its identity is derived from some general expectation of "college" rather than a famous specific example. Clarion University is not an elite school. Few of the students have heard of Williams—or Kenyon. The town doesn't even have one Italian restaurant.

Understood in this context, a second-rate university is pleased to think of itself as staging a local version of the same old national play: Higher Education. Everywhere the performance is based on a solid script, featuring responsible administrators, hard-working faculty, and earnest students. Moreover, we in the cast all know that there are good reasons why the play has been so long running (since 1867, in Clarion's case). So all wish only—well, what? That there would be a wider audience? It would seem so. The idea of some audience other than oneself (apart from the state legislature) is difficult to get rid of. Furthermore, these days even the most local players are bound to be affected by the widespread uncertainty about what exactly should be going on in any one academic production. So another thing to say about a second-rate university is that it is implicated very deeply in a fundamental contradiction: at the same time much of the official energy is intent on keeping the curtain down, much of the rest is bent on hoisting it up.

But only so far, and then only according to certain discursive rules. One is that the institution may be compared on a national scale with other universities only at great risk. For example, in 1990 a report by *Money* magazine ranked Clarion University as one of the top 50 "best buys" among public colleges in the United States. This fact was promptly and prominently mentioned in all university publicity. Alas, in its 1991 report, *Money* failed to mention Clarion at all in its 100 best college buys. National recognition is fickle. In my article, I was interested in examining why, for universities such as Clarion, such recognition is in fact nonexistent.[2]

Argue this, however, and locally one is only going to be more deeply imperiled by the contradiction. In a second departmental open letter, another colleague, taking his usual high road, wrote a righteous paragraph in which my villainous byways lay below, strewn with bodies: student teachers embarrassed, freshpersons confused, and Clarion graduates appalled by the sudden publicity when the *Pittsburgh Press* got wind of the article. "*You* made Clarion the issue," he thundered, in what I took to be the very voice of provinciality, red-faced with the phenomenon it decried. A third thing about second-rate universities follows from the second: unable to produce the conditions for their own wider visibility, they come to resent any conditions, while they continue to long for the right set.

What would be the right set? A column mocking me in the student newspaper purported to settle the issue: "Clarion University is legislatively mandated to serve a region and not an economic and intellectual elite." Fair enough, one supposes—and would that any university could live by legislative mandate alone. Instead, "regional" ones abide according to standards and criteria held by national elites. The student hastened immediately to negatively register them: "Clarion is not, and never has been, a richly-endowed research institution." The very editor of the newspaper began the year by positively registering them. During his summer journalistic sojourn, he had informed us, not only did he discover that Clarion students are getting "a good education," but "this education is on an even keel with some of the other big name schools around the country."

Other? But isn't his point that Clarion is not a "big name" school? Otherwise, there would be no sense to his prouder point that "to be blatantly obvious, I ended up teaching them [the other big name schools] a few things." What kind of writing is this? Through the analphabetic haze, what sorts of anxieties are being expressed? I believe the most prominent one is of a piece with that expressed by my colleagues above: institutional identity at a Clarion abides by being divided against itself. On the one hand, we are bid to be "Clarion proud." On the other hand, we secretly wonder if sometime between 1990 and 1991 *Money* got hold of the student newspaper. A few weeks later during that fateful year, a faculty member wrote in decrying that his earlier letter was rendered intelligible because "PhDs" had been taken to be an abbreviation for "Phasing." One reads this sort of thing and fears for the legislative mandate itself.

1.

The pride of second-rate universities is an insecure thing, because it is situated at the pleasure of much larger, wealthier, and altogether more sovereign institutions from which we must distinguish ourselves while participating in the same discourse (of scholarship; interdisciplinary concerns; multicultural agendas; and so on) by which they, in turn, realize themselves. How do we distinguish ourselves? We teach. Who? Well, students who don't know what a Ph.D. is. Most American college students, after all, don't come from homes where a parent or a relative has a Ph.D. Somebody has to teach these students, especially if they're the first in their families to attend college. Yet what happens when their teachers attend regional or national conferences in their respective disciplines? They discover that their students effectively don't exist because the issues that vitalize the conferences have virtually nothing to do with them.

During the fall semester of the departmental open letter, I chanced to attend a conference in Chicago. There a woman from Oberlin gave an excellent paper which expressed the follies of teaching politically-correct texts to students who know they're politically correct. Her example was a novel by an author who has a Sudanese father and an English mother. Her students missed how trenchant is the book's postcolonial critique because the photo of the author on the back cover made it obvious to them he was just another Western white man. They didn't like the book at all. Listening to this presentation, I couldn't help but think that, for my students, the photo would provide one of the few reassuring reasons why they might like the book. Their backgrounds contain few representations of the "Third World." In 1991, they were only just beginning to learn what political correctness was; I'm still not sure to this day they know it other than as a stance that someone else has, such as students from Oberlin, perhaps, wherever that is.

Of course, one is always presumably free to give one's own paper at any conference about one's own follies. Nonetheless, how not to return from one of some national scope without the feeling that some experience is authorized because some is not? It's no easy thing to be a second-rate university because the more general discourse of American higher education flattens out the vast exclusions and purports to extend an available rhetoric to any and all institutions. On this basis *there are no second-rate universities*. No matter that everybody knows the number of acclaimed elite ones who write the lines and direct the show, at once behind the scenes and right up front; these in turn recreate, reproduce, and diffuse the power of economic elites. As usual, it is one central burden of standard rhetorical options to efface what "everybody knows." I heard it remarked that I could have avoided a lot of trouble for myself if I'd merely been politically correct. Clarion is not second-rate. It is *differently rated*.

"I still don't understand why you had to mention Clarion," my dean kept saying to me the one time we spoke, most agreeably, about my infamous article. Once again, a Clarion is, specifically, Clarion in one fundamental sense because it can't be mentioned. Elites, on the other hand, are elites because they can be mentioned—indeed, are mentioned so often, in so many contexts, that citation of "Harvard," for example, can be indifferent about the material institution. One of the curiosities around the controversy concerning the strike of Yale graduate teaching assistants—to take a recent example—is that it threatened to ground prestige in the commonplaces of literal working conditions. Citing a local professor who characterized the students as "among the blessed of the earth," Michael Bérubé brings us back to the point: "They are not, after all, any garden-variety cheap labor; they are cheap labor *at Yale*" (*Employment*, 51).

A Clarion cannot afford to be so casually cited, and must remain mired in literalities. So how to explain that my article was a deliberate effort to intervene in the conventional discourse whereby, first of all, Clarion can't be so much as mentioned? I wanted to reveal, specifically, how its unmentionable status is appropriated by the encompassing system of institutional hierarchies (including how even something scandalous at a Clarion can be charming or piquant at a Kenyon). One reads about higher education today amazed at how the names still have to be changed to protect the actual.

If its authority isn't depersonalized and unspecified, it's often falsely designated. The new academic magazine, *Lingua Franca*, apparently designed to counter the perceived blandness of the *Chronicle of Higher Education*, regularly contains pieces written by pseudonymous academics. Similarly, even during a period of strenuous, thorough professional critique, articles in books feature pseudonyms. See, for example, the brief contribution to the recent *Left Politics and the Literary Profession*, "Somewhere Off the Coast of Academia," by one "Robert Rich." He sketches a grim, sardonic portrait of present academic life, e.g. "The slightest sign of individual difference draws a show of force. One is constantly watched, followed, under surveillance, and the subject of reports" (291).[3] Is the reason that he is identified as "the pseudonym of a teacher at a large western university" merely because he fears for his tenure? Examples such as Danell Jones's account of his disillusionment with Rocky Mountain College remain extremely unusual (and even here seems possible because Jones only stayed a year and got another position at the University of Denver).

I'm reminded once again of a favorite statement by Michel Foucault: "People know what they do; they frequently know why they do what they do; but what they don't know is what they do does" (cited in Dreyfus and Rabinow, 187). Among many of the things this suppresssion of institutional affiliation does, I think, is to consolidate the very hierarchical structure it's ostensibly set free to question. In fact, "Robert Rich" doesn't question this structure. He isn't aware of it. He just participates in it. Granted, one has to participate in the structure even when one means to disclose its silences, its secret ruses, and its human costs. No discursive position is going to cease being, as they say at conferences, "vexed"; Gayatri Spivak expresses, I think, one of the profound theoretical truths when she maintains as follows: "Persistently to critique a structure that one cannot not (wish to) inhabit is the deconstructive stance" (795). Nonetheless, the structure of institutional hierarchy significantly perpetuates itself because it will accommodate a critique from certain favored institutional sites only.

Even more crucial is the function of an evaluative vocabulary. There simply isn't any public one apart from the guidebook and magazine ratings of American universities designed for high school graduates. "What's the difference between 'second-rate' and 'second-tier?'" a Pittsburgh reporter asked me during the fall after the publication of my article. I wanted to reply that it was the difference between plain speaking and academic bullshit. Perhaps this would have been too easy, although an inescapable part of any thing is the language used to describe it, and few people other than academics have good reason to be sensitive about the fact. A woman from a college in Vermont I'd never heard of wrote me and gave its address in conclusion as on "University Drive," only to write in the margin, "Sometimes the address is the last straw." Perhaps no professional more than an academic falls into the gap between an institution's hushed, mundane frailties and its lofty, timeless occasions. Sometimes all you can do is plunge.

After the publication of "On Teaching at a Second-Rate University," I heard from many who had hit bottom and splattered. Let me continue with more from this same woman: "For most of us, it was over long ago. In a profession obsessed with elitism and correct sympathies, most of us are buried by the pretensions of the nouveau elite research schools. . . . The few who are successful in the academy fear that failure is contagious and they do their best to smother us. The genuine failures revel in their superiority as 'the real teachers.'" I have to assume that I'm being true to the spirit of the communication in quoting from it. This is a letter that protests against having to be "personal" even while it remains so. How her institution is ranked is the single most important fact of this woman's professional life. Part of the pain of having hit bottom, I take it, is that everybody around is still acting as if they're on top.

Just so, part of the experience of being an academic, anywhere at all in the United States, may be that there is a daily, steady, gaseous pressure by means of which any institution expands its own prestige. Of course nobody likes to be thought second-rate. This doesn't mean everybody needs to be thought first-rate, or just, well, "differently rated." I couldn't very well have been surprised years ago to the local reaction to my article, once enough xeroxed copies of it made their way around. (It was as if, via photocopying, the campus had not only created a very personal, hand-to-hand foundation for the article's reception, but reauthored it as a communal enterprise. Most read the same copy, complete with underlinings, and nobody knew who made the original.) I was astonished the day a man with whom I've taught for many years accosted me with my only mistake: I should have called Clarion third-rate!

People react differently to pretense. How an academic reacts may very well determine what sort of career he or she is likely to have. Another day I met another old colleague whose "take" on my infamy wasn't so clear. I reminded him of the party a few years ago when our group fell into a how-did-you-come-to-Clarion mood. In the midst of the usual reasons, he had suddenly blurted: "We're here because we couldn't get jobs anywhere else." I had howled. The comment was hardly intended to be a balanced assessment. What delighted me instead is how the words flew in the face of, well, balanced assessments. (These always stress *choice*.) Blunt evaluative principles have been edited out of such assessments. Hence, into the voided space flows both a covert self-importance and an even more covert resentment. Must one's own institutionalized second-ratedness be something one never quite sees? When does it lose its character as a *consigned* thing, and take on the coloration of something more personally held? How many fail to realize how such duplicities function to consolidate the larger interests of institutional politics?

Consider the difference between evaluation and recognition. A Clarion has every reason to be vitally interested in the distinction, yet possesses no discursive power to alter how it is weighed. Hence, the following characterization of Clarion as an "invisible college" (as the headline of a subsequent profile on me in the *Chronicle of Higher Education* had it) in a letter-to-the-editor by one Gerald Phillips, a professor from the area's major research institution, Penn State: "Its faculty, with some notable exceptions, are quite dedicated to teaching undergraduate students, and, for the most part, do a fine job of it. Some of its faculty also do research and publish the results and are given appropriate credit for it" (B3). How does the professor know? Of course he doesn't, in any specific way. What he does know is how to give evaluation the character of a recognition without passing through the stage of description. So it goes with second-rate universities, over and over again: recognized in order to be categorized, and then categorized in order to be dismissed or patronized. "Their faculties are dedicated to their teaching tasks," the Penn State professor propounded, "as they are defined for them by policy and circumstances."[4]

In other words, all is well there as long as faculty members do what they're told. Do they, in fact? I believe one reason for the notoriety of my article is that it suggests some faculty aren't as content as they're mandated to be with teaching at places where they're supposed to do nothing else. I don't say I'm not. In fact, I don't say anything about teaching—and this proved to be sufficient provocation. The Penn State professor, of course, keeps mentioning teaching because at his own "highly visible" institution the important thing is doing research. Of such a virtually unexamined hierarchy of value is the whole enterprise of American higher education constructed, even if one rarely gets to see it expressed so crudely.[5] The incoherence of a system where research did *not* have more power and prestige than teaching might be surpassed by the threat to a system where all activity in the lower ranks is not as dedicated to teaching as it's supposed to be.

Criticism of the power of research culture has become more widespread in more recent years. (For a sample of the range of this critique, see Damrosh or Ziolkowski.) Yet, as Zelda Gamson concludes, not only have attacks "not seriously affected the schools in which the culture was created." There is more: "The stratification system in the academy is stronger than ever" (73). In terms of this stratification, it's essential that most American universities remain "invisible," or, what is the same thing, *known* simply in terms of their teaching.

Consequently, the larger public can proceed without really understanding very much about these universities at all. This suits the universities just fine. The "controversy" at Clarion over my article, for example, was that there *was* a controversy in the first place. In fact, no "debate" ensued. I scarcely expected that there would be. Indeed, I didn't even think anybody would so much as read the article. The library stopped subscribing to *South Atlantic Quarterly* years ago. Late that summer, one respondent—from a first-rate institution—had written of the magazine to me as "one of the most spectacularly reputable journals going." If so, would not simply getting published in it constitute something of the article's claim? Instead, few on my own campus appeared to have heard of the magazine. A colleague from another department left one morning with my copy of it in a plain brown envelope.

Instead of debate there was fear. "There's no forum to discuss any of this in the department," another colleague confided to me one day. He seemed afraid. Of what? Unpacking what "any of this" referred to? My impression was that students, in contrast to faculty, were bemused. "Woefully provincial" I had characterized these students. "Woefully provincial" broadly smiled one one day, bouncing into class most unwoefully. In any event, the public outcry failed to develop further. The publicity, if not my local infamy, was over in a couple of weeks. We were all grateful, I think, to resume the business of forming campus-wide committees in order to implement the 12 Strategic Planning Goals and to complete the survey from the Faculty Development Action Plan Grant.

2.

How much fear is there at campuses throughout the rest of the country? Often, reading letters I continued to receive through the semester, there seemed to me so much fear elsewhere that Clarion came to appear as a forum. One man from another Pennsylvania state university actually asked me to write a letter stating I didn't know him, lest he be mistaken for someone mentioned in my article! Probably this was too highly timorous an instance, and yet consider the following comment from another man at a Texas university (one I'd never heard of) about it and others in his experience: "No one cares if you publish at these places except that they become conscience stricken, jealous, and, then, hostile if you do. I've published *more* because I work in such places but have also probably suffered more. Students are of low quality here and this goes (generally) hand in hand with the faculty." He mentions that he's won numerous teaching awards.

Nothing surprised me more about these professors than several who assured me that they taught at places less favored than Clarion. "As one who has slipped well below your 'second rate university,'" one introduced herself. Another, from somewhere in Alabama, mentioned an employment record of six institutions in nearly fifteen years, "none as good as Clarion (or certainly no better)." I had not meant my use of the term, "second-rate," to represent more than an affective category. Even so much as the addition of regional factors (as more than one correspondent noted) complicates how any one university may be evaluated, and of course probably any one can be made to appear either better or worse depending upon some other placed alongside it; a placement is seldom made at all except in one's favor, as we note with respect to the citation of Williams College by the Kenyon professor, above. Nonetheless, there are clearly vast deeps of inky prestige into which it would be fruitless to inquire. "We're a good second-rate university," pronounced still another colleague one day to me. I nodded. We both felt we knew plenty which weren't so good. I'm not sure how many we knew which were barely universities, but they exist in great number, and real people teach at them.[6]

How many of them resent those at their more visible counterparts? One woman reminded me that educational research conclusively demonstrates institutional prestige to be the most important single factor in securing one's first job. "It still wrenches my guts when I come across simpletons in the field at Ivy League schools who got their jobs because they had an influential adviser or the right graduate degree," wrote a man in Virginia. He said he's published books and numerous articles. Is it these that enable him to have the confidence of his bitterness, on the basis of which he assured me: "You are not the only one out in the academic Gulag?" Would the man have felt this way had he been content simply to teach? What *is* it to be content to teach? Not to read anything, not to go to conferences, not to have professional ambitions?

That is, what is it to teach not exclusively in relation to one's students or even one's own colleagues but to the standards of the promotion committee, much less those of the whole discipline? One doesn't, after all, just "teach." The teaching is situated in a broad professional continuum where it is subject to any number of valuations relative to other activities. (See the chapter, "High Flying at Low levels," in Caesar, *Writing*.) Of course one may choose to teach. People who hold forth on the self-sufficient rewards of teaching usually define it as a matter of choice. But then what is choice?

Certainly not something free from its own mystifications. If it were, James Phelan, for one, in his journal of fifteen months of professional life, wouldn't be able, on the one hand, to bemoan that so many academics have so little choice about where to live, while, on the other hand, remark that "professors are all finally free agents" (195).[7] One can only wonder what the discipline would look like if some of these people who only teach, under the exclusion of all other sources of value, published their own stories.

Out of graduate school, Phelan came in second at Berkeley. The people about whom I'm speaking, however, never had a chance at Ohio State (where Phelan came in first) and they don't appear to feel the insufficiency of teaching because they aren't any good at it. They just don't have any choice. "I don't expect to do much better in my career," wrote a man from Louisiana, "as a realist at forty, despite almost twenty publications, membership in two NEH Summer Seminars, postdoctoral coursework to update on technical writing, computers, etc." "No one ever got out of here," wrote another to me from Nebraska, "as that character says in Dante. In eighteen years, I have never seen anyone move on except through death or retirement." Phelan's *Beyond the Tenure Track*, on the other hand, details a record of activity staged in an entirely different theatre before an entirely different audience. He's expected to be free to move—in a professional network of friends and associates, at conferences throughout the country, and to another position, if he can get it.

But of course, one could retort, this is all nothing new. Teaching is disvalued? Everybody Knows. Some universities have more prestige than others? Tell me another. Academic life is insecure? Say it isn't so! The surest way to discount something is to assert its sheer self-evidentness. In fact these issues seem to me the product of everybody purporting to know on the basis of not wanting to know. Take elite universities: how is one supposed to regard them if one is positioned institutionally below them? It might depend upon how far below. At second-rate universities, though, my feeling is that the individual is simply not supposed to regard them at all. Hence, for example, the Clarion student who once weighed in to the student newspaper with her opinion that my "main concern is to gaze rapturously at people who happen to work at institutions with more name recognition." How to reply? By asking: who, in fact, actually controls the gaze? Or by wondering: who defines sight? To have to be accused of being contaminated in order to ask these questions illustrates one way through which the remorseless hierarchy of American higher education perpetuates itself. The student

can be forgiven, I suppose, for just not wanting to hear about this
hierarchy, unless as a source of envy.

One day during the end of the semester I received a letter from
a man who taught at an American institution not even located on
the U.S. mainland. He had read his *Chronicle* and "was particularly interested in your comments defining a caste system of universities, with the idea that 'you are where you teach.'" Only
recently, the man went on to say, had he become aware of "the
hidden implications of being a part of a second-rate institution. . . .
The problems I see here are aggrievated by the official pretense of
the university hierarchy, that this university is somehow on par
with mainland campuses." "Increasingly," he concluded, "I have the
feeling that I must escape from this rather pathological milieu or
suffer a slow poisoning of my career."

How to respond? Everybody knows? He didn't. Should he? Perhaps—years later. Now rereading these letters reminds me of nothing so much as reading the high school teachers who contribute
hopeful pieces in the past couple of years to the Modern Language
Association's annual issue of *Profession* or, better, the professors who
describe work in county jails or as full-time adjuncts in the pages of
On the Market, a new collection of essays by the youngest members
of the generation. They are, as Bérubé writes, "being squeezed by a
system whose ideal image of itself promotes theoretically sophisticated, interdisciplinary work in extraliterary studies but whose
material basis is shrinking as fast as its superstructure is expand-
ing" (*Employment*, 101). But years later, it seems, even a heightened
consciousness of career horizons does not necessarily lead to realistic
expectations on the part of those lucky enough to land a ride on the
tenure track at "invisible" or "comprehensive" institutions that we
still don't even know what to call because "the system" has a vested
interest in promoting a lack of interest in them.

My own conviction is that, whether off the U.S. mainland or in
the heart of the Midwest, these institutions are at the very least
mysterious places, far from being populated by faculty who have
"chosen" to be there or who are happy to be teaching because it has
been legislatively mandated that this is all they can be happy
doing. Despite the consoling mythology of unified "community" that
has also been accorded them, these institutions may contain experience so raw, diverse, and either blasted or unregenerate that
even their first-rate counterparts could not easily accommodate it.
At one point, my man in Texas stated: "We're losers, all (and we
know it?)." How substantial an investment does this individual, or
any individual, make in the question mark? Another correspondent

phrased it this way: "Where did we find it necessary to construct institutional non-being (or slums, I suppose)?" I would put the question still another way: having constructed institutional non-being, where is the value given to its knowledge of itself?

Kathleen Woodward has an interesting essay-review on some recent memoirs that dramatize a state she terms, "bureaucratic panic," produced "by deadlines and other inflexible requirements of a bureaucracy" (60). None of her examples is from academic life, despite the fact that it might easily seem this particular bureau-cratic mode of being illustrates at least as well as any other the way in which the positional and the personal fail to equate. How can we explain the absence of academic instances? Of course a number of reasons could be suggested. It seems to me that one is particularly compelling: bureaucratic panic, not to mention disso-nance between the personal and the positional, exists to be recu-perated by first-rate institutions alone.

An enormous interest continues on the part of the contemporary critical or poststructuralist theory in marginal sites, postcolonial conditions, and even indeterminate or decentered identities. (I make this point more forcefully both in Chapter Three and in Chapter Seven.) Here let me be content to note that others have seen the linkage. For example, Stephen Slemon in a critique of postcolonialism writes as follows: "I cannot help but noticing [that] . . . our theoreti-cal masters in Paris and Oxford are read and referenced by exem-plary theorists of the local . . . but these metropolitan theorists seldom reference these cultural and theoretical mediators in turn" (31).

Of course David Bromwich (speaking more generally on the writhings of "academic culture") is right: "To see ourselves as *na-tives under seige* would lend credibility as well to the poignant evocations of 'community' from university presidents and other incapacitated local chieftains. The perspective of colonial victims could be, if not the light at the end of the tunnel, certainly an apt and acceptable light in the tunnel itself" (232). But it needs to be recognized that this "perspective" has always been immanent (if not actually lit until recently) in the very construction of the tun-nel. Bromwich's "ourselves" comprises an already divided constitu-ency, and this division now becomes theorized in the 90s as a displaced form of an aging academy's (self) consciousness of its own totality. Its power silences not only ethnic minorities but also de-graded cultural locations.

Another way to desribe this consciousness: being embedded; that is, we are the product of our constraints; we are always al-ready in place; we are inconceivable, even to ourselves, apart from

our professional circumstances. As Stanley Fish states in his introduction to *Doing What Comes Naturally*: "Being embedded means
just that, being embedded *always*, and one does not escape
embeddedness by acknowledging, as I do, that it is itself a frac-
tured, fissured, volatile condition" (32). So (at any rate) it looks
from Duke. (Where of course all sorts of dissonance between the
personal and the positional have famously emanated; for an account, see Begley.) From a less lofty vantage, embeddedness looks
monolithic, seamless, and stagnant. Or to put this differently, one
can be more than half in love with easeful margins of any sort if
one does not occupy the institutional space of one.

The question of how directly I can write out my own personal
marginality will ceaselessly occupy me throughout this book. What
I fear far more than charges of bitterness or bad faith is the prospect of [always] already having my experience simply effaced, before its own fateful appropriation by more "metropolitan" centers,
full of more powerfully embedded others of all sorts. Doubtless it's
true that marginality can be written of only insofar as it participates in the far more impersonal, not to say invisible, network of
theoretical presuming and institutional positioning. (This is not to
consider the case of marginality rewritten as subjection. For a
searching consideration, see Butler.) But neither theory nor institution says everything about how marginality—especially when it
fails to be, in the current idiom, "enabling"—can be written. I don't
agree with James Sosnoski with respect to "the autobiographical
mode," which he claims "does not work well as a critique of power
relations" (*Token Professionals*, xxix).

For one thing, the nature of anyone's marginality changes,
depending upon how many voices (some similar to yours, some not)
you can hear. (Again, I would refer to the rather astonishing range
in the Boufis and Olsen collection.) Speaking of "invested principles
and privileges" idealized behind the figure he terms "the giver of
seriousness," James Kincaid puts the matter succinctly: "Different
tones lay out different maps" (12). Another thing: the potential or
actual comedy (just to name one route) of anybody's peculiar
embeddedness may not result in escape; it can result in renewal,
as a reader of Emily Toth's advice will discover, if nowhere else. In
my own experience, I couldn't have known when I left Clarion for
that fall conference years ago that the most direct moment of open
hostility I'd encounter about my article would take place while I
was signing into a Chicago hotel. A woman (who had evidently
heard me introduce myself to someone else) suddenly stepped up

and burst out: "My husband teaches at Clarion. I think your article was [unintelligible] and insensitive." She stalked away before I could reply. Since what I thought she'd said was "inappropriate," I wanted to ask her if she didn't know any fiercer words.

3.

Let me conclude with another story. By the time I left Clarion, I thought all the furor was over. Certainly my apprehension was. The whole semester really hadn't been so bad. Only the action of my circulatory chair had rattled me. But the open letters had been fun; I like to think they'll go down as highlights in the unrecorded annals of the department, along with the departmental meeting decades before when a senior man suddenly stood up and wished eternal damnation on our old chair, or the summer letter of resignation years later sent to everyone by another chair, who promptly allowed himself to be persuaded to reconsider and recind at the first fall department meeting. What had bothered me most was the thought that I'd be fired—or at least that the administration would move against me in some way. One friend maintained, "The president couldn't do anything to a full professor if she tripped over you having sex with a dog outside her office." "But only if it could be proven that the animal had consented," I cautioned, trying not to be so worried. In fact, I was not the hero of my own experience. I was afraid. All praise to tenure, though. There was no official response.

So why this late fall day did I instantly freeze, once inside my door, when a letter fell onto the kitchen counter? "Office of the President," it read. I was unusually relaxed this day. This is when the blow always falls. There could be no doubt now what was inside the envelope. The administrative logic was suddenly clear: wait till all the publicity had died down and then make your move. I feared I'd misplaced the name of a certain lawyer. I wondered if I could find the reply from the American Civil Liberties Union to my letter of inquiry. It finally had to be admitted: you simply *can't* write an article entitled, "On Teaching at a Second-Rate University," and, well, get away with it.

Would I be suspended first? I stared at the envelope and ran through in my mind all the discussion many weeks previously that my wife and I had about what to do if this should happen. Had we concluded suspension would be for the best? I decided to make some soup before opening the envelope. There was only chicken noodle

available. Sometimes you don't want chicken noodle. So what the
hell: I opened the envelope and read the following first paragraph:

> "Being part of the Clarion university family is very special
> to us all. We share pride in our accomplishments, confidence
> in our future, and a common desire to serve our institution
> and its tradition. To enhance that tradition, we are em-
> barking on a new business opportunity . . . the Clarion
> University VISA Credit Card."

Did somebody say something about a larger premise or about
community? I smiled. I heated up some soup. No matter where in
the academic world you are, you just can't beat all this talk of
power. You can't *fix* it. Even when you think you're most embedded
(if not endangered), the energies of American higher education, not
to say capitalism itself, will find a way out for you. This in part is
what being embedded means. Some position amid the most remorseless hierarchy is never completely stable. Identity can always
be recreated in another register, and the rigors of an unfortunate
categorization can be reborn as a first-rate opportunity.

But of course the rest of what being embedded means abides
in the familiar, daily ways: saying hello to colleagues in the hall
between classes; keeping office hours so students can say hello to
you; and just generally being a member of a department. After the
open letters exchanged with two of my erstwhile colleagues, I grew
less sure about whether I'd been written out of the department or
had written myself back in. Who decides, anyway—in actual social
fact, I mean? Perhaps the nicest thing about being a member of a
department is that nobody has the power to decide.

There is only the official compact: with tenure, you're part of
your department until death or retirement do you part, no matter
what your colleagues really think of you. You can always go to
meetings. You can always vote. I did both during the following
spring semester, without ceasing to wonder if I should have done
either, much less exactly what I was doing in the first place. If the
analogy of a department to a marriage is an almost inescapable
one, then there's probably much good it makes available especially
during those periods when the familiar becomes strange once more.
Or maybe best of all during those periods when the nuptial origins
appear almost entirely gone and the bonds seem to endure more for
the good of everybody else than for the principal parties.

CHAPTER TWO

᪐

Electing a Department:
Differences, Fictions, and a Narrative

"If I were to make a critical comment on the English department, I would say that it is not enough like the media representation of it."

— Stanley Fish on the Duke English department

"No word of this meeting is to be spoken outside this room." So spake my last chair both at the beginning and the end of the biggest department meeting in many years. All but one of twenty-one permanent, tenure-track members were present. Our occasion was to choose candidates for two new positions. The Search Committee had labored long and hard. Everybody was a-buzz with anticipation. The meeting had even drawn me, for only the second time that year. What is an academic department? In a very real sense, it is the story of why a senior member would disdain its formal deliberations; why its hiring usually proves so contentious; and why a chair would be moved to mark all business as strictly private.

One thing needs to be stressed about this narrative: it is never told in specific terms. "In the department," begins Nicolai Gogol's great story, "The Overcoat"—but then the narrator waivers: "but perhaps it is just as well not to say which department. There is

39

nothing more touchy and ill-tempered than departments, regiments, government offices, and indeed any kind of official body" (5). Any academic department is no different. The only departments that receive public representation are those, such as Duke's, whose members or whose institutions already enjoy enough renown that they have specificity to waste.[1] Even in these cases there are limits; we never expect to learn what Fredric Jameson really thinks of Frank Lentricchia's divorce. The following account would be different if I had made the same discreet choice as Gogol's narrator, who "in order to avoid all sorts of unpleasant misunderstandings," concludes that "we shall refer to the department in question as *a certain department.*"

How much different? To some, not much. Nobody in my department commands a national reputation. No one outside my department could recognize anybody referred to here, or would care to. Indeed, to some we will all variously appear familiar enough in some stereotypical sense, and to read a specific tale of our deliberations will appear the stuff of banality rather than transgression. To others, however, the following pages will represent a breach of discretion. The actual department business of real departments is properly conducted in private, and a public narrative of even one hiring decision is neither responsible nor ethical. How much difference will such a narrative make? Perhaps it depends upon what sort of inquiry it is designed to serve.

It might be more accurate to characterize the following pages as an exploration into the nature of academic departments with a narrative embedded in it. The argument is that a department as a social entity has been continually repressed in educational discourse; indeed, this is why we lack narratives. Two things especially result from this repression. First, the necesssary fiction of a department can be stabilized as a structure, recreated ultimately in the interests of the research university model that initiated the modern conception of a department. Secondly, the social foundation of this structure fails to be granted any discursive existence, because all authority derives from the elite model, founded on scholarship.

It may be the case that all departments suffer from this repression; hence the reason—to take a recent example—why in his latest study James Sosnoski must sort through so many varied definitions of the term, "discipline," as if it had strictly to do with either intellectual work or bureaucratic rule. (See *Modern Skeletons*, 28–42.) Departments such as my own, however, suffer most because they abide in institutions that cannot support research and therefore are unable to reconcile their professional identity with their social one. Only this latter identity gives my department its life, even if the former provides its occasion.

But how to express its business as a narrative? Immediately there's the question of whose story it is—and the prospect that there are as many versions of any one department as there are members of it. Everybody has heard of departments whose members are at such complete odds with one another that they can't even agree when to have a meeting. I heard of another this past year, some of whose members communicate which each other only by e-mail. "We're not that bad," assured the man who told this to my friend. "We all talk to each other in our department." Nonetheless, one can be fairly certain that if each of the people in this virtual department were to try to relate the story of so much as a single year, all would be astonished at the previously unspoken differences among them. So individual differences must be acknowledged and some risk taken if one wants to open up the conditions by which the basic organizational units of an academic discipline are comprehended: departmental truth is not only muffled and inward but deeply personal. In order to give one's own department as the story of one vote, and to give one vote as the story of the department, much is going to be told that will sound like sheer fiction.

Exactly what sorts of social organizations are departments? Why do so many fall by the wayside along the high road of disciplinarity? Electing a department does not involve a direct, explicit consideration of such questions by its members, even if the questions are lodged at the center of virtually any departmental deliberation. Indeed, it is probably the essence of the election process that such a consideration cannot take place, and in this respect (it seems to me) a narrative of electing a department accords with our deepest sense of all narratives arising from academic life. They are simultaneously heard in two registers: banal and exceptional, impeccably deferred and irredeemably blunt.

1.

It seemed a forgone conclusion: the local favorite for one of the positions was the lover and companion of one of the two most powerful people in the department. She had a glowing letter of recommendation in her file from the other. In addition, the woman had been teaching composition in the department off and on for a number of years and enjoyed easy social contact with the majority of members. Finally, all seemed agreed that she was a good teacher and that she had conducted her formal job interview with her usual poise. Therefore, it almost appeared vindictive to point out that, among other imperfections, she had not had one graduate course in the area, had never taught a course in it, and had written her dissertation in an entirely different area. I pointed these things out at the meeting anyway.

A few others also wondered about what claims for specialization we were being offered. More spoke in the woman's favor—all discretely ignoring her lack of credentials and emphasizing instead her interview performance. There was really only one other candidate, very well qualified, even if in the context of the meeting she finally had to matter less for herself than as a locus for principled opposition to the local favorite. At last we voted. A tie, with two abstentions. Another vote. Another tie, with no abstentions. We were out of time and one vote short of the absolute majority department rules stipulated. A special vote was quickly announced two days hence, ballots to be cast in a box on the department secretary's desk.

What story of the department had transpired to this point? In one respect, it is a narrative having to do with the enormous recent increase in temporary, part-time faculty. Whatever principles of sociality obtain, it is difficult to ignore adjuncts at the departmental coffeepot. One of the cruelest academic stories I know is of an "adjunct" who thought she was on friendly terms with a permanent member until he said one day, "I really don't want to talk to you because adjuncts are always leaving." Tenured people, in my experience, are capable of talking more frankly to those less secure than to their own colleagues (in large departments, this includes grad students), and often fight ferociously for non-tenured friends, if a spot on the tenure track opens up. In this particular election, the spot had been created by the simple procedure of adding the local favorite to the three already selected by the search committee.

In terms of my emphasis, her addition more sharply reformulated the conflict between two quite separate visions: the department as a professional organization and a social one. Indeed, given the way a department such as my own is inscribed in the institutional hierarchy of American higher education, this conflict is inescapable. Supporters of the local favorite might not agree, of course. Undoubtedly supporters of the local favorite never agree—rightly

or wrongly—that the person is finally being considered solely for
social reasons, and of course this may not always be the case, even
if in departments such as mine it is almost guaranteed to be so.
More interesting, though, is the fact that social reasons must remain unenunciated, even among a group of people for whom they
are decisive.

Of course in one sense this is as it should be. Few departments
labor without the illusion that new members are chosen on the
basis of criteria safely removed from the conviction that certain
people are just not "one of us," as I recall a colleague blurting out
years ago during another meeting. In another sense, however, the
repression of the social exacts a terrible cost, because even a candidate not worth the name must be publicly accountable as a good
teacher, a sound scholar, or a knowledgeable theorist. There is no
other official vocabulary. Thus, the moment of the social imperative
always marks any department's division from itself. It shouldn't
ever happen from a strict professional vantage that the department
would be caught in the throes of its affection for a local candidate.
My guess is that it happens all the time—everywhere.

Clarion's difference from Harvard or Duke lies in the fact that
departments at these distinguished institutions don't have to face
this division, over and over again. There, local favorites are exceptions—if not (one trusts) exceptional. Hence, for example, Harvard's
famous dean, Henry Rosovsky, is quite clear: Harvard staffs its
departments according to who is the best in the world in any field.[2]
It is left to most other universities to manage their own versions
of this lofty standard. The official conception of the department
handed down to them by the dynamic, ambitious research model
ignores how few can approximate it and disdains any other idea,
especially a social one. To Rosovsky, the social remains a suspect,
if not degraded, realm of "petty jealousy." Or, to take another more
recent example, the social has to be almost ignored—if not entirely
unlamented—in David Dambrosch's account of the sovereign figure
of the individual scholar, one who works alone and belongs to the
department only in the most nominal fashion.

Clarion's local favorites, on the other hand, are not exceptional
because the department is not in place to define itself exclusively
as a disciplinary entity. Local favorites are instead a constitutive
feature of our departmental composition. The pain is that each
time we elect someone into the department, the decisive role of
social pressures cannot be admitted—although, each time, it must
somehow be assessed. Although the results haven't always been

unhappy for the English department, the process never transpires without bitterness, resentment, and renewed factionalism. To put the ultimate consequence still more crudely: the department finally *is* this division between the professional and the social.

Granted, few will dispute our authority to teach topic sentences, the Pearl poet, and slave narratives—although many members were alarmed a few years ago when, at one of those meetings convened so that the administration could "engage in dialogue," the new dean instructed the department to have a proposed position in medieval literature reborn as one in cultural studies so that we would have a better chance to consider minority candidates. Nevertheless, as a department we are not ultimately a group of professionals who "profess" such subjects as much as a group of individuals who have to relate to each other, day by day, in terms of them.

Why write of all this specifically? I was enjoined not to. Let me begin to answer this question by reformulating it: why be enjoined not to? And then to pose a further question: whose interests are being served by everybody being so enjoined? Those of the department, considered as a family? Gordon Hutner refers to "the disguised dream of a nuclear family that haunts every department meeting ever called" (76). But a chair is not a father, nor do the rest of the members of a department bond or dispute among themselves as siblings. My department was more familial when I joined it over twenty–five years ago, and immediately fell under the tyranny of an old chair whom just about everyone feared, hated, and loved to tell incredible stories about. I felt enlisted into a Freudian Band of Brothers (there were only two women) before the parricidal deed had been done. It never was, though. Our father's end came rather lamely and sadly. He just crept away like the old bachelor he was, and we children were left without any clear image of how to reproduce his power.

The peculiar position of any chair cannot be put better than Ohmann: "The chairman's power comes from the multiversity in which departments find themselves, and it is necessary because decisions have to pass back and forth between a managerial and a professional setting" (218). There is a sense in which a chair is structurally compromised. At once representative of the "remotest arm" of the administration (as Ohmann goes on to explain) and the inner recesses of the department, it's often not clear in whose name a chair speaks. Whether or not enjoining us not to speak outside was intended by the chair simply to encourage discussion, discussion was in fact discouragingly brief and restrained. Energies at variance with fictions of professionalism were free to continue, and to issue their own challenge in terms of the upcoming vote. Everybody knew what seethed beneath the rules. In whose name, finally, were we being asked to forget?

Worst of all, it seemed to me we were being asked this day to make over our own departmental interests, such as they could be made manifest, in the image of the institution. Of course in many ways the interests of the part and the whole are identical; one could even claim that a department *has* no interests apart from the larger ones of its institution.[3] What I want to claim myself is that the category of the social marks the limits of mutual interest. The administration can only be concerned about the members of a department getting along with each other insofar as its administrative functioning is threatened. The members themselves, on the other hand, not only know far more intimately how this functioning is dependent upon getting along; they know how sometimes sheer getting along is more important—bureaucratic license or disciplinary integrity be damned. This vote was one such time. Once again, the English department had to decide on its own reason for being.

I've failed to emphasize how excited I'd grown at the prospect. "All bets are off," somebody said. Others knew for how many years all bets had been settled and all important decisions based on the same two factions. Could these factions have at last dissipated, as rumored? Only in the last couple of years had a significant number of new people come into the department. "It's a new department now," people had taken to exclaiming, always with a certain wonderment. Everybody sensed that no vote so much this one over hiring a local favorite would reveal how new the department really had become. Before the meeting, I even thought of my old retired colleague, and how he used to relish the infrequent times when business as usual was going to fail. "God, how I love chaos, Terry. It's all we can hope for."

Perhaps those ready to vote for the local favorite were in thrall of similar energies. Ohmann begins his chapter on English departments by citing Shaw's aphorism about all professions as conspiracies against the laity, and then compares English departments to "the conspirators' cell groups" (209). He means the conspiracy to be directed at the public. What about a conspiracy directed at the department's own disciplinary self-image, as dictated by the public? Maybe from the outside it doesn't make sense why a department would settle for mediocrity, familiarity, and other unworthy

professional goals, each heedless of the official imperative for
unremiting innovation in all things. (The number of untold departmental narratives about the consequences of forced compliance to
affirmative action guidelines must be legion.) From the inside,
however, where these sorts of things can be casually misrepresented, where inertia sometimes feels sweet, and where few care to
hear about new knives, much less "cutting edges," it can be, I'm
convinced, deeply satisfying to bond once more against the vast,
threatening outside, and to hell with administrative directives about
multiculturalism, disciplinary ones about the latest theory from
Duke, or political ones about outcomes' assessments.

Exactly what *unites* a group? At root, certain proscribed ways
of negotiating with the outside so that the group can perpetuate its
identity. The peculiar groups that are academic departments have
their respective identities so consummately rationalized, on the
other hand, that a species of fatigued formality quite typically transpires with respect to the outside. Donald Barthelme has a lovely
story, "The New Member," about this operation. Members of an
unnamed committee begin their meeting by taking note of a man
looking in from outside a window. Immediately the meeting comes
to be about the group's fascination with this man, or perhaps rather
its inability to direct its attention to the "pressing items" of the
agenda. The only item they really get to is "the Worth girl." One
man moves she be hit by a car. Another woman moves that the
Worth girl fall in love with the man outside. Eventually all agree
to invite him in, whereupon he states, no, he has no grievance, he
just wants to " 'be with somebody' " (184). The committee understands. A motion is soon forthcoming to make the man a member.
The motion passes easily. The man sits down and begins to an-
nounce, among other things, that everyone has to wear overalls; no
one can wear nose rings; and gatherings of one or more persons are
prohibited.

What Barthelme presents is an exquisitely incoherent dance of
social energy, collapsed into formalism. The old members need a
new member not so much to change the rules as to reinvigorate
themselves in relation to each other. (This, in turn, is the point of
having rules.) I suppose the need arises in any group grown idle
about its energies. Was this the case in my own department at the
time of the vote for its own new member? Perhaps there are times
in the history of a group when only a new member can reveal how
old everybody is. My truest objection to the local favorite was that
she wasn't new. Indeed, so well integrated into the department was

she (and not only because of her relationship to one of its most powerful members), that you could hardly see around her. Consequently, a vote against her appeared to me as a vote for the Outside itself. What story could a department tell itself that was willing to renounce its need for an outside?

Of course there are always plenty of official narratives to be constructed each year for versions of outsides. In large part, even the day-to-day business of a department consists in its mutual commitment to the necessity for such narratives. Everybody has to write teaching observations on everybody else according to the bargaining agreement, committees have to report at meetings to the department as a whole, the chair has to draw up curriculum and pedagogical stories for the administration to hear—to mention these only. (Last year much departmental time was invested in a grand narrative called the NCATE report, required each ten years for certification on the national level. I had to ask the chair what the letters stood for, and she had to ask somebody else.) But all these narratives are really registers of a deeper, if wider, interiority whereby a department simultaneously recreates an institution and is recreated by it. Hiring raises the possibility of another story.

But what story? Normally in most departments, I suppose, the plot lines hardly get established as something very different. Any recruitment remains embedded in the institution. It's still conducted along disciplinary lines—even if during the past decade recruitment is now subject wholly to being initiated or terminated according to affirmative action guidelines. Yet a new member might not fit—or might fit in unusually provocative ways. A group has every right to be excited at the prospect. I couldn't help but sit amid mine the afternoon of the vote and wonder precisely how I belonged myself. I had once been friends of a sort with the local favorite, for example. What sense did this make now, much less the reasons why we were no longer friends? I knew of a position in another department where a friend of mine was the local but not, evidently, the favorite. How different was this man's situation? How different is any department from another? Does every departmental narrative have to refract into its most individual, personal plot lines? Was my own lack of sympathy to the social currents energizing our favorite merely because, in the end, I didn't feel part of them— whether as a colleague or as a scholar, it made no real differece?

One can be a member of a larger department (not to say a more prestigious one), and far more easily remain apart, I think, from the pressure of such questions. Hence, for example, in his recent memoir Frank Lentricchia can write as follows: "I teach English at a distinguished university, which is like all English departments I have known or heard about, we have virtually nothing in common, not even literature" (11). Lentricchia can be forgiven for being unable to broaden his social, if not discursive, base. The circumstances in which most academics labor, however, are far more unforgiving. An old friend likes to recall the first job of her and her husband at one of the best small liberal arts schools in the country. Early in the year, they attended a concert. A couple from his department sat next to them. At intermission, the man confessed to being bored and suggested they all retire to his house for a drink. My friend and her husband looked at each other. Alas, they demurred. The story of how he lost his job over this incident is too intricate (and unbelievable) to tell. "We should have known better," my friend concludes. True. Embedded within the professionalized departmental narrative we should all know better. The basic point of this latter narrative, however, is that what we would know should remain uncontaminated by the debased social realm of the anecdotal, which is irrelevant to the discipline.

For a time in a foreign country I taught with a man who came from a junior college in the South. "We like each other," he used to say of his department, "we do lots of things together." Periodically I asked him to repeat how collectively happy everybody was, so unbelievable did it seem to me. Could it only happen in a junior college, consigned to a lowly position in academic ranking? (Or else it could only happen long ago, and then probably only through the efforts of an exuberant chair; see Spilka, who offers the sort of richly ancedotal account that *College English* would not very likely publish today, when we might be presumed to know better, about the profession, if not ourselves.) One admits how much sociality matters (because research does not) only very grudgingly. More recently at a conference I met a woman from another junior college. I asked her how many courses she taught. She said five. "It's all right, we have fun together. We don't have the pressures you do because we don't have any 'airs.' "

One could hazard an axiom: the more institutionally low, the more departmentally happy. And yet people will not necessarily like each other because they have only themselves or lack some official basis on which to compete; for one thing, there will always have to be elections to hire new members. The following formulation seems better: the more illusions (warranted or not) about scholarship, the less acknowledgement about the significance of sociality.

Therefore, most departments regularly purchase the first at the expense of the second—as no one will have to remind the dour Lentricchia (or even the misunderstood Stanley Fish, his former chairman). Alas, though, groups of people need occasions in order to be revealed to themselves as groups, if not to experience themselves in this way. My department (as opposed to its factions) has always been poor in such occasions. I stopped going to the few sporadic ones, including the Christmas party some years ago when a drunken colleague arrived late and proceeded to vomit on her hostess's rug. Everyone agreed afterwards that the event was at least a lot more fun than anything that ever happens at a department meeting.

2.

After such incoherence, what story? Can the real one about any department be told as merely how someone in the group relates to the others? Or is the deeper narrative instead the recurrent hope, manifest in a number of different ways, and only fitfully collective, that one day a new member will come along to make good all the unused, stale, or disvalued social possibilities? Granted, such concerns about a department could not be more different than, say, those of James Phelan, when he laments the Duke phenomenon of securing preeminence by hiring away top people and speaks of the necessity for a "better model." It involves "people with diverse interests and expertise who share more fundamental beliefs about education, critical discourse, and inquiry" (196). The telling thing to me is that Phelan is apparently under no pressure to line up this wish over against the disturbing moment when he meets a colleague and they just "have a good talk," much to Phelan's amazement that such a thing so rarely happens (48).

Such things probably happen more often in my own department, because we're not subject to the research demands of Phelan's (which is the first thing he and his colleague begin to talk about). "How is your research going?" is not, after all, a question designed to elicit profound human contact. Indeed, it could easily be argued that the purpose of an academic department is to inhibit such contact, as meetings transpire over each year's budget; each semester's course schedule; and the constitution of standing and ad hoc committees. These are almost exclusively the terms in which Joel Colton discusses "The Role of the Department in the Groves of Academe" in *The Academic Handbook*. It is not his concern if someone refuses to

post office hours, if nobody wants to chair the evaluation committee, or if there simply are no curricular dreams to be dreamed this
year.[4] Colton begins by noting the common wisdom once expressed
by a popular faculty member, speaking to students and extolling
the virtues of an academic career. He is asked if there are any
disadvantages. "Yes," the professor replies, "the colleagues in one's
own department" (261). In such a context, how not to long for
Phelan's notion of a department?

There are two basic reasons why not. First, Phelan's vision is
simply false. People in an academic department are defined in terms
of their commitment to their discipline, not each other. Hence they
are academics in the first place (and only committed to each other
in some other way after the fact). Hence also, Phelan himself rarely
gets together with any of his colleagues in order to share fundamental beliefs. The Ohio State English department may have fewer
parties than the Clarion English department. He mentions only a
few people who have his same intellectual interests. What Phelan
does he does alone. There really *is* no stable structural analogy for
how his real activity participates in the larger life of his department, especially insofar as the activity not only consists of solitary
worrying—about his classes, giving papers, and publishing a book—
but about aspiring to join another department (eventually his own
chair has to be told), albeit as the occupant of an endowed chair.

Second, Phelan's vision lacks political nuance. We don't need
better models of departments. We need better fictions. The reason
we don't get them is because of institutional hierarchy. An institution such as Ohio State simply transmits the organizing logic of
elite institutions, founded on a research imperative whereby each
member of a department is comprehended not as a social being but
as a scholar who works alone. (Again, Demrosch is eloquent on this
point.) Phelan sentimentalizes community not only because he lacks
it but because he isn't mandated to have any. Of course nobody else
is either. Yet what this means in practice is that large, doctoral
universities effectively set the terms anyway. Compare to Phelan
the Penn State professor in a letter to the *Chronicle of Higher
Education* about how my university is different from his: "There is
a kind of unity of mission on that campus. The faculty is not com-
posed of independent scholarly entrepreneurs. It is more united
than the diverse faculty at our cumbersome multiversity" (B3).
Penn State, in other words, gets to say what Clarion is, and not
vice versa. Consigned to an "organic" realm, Clarion speaks only to
itself and for itself. No wonder it opts for local favorites.

Let me enlarge on this last point by citing a remark from a recent article of Gerald Graff's. He has been emphasizing how disabled academics are from explaining what they do to anybody else by the fact that they teach in isolation from each other. One problem that follows: even students are excluded from a larger conversation and prevented from understanding the intellectual allegiances or identities of their professors. " 'You call yourself a Marxist-feminist, but you sound like just a bourgeois liberal to me.' This contesting of identifications takes place frequently at our academic conferences but rarely in our classrooms" ("Academic Writing," 16).[5] More to my purpose, such contesting rarely takes place in our halls, or our coffee lounges, or our department meetings. Undoubtedly it should. But it doesn't—and instead conferences seem to proliferate especially at the regional or even local level. Could this be because departments have become more constricted? What is a haplessly socialized member of one to do, for all manner of invigoration, but go to a conference? Graff's line appears scarcely conceivable anywhere else. Therefore, the best, most searching and consoling stories available to the profession at the present time may no longer be the product of departments, but of conferences.

Meanwhile, we fail to get better fictions about departments because the focus for an academic discipline continues to be lodged at the departmental level. This serves the interests of research institutions who in fact secure their preeminence by a disciplinary organization based on linkages among departments rather than membership in any one. (Berkeley hires from Yale and vice versa. It is no surprise that Pehlan, from Chicago, once came in second at Berkeley. He still makes all his important professional moves at conferences, and from there emerge all his candid conversations.) One way this organization consolidates itself is precisely through conferences; they're expensive to attend, feature papers expressive of the latest fashions, and encourage in all sorts of ways the maintenance of institutional boundaries based on status. (To be from a place no one has heard of seldom elicits conversation at the cash bar.) However, more conferences—even, now, organized by universities which enjoy little status—don't necessarily open up the possibilities for who gets to deliver papers at the MLA or the English Institute (even if they do offer opportunities for recuperating lost, idle, or stagnant sociality back home).[6] English may not be the only discipline to be fast approaching a time when more conferences only mean more people in attendance meeting still more people, who used to be the people who stayed home and didn't go to conferences.

Perhaps the social actuality of a department may finally not be intelligible except in terms either larger or smaller than those of the disciplinary or administrative unit. Most may never experience themselves in larger terms. Most may not want to. (At any conference one is guaranteed to hear about these.) What difference does it make to such a department to be mindful of another whose whole identity is founded upon easy access to a wider professional world? Academic departments at the majority of universities throughout the United States function as small, intricate units only nominally related to this world. Members in these departments may read about it. Their universities lack the resources to enable them to contribute to it; instead, only highly localized versions of the values of the great world are possible. At one point in Molly Hite's *Class Porn*, the heroine hears a tenured member exclaim about another man on their committee that he's a "great guy," and then she thinks as follows: "It's one of the conventions of our committee that when you mention the name of somebody on it you're supposed to be overcome with emotion. The emotions differ hierarchically, of course. When my name is mentioned, for instance, presumably everybody laughs" (145). She's just a lowly lecturer without her dissertation finished. People who lack a Ph.D. lack even the recognition of another university.

Hite's amusing novel is not an example of what I mean by a better fiction about departmental life. For one thing, Eleanor Nyland renounces it by the end. Renunciation happens recurrently in academic novels—and, if it doesn't, academic life has been sorely tested, usually by erotic horizons heretofore unimagined. (But this may be changing; see Bagley.) Stories that trace the precise lineaments of a department's own narrow bounds in order to embrace them are, on the other hand, far more rare, harsh, and precious. I think of them as fictions of friendship. Friendship really doesn't have anything to do with departments at all, and may more often function in them as yet another threat to their social coherence; even friends, as in my own late instance, have to vote.[7] Nevertheless, to friends, the sheer *conspiracy* of professional life is eased. Friendship is probably the best, most humanizing possibility available to most of us in departments, because it promises the story neither of structure nor hierarchy, although inescapably implicated in each.

Let me conclude this chapter with one of the finest academic fictions I know: Bernard Malamud's "Rembrandt's Hat." Arkin, an art historian, is a dozen years younger than Rubin, a sculptor, at the New York art school where both teach. They're friendly, but not friends. They become enemies after the day when Arkin admiringly compares one of Rubin's many odd hats to one from a middle-aged self-portrait of Rembrandt. After that, Rubin ceases to wear the hat and appears to Arkin to be avoiding him. Months pass. One day Arkin happens into Rubin's studio. There's really only one piece that he likes. Another day, while showing some slides, he sees that the hat Rubin wore months earlier more resembled that of a cook at a diner than Rembrandt's. Later he returns to the sculptor's studio, congratulates him on the fine piece, and apologizes for mixing up the hats so long ago. Rubin accepts the apology, but the two men become no more than cordial to each other. Once, Arkin spots Rubin regarding himself in the bathroom mirror in a white cap that now really does appear to resemble Rembrandt's hat.

What seems to me especially beautiful about this story is how the air of a very peculiar human contact—close, fragile, intolerably slight and painfully interiorized—lifts off its plot. Where else but in an academic department could Rubin have taken the exact kind of offense he does, and who else but an academic such as Arkin could have expressed it with such apparent casualness? There are departments in which people teach together for decades and yet fail to achieve as much clarification of their mutual feelings for each other as Malamud's narrative provides his two characters. How necessary is it to us for others to tell us who we are? Or are we content to think we know already? In the end, the distinctive thing about the stories possible in any department, unlike those in a marriage, may be that they must remain partial, blunted, baffled, or just silenced. Beyond the estimidable professional reasons (as well as the obvious danger of litigation), I'm not sure why this should be so—unless there are embodied in academic attire such depths of self-regard that no disciplinary formation, no administrative directive, and no social group can be divised to organize, address, or confront them.

3.

About the department vote: when the third round was counted, two days later, the local favorite was defeated, 11–9. One member continued to abstain. There was speculation. Few really knew why he did. Another member switched his or her vote. More speculation. No one could be absolutely certain who. The new member returned her signed contract in time to permit the fact to be announced at the last meeting of the semester. No expression of opinion was heard.

CHAPTER THREE

வ்‌

The Politics of
Institutional Affiliation

Sessions at professional conventions, unlike department meetings, are occasions for lots of talk. You find one of the hotel's conference rooms, sit down, and begin to imagine if a paper about to be delivered by one of three people sitting up front behind a table with a pitcher of water on it will live up to its promising title. Or perhaps, as everyone settles among the rows of chairs, you strike up a conversation if there's somebody sitting next to you. There's an air in the room combining the careful solemnity prior to a religious service with the studied casualness before a sit-down dinner. You try to chat more breezily than you normally would with a colleague back home.

Once at the annual national meeting the Modern Language Association (MLA)—by far the largest organization in the profession—I chanced to speak with a man for nearly a minute before we each suddenly realized that we had known each other as undergraduates. We had failed to stare first at our respective badges. Arguably much of what's most vital at a conference has very little to do with the official agenda. In this respect, sessions again differ from department meetings (though not so much religious services), where there is only the agenda, and it can't be questioned, whatever is said about it—or anything else, either before or after the meeting.

The most compelling thing for me at a recent MLA meeting in Chicago had nothing to do with the program. Or rather—especially after having written on attending the MLA to find I could only extricate with great difficulty the not-MLA from the MLA—I should

55

say that the most compelling thing was something the program has nothing to do with. (See Caesar, *Conspiring*.) Yet, it is very much to my point that this something should be representative of a whole host of things that the MLA supposes itself to have very much to do with: political agency, for example, or marginality and heterogeneity. How could what's at stake in the incident I want to relate have so far eluded professional consideration? This is the question I want to raise, and therefore this chapter will be about the political importance of institutional affiliation.

Before proceeding further, a disclaimer: I have no direct experience with either of the conventions of the other two major professional organizations in English: the NCTE (National Council of Teachers of English) and the CCCC (Conference on College Composition and Communication). People who have such experience assure me that the atmosphere at both is not nearly so politically fraught and stratified as at the MLA. Sessions are organized differently, with more round-table discussion sections. There are far more opportunities for speakers from second-rate schools. So-called independent scholars (without any institutional affiliation) are more prominent. They are even *high-school teachers* about. What to say? Maybe so. But I'm inclined to feel unconvinced, or at least to suspect that the counter-narrative each of these organizations provides to the MLA begins with a presumed banishing of hierarchy that only proceeds to get reconstituted in different ways.

One way is revealed, for example, by a special insert, "Forum," in the middle of a recent issue of the important journal, *College Composition and Communication*. Granted, that these pages appear at all is remarkable; one could not likely imagine just an insert in the pages of *PMLA*.[1] The first piece celebrates a workshop held at the last CCCC on collective bargaining and coalition-building to combat the nontenured future of academic employment. The last piece is an "Adjunct Faculty Manifesto," which concludes with a ringing cry for collective action over such issues as job security, fair compensation, and professional support. This is all well and good, and another example of the more typical discourse to be found at these other two organizations than at the MLA. (Although not if Cary Nelson has any say in it; see his *Manifesto* for a wide-ranging critique of the organization.) But what relation does this discourse have with that of the first article in the same issue, which studies the response of two different writing programs at two different campuses to the state system president's call to remove remedial courses from all campuses? These two campuses are given pseudnonymous names.[2] Why can't they be directly named? The following chapter examines the consequences.

1.

One of the first Chicago sessions I attended featured four papers, plus a respondent. Clearly it was going to have to be one of those panels where each speaker has been cautioned to take no more than twelve minutes. The first speaker held forth for slightly over twenty. Before the second could begin, a man stood up from a back row, protested that the first speaker had taken "ten more minutes than he should have," opined that he had said "many silly things," and demanded to know "if I'm going to be permitted to ask a question or two." The session chair provided a fair imitation of poise as he replied that the appropriate "time for questions" will only be after all the papers have been read.

The next speaker took nearly twenty-five minutes. (I checked my watch.) The third expired in no less than twenty-two minutes. I didn't time the fourth, who amazed all by flourishing several concluding pages she assured us she would no longer read and thereby finished in something suspiciously close to twelve minutes. The respondent (who liked the last paper best) took less than ten. By this time the session, which had begun late, was nearly fifteen minutes over its scheduled time period.

Up jumped the man who had earlier protested. "Am I permitted to read my own paper?" Murmurs could be heard in the audience. "I respectfully request to be allowed to deliver a paper at this session next year." How could embarrassment not have been felt? "I want to know what the system is that permitted these people to be chosen." Outrage? The chair said nothing. "I know no one in this room supports me," continued the protestor about next year's possible paper, "but may I have one second?" None was forthcoming. "I want to have my views heard." No one asked him to clarify what they were. Eventually he sat down.

There were a couple of desultory questions before the session adjourned. The protestor—just to continue to call him this—didn't leave as hurriedly as one might have expected. He did leave before I could spot where he was from, although not before he spoke to a man at the door who was conversing with another man. All I could catch of the reply was, "Yes, but it doesn't work that way," uttered with a nicely flicked contempt—and then I remembered that before the session changed rooms, I had chanced to sit behind this man and overhear his enthusiastic description to someone else about the two books, no less, that he was editing.

Later, downstairs in the hotel lobby, I sat among a group which included three of the session's speakers. Nobody mentioned the protestor. I wanted to. I didn't, even after being astonished at one point to look up and see him (alone) walk by my chair. It was almost possible to make out his badge. I wanted to speak to him, but he was gone before I could decide exactly what to say. Would the occasion present itself again? I immediately hoped so. You never quite know whom you're going to meet at an annual gathering over well over 10,000 people, or when. But the man was never again to be seen during the course of the next two days.

To a discipline more than smitten by margins of all sorts, his behavior at the session could not be more illuminating of some of its most central practices. One of them is the fact that sessions are for speakers, not listeners. At the MLA, all in the audience are duly expected to sit quietly while still another session chair, having flourished "the period for discussion," proceeds to do nothing if each speaker systematically uses up too much time. What do they do at the NCTE? Ms. Mentor suggests a variety of desperate measures, ranging from passing a notecard to putting handcream on your hands. (See Tate, 49.) It must be admitted: to be able to read a paper is an honor. To read a paper is to be given a license to perform. The license, in turn, is certified by the unspoken values of the very profession, whereby production is simply more important than consumption. The MLA needs its annual thousands. But from the perspective of the sessions to which they throng, the convention is not for most of them, and instead for those few to whom the rest come to hear. Speakers may have to be mindful of constraints, but finally they can take the time they need, and take it from their hearers, who have no voice and only nominal status.

Of course it could be claimed that my distinction is too sharp. The audience doesn't require a voice, or rather merely agrees to have it transformed on the occasion of a session into that of some others, whom the audience is pleased to attend as if witnessing its own exteriorized, esteemed self. (See Goffman's fine essay, "The Lecture," in *Forms*.) Therefore, listening is not at all the passive, unproductive activity it might first appear to be. Everybody knows its value. (Except perhaps those who avoid the MLA.) Indeed, its value doesn't have to be mentioned, even if there is a certain division within it, as illustrated by the prototypical speaker who, hav-

ing finished, "can begin to enjoy the convention now that my paper
is over."

The protestor at my session, however, mocked this sort of logic.
He wanted to *speak*—immediately. Worse, he had "views," considerably at variance with those which had already been formally
articulated. Ideally, what should he have been told? To wait for a
discussion period, when what he feared was that this period was
only going to be progressively de-realized? To understand that he
was in attendance as a member of a group, which was consolidated
not only because of its interests but its values? Should he have
been instructed specifically on one of these: it is far more significant
for any speaker to take ten minutes or more of allotted time than
for any listener to take so much as one minute to object in any
way? But eventually, it seems to me, we reach a harsher truth.
This man could ultimately only be told one thing: he doesn't belong
at the MLA in the first place. How can you have any business at
all at the MLA if you don't know when to *sit still*?

The easiest reading of the protestor's behavior is that he was
the very embodiment of a professional scandal: someone who's never
been to an MLA. At least it's a scandal from the point of view of the
Modern Language Association, and no matter that in every English
department throughout the country, doubtlessly including those with
prominent members at every convention, there are people who don't
belong to the association and never go to the convention. Granting
the scandal, there could well be claimed an even harsher truth about
the man: he doesn't belong in the profession at all. Has anyone ever
proposed the following question for a special session: *do* you belong
in the profession if you are not a member of the MLA? Since one
would have to be a member in order to attend such a session, and
certainly to deliver a paper, the question is probably self-defeating.

Nonetheless, if you don't know how to act at the MLA convention (or lack the discretion to keep your mouth shut if you don't),
then how should "the profession" be characterized in your case?
How should you be characterized in terms of it? If you need to be
told that no one session continues with the same subject from one
year to the next, then what might constitute some still more el-
ementary, zero degree of professional knowledge? Some intelligence
concerning the fact of scholarly eminence; the importance of personal associations; and the power of institutional affiliation? But
how can you abide in the profession—forget the MLA—apart from
such knowledge about such things?[3] I doubt if anybody has to be
told about them at the NCTE or CCCC.

After such knowledge, what forgiveness? From a properly professional point of view, should the protestor's action not be judged to be unforgivable? The most compelling thing about him is not so much that he didn't "know enough" about "how things work." So utterly heedless of all he did or didn't know, he suggests that we, by contrast, know too much. What the man at the door who spoke to him, for example, apparently knew was that he's beneath contempt. But why? Because he had no power? Or because he just didn't know how to get it, and so had to behave too crudely in his desire to do so?

The rest of us remain who we are, presumably, because we either have power or we don't; if we don't, then we make the best of it; attend to those who do; take what we can; and do with it what we will back home. And insofar as what *sort* of power is concerned—professional, disciplinary, discursive, political, racial, and so on—we can all at least agree to convene, in large part, around this very question. What the protestor at my session reveals, though, is that there remains all the while a far more literal, even brutal operation going on in the very organization and disposition of the convening. The great majority of those who come together are consigned to the same position; are expected to embrace the same standard of behavior; are presumed to adhere to the same unspoken values over what transpires at a representative session; and are expected to stay respectful about the dynamics of what the badge of each one proclaims: institutional affiliation.

Does it matter in some specific way where the protestor was from? My feeling is that it does. But in any case the scandal is that it didn't appear to matter *to him*. All the session speakers may not have been from what are normally taken to be first-rate universities, but each one was from somewhere more widely known than I suppose his institution to be. Since I never learned, there abides a kind of lovely institutional aporia in my experience. This seems to me just as it should be, and it follows, I believe, from the fact that most people attending the MLA that year or next year could select—whatever the discriminations that could be variously made among the institutions in the following list—the one institution that no one would take as first-rate: Yale, Northwestern, Pittsburgh, Michigan, Duke, Harvard, Toronto, CCNY, Irvine, Kalamazoo College, Cornell.

I compile the list from the contributors to *Profession 90*, the annual periodical sponsored by the MLA. It's interesting to compare these institutions to the ones represented by the few pages of "Forum" letters in the magazine. The institutions from which these

letters most typically come are not, in turn, the same as those of
the contributors to any issue of *PMLA* itself. Finally, the institutional mechanics at MLA convention sessions conform well enough
to this same profile: though every single paper is not read by someone from a first-rate institution, most are. How many, in turn, are
heard by people from Kalamazoo or the institution where the protestor is from? At such places, papers of comparable learning or
sophistication would be far less likely to be produced, even if they
were somehow institutionally empowered to be considered for some
session, which they aren't.

Why has this obvious state of affairs gone unremarked upon?
Of course, this is not entirely the case. Just to stay within the
framwork of the Modern Language Association, consider, for example, a recent letter by Samuel Schuman in response to a *PMLA*
Forum on the Teaching of Literature. Schuman notes that all the
authors but one (who is from Westchester Community College), are
from research universities. Nothing unusual here, he continues,
"but in this particular case, the omission [of liberal arts colleges or
regional comprehensive universities] seems embarrassing, reveal-
ing, even silly. . . . It would have been wise to have included us in
this discussion" (441). Why were institutions such as Schuman's
(who teaches at a branch campus of the University of Minnesota)
not included?

Schuman knows the answer. The answer is simply: the very
question is too obvious. Everybody knows (presumably) there are
"major research institutions" in which professors have teaching
loads of two or three courses a year rather than seven or eight, or
where they expect regular leaves or release time and enjoy generous administrative support for research or conference expenses,
while generally benefiting from a myriad of enabling conditions
(graduate students to do research, secretaries to type the papers)
in order to secure possession of the most productive edge of the
discipline. Yet, if the theory so prominent at the MLA for well over
a decade now has offered anything, it's a provocation to weigh the
persistance of hierarchies in any sort of discourse and to consider
the fact that knowledge is motivated by desires for power and
authority. What is obvious to some *is* obvious, that is, because it's
not obvious to others (who must appear, as Schuman writes, above,
"curmudgeonly, out of fashion, irrelevant," in pointing this out).
Indeed, it is my own conviction that what "everybody knows" about
the politics of institutional affiliation in the profession has scarcely
begun to be articulated, and publicly barely at all.

Such silence may be one explanation for my protestor; it is as if in his very heedlessness he marks the space occupied by vast numbers of MLA members (to imagine these only) who really know very little about how anything "works," because such knowledge is enunciated elsewhere, where it continues to be the property of exclusive institutional communities. Moreover, this knowledge is appropriated and consolidated on the basis of the ignorance of those who do not belong to these communities, as eager to join as many who are excluded from them might be. How widely is it supposed to be known—by anyone—that most MLA sessions are the result of prior arrangement among the principals? Of course this state of affairs is not a happy one. It is especially unhappy if it can be comprehended as, arguably, the most fundamental structural feature of the profession. Nobody likes to consider the hegemony of first-rate universities or even to characterize the subjugated status of second-rate ones.

2.

I left Chicago more convinced than ever that the very discourse of profession has at last come to be affected by hierarchy—not openly (would this eventually result in an MLA convention where the badges had only the names of individuals and not institutions?), but in the displaced form of the ubiquitous concerns of race, class, and gender. Subsequent years have only cemented the displacement. Consider, for example, the following commentary by a most representative feminist critic about an equally typical post-colonial (the critic's own category is "deterritorialized") text, by a Carribean woman: "Cliff constitutes a kind of collective history based on gender as well as on race and class. It is a history of women who are threatened variously and complexly by forces ranging from an American drug company to the masculinist proponents of certain nationalist liberation struggles. This kind of epistemological shift helps to enact a politics of identity that is flexible enough to encompass the ironies and contradictions of the modern world system" (Kaplan, 197).

In other words, Cliff's identity is *productive*. Her credentials as a victim are impeccable, and her own discursive register of them participates in the most advanced species of "feminist poetics," founded on race and class. Indeed, these days, almost anyone, man or woman, can expect to get into print with the sort of thing represented (to take another example) by Shirley Geok-Lin Lim. She recalls how she once cherished *The Art of Versification and the Technicalities of Poetry*, by one R. F. Brewer, and now realizes how the precious text "unweighted the imperialism in English poetry." The English themselves had to learn the English language, not only twelve year-old girls growing up in Malacca. English poetry was "socially constructed" (193). Just so, all the moves of race, class, and gender at conferences or in journals these days are designed to reveal the socio-political constructedness of everything, which is, in turn, one reason why political correctness has become such an intractable problem.[4]

In stark contrast, institutional identity is static and unitary. It carries no principle of conversion into race, gender, or class, and it lacks some ideological rationale for why such a principle should be mentioned at all. Either you teach at Cornell or you don't, we might say. If you do, you see yourself in terms of Yale or Rutgers. If you don't, then you read articles or hear papers by people from Cornell while your institution's basketball team plays with Glenville State or Mount St. Mary College and you wish you could at least meet someone from Rutgers at the departmental coffee pot. There (at least in theory) you could talk about how ironic or awful it is that the margins of organizations and discourses everywhere are occupied by politically subordinated groups.

Of course all sorts of distinctions and qualifications need to be made regarding the above displacement. For example, there are undoubtedly people at Cornell who think Rutgers is second-rate (and probably even vice-versa). All such discriminations are precisely my point. There is an acute, subtle, elusive politics to institutional affiliation which is far from static, and needs to be continually renegotiated, even by those who set the terms. For instance, someone from Kalamazoo College can conceivably get published in *Profession 90*—or its editors can deem it necessary that such an institution have some representation.[5] Even back at the MLA itself, the sheer impossibility of changing jobs or the vast decrease in advertising new ones by now spills over from halls at each year's Mariott or the Hyatt and into the session rooms, in the form of occasional sessions on such topics as "MLAienation" (to cite just one from Toronto a couple of years ago). How can one adequately describe the effect of such pressures, not to say attribute them all to a structure of institutional hierarchy, on the model of a structure of colonialism or phallocentrism?

Furthermore, how can one adequately describe excluded energies when they no longer feel marginal—if only because the discourse of what is centrally expressed continues to be certified by agendas that purport to represent the subversive; the politically neglected; the "untotalizable"; the somehow delegitimized? Let me state what I'm suggesting as bluntly as I can: part of the reason race, gender, and class have become such overwhelming professional concerns is because the politics of institutional affiliation within the profession have not. Instead, these politics have functioned as a mute background against which wider, more abstract, and ostensibly less self-interested questions have been staged.

From a strictly theoretical point of view, there should be nothing surprising about this. I take one of the enabling formulations of deconstructive practice to be stated by Barbara Johnson in her introduction to *The Critical Difference*: "The differences *between* entities (prose and poetry; man and woman; literature and theory; guilt and innocence) are shown to be based on a repression of differences *within* entities, ways in which an entity differs from itself" (x–xi). The differences between first-rate and second-rate universities possess the power that they do because it is arguably just as important for the first-rate institutions to banish the second-rate in themselves as it is for the second-rate ones to transform themselves into something first-rate. ("Major research institution" is of course a euphemism. Nobody speaks of a "minor research institution.") Institutional hierarchies represent the fundamental way by which the University of Pennsylvania and Clarion University of Pennsylvania, respectively, advance their own internal differences in terms of exterior differences from each other. In this sense, each institution is as inconceivable without the other as Kenyon College is from Williams (in which differences between entities are not suppressed).[6]

One reason the MLA must be understood, in turn, as inconceivable without badges that give institutional affiliation is because differences among institutions must be put in play as a, if not the, constituent feature of their very existence as each self-imagined entities. (For a view of another national practice see Caesar, "Ocean.") In a very real sense, the MLA is *for* institutions—rather than the individuals who are alternately subsumed into their prestige or lost to their lack of it. Of course all sorts of asymmetries between institution and individual are possible, as well as any number of similarities between specific institutions whose differences cannot be completely controlled (Johnson is quite clear on this point) by any system of representation. No one source of power—the National Endowment for the Humanities, White

Males, the Marketplace, Patriarchy—dictates them all. My point is that the system of representation which makes the play of institutional differences possible is not itself on any discursive agenda within the profession, at least for this particular reason.

Why not? It would be too crude to say because the profession is controlled by first-rate institutions—even when it could be argued that the basic way in which the control is maintained is by interrogating the ideological composition of "control" and theorizing the avenues (fashionable authorities and so on) by which this interrogation must be pursued. But it does not appear quite so crude if the same contention is made when the occasion is the representation of South Africa in a recent *PMLA* special issue on Colonialism and the Postcolonial Condition. In the course of replying to a professor from Queen's University, a professor from a South African university cautions thus: "North American academics should remember that the real resources and power at their disposal are those related to the material conditions of the production of 'knowledge' in the form of scholarly publications" (Dovey, "Letter," 1049). The South African professor forebears mentioning that the Canadian one is careful to acknowledge the financial assistance of her institution's Office of Research Services.

Would it be too crude to "resituate" (as they say at the MLA) the correspondence? Fresh from the spectacle of the annual convention, it is often very difficult not to be struck by the happy consequences in the production of knowledge at a session on, for example, "Ideology," in which you know, even before you look, that the speakers are going to be from, let's say, Brown, Syracuse, and Cornell. This was in fact the actual case of a real session on this subject at Chicago. It is impossible, I believe, not to wonder how different such a session would have been if the speakers had been from institutions as ignoble as these three are estimable? Very little about my argument matters if there would be no difference. It's the sort of consequence that moves Michael Bèrubè in a recent review of books on the state of the academy to fault David Damrosch thus: "But for a great number of American college teachers at places unlike Columbia University, I fear, *We Scholars* will read like a postcard from the volcano—moving, urgent, but finally unintelligible" ("Abuses," 156).

In any case, at this session on Ideology no one asked anything about intelligibility or anything else, from the basis of a different institutional position. (Presumably this is the sort of thing that goes on regularly at NCTE or CCCC, if only because the greater proximity to the classroom of each respective convention's concerns broadens, or flattens, the institutional base.) We all remained in our places, politely listening while one speaker in particular, Ellen Rooney, developed the argument of her book on pluralism about how "the power of pluralism" not only requires exclusion but the effacement of the possibilities of effacing the exclusion. Everybody clapped. I think she allowed that, although we can't do much about the necessary moment of exclusion, we can re-order hierarchies. Is the reason nobody talks about institutional politics because it marks the figure of exclusion which all the other pluralized, hierarchized terms depend upon?

I cite Rooney's particular presentation not so much because I believe it reveals the inescapability of institutional politics. Most any MLA session would. Rooney's, however, is an example of its peculiar logic. First of all, if institutional difference is not itself the sign for exclusion, it can only function on the basis of exclusion, and there is always somewhere that is going to get excluded. Secondly, the specific grounds for exclusion matter less than the structural operation itself. Therefore, the difficulty of sorting out first-from second-rate institutions doesn't really matter very much, and can be safely consigned to personal, anecdotal, and impressionistic levels. Or else to corporate thought experiments; for an unusually bold example, see Chester Finn's typology of "brand-name," "mass-provider," and "convenience" institutions, in the interests of improved service to the "post-secondary marketplace."

A third thing about Rooney's presentation is arguably the most decisive one: theoretical study of exclusion concentrates on it in a circumspectly abstract way, nuanced (or "inflected") by a certain approved political investment (Rooney's is feminism) but not limited to it, lest the structural framework itself be prematurely, not to say naively, grounded and foreclosed. Perhaps the fundamental threat a discourse on institutional politics has for the theoretical hegemony of the profession is that it suggests the grand, progressive thematic of exclusion is founded on institutional prestige; academic ambition; personal bickering; organizational resentment; status anxiety; and all sorts of other horrors that need instead to be redeemed at another level.

Rooney spoke at one point of the profession's "irreducable discontinuities." I would put the point in the following way: as long as we keep the discontinuities irreducable, they can be productive. Productive, that is, for those who have the institutional privilege and the real resources to theorize them. This privilege can, in turn, amount to something so apparently simple as being able to deliver a paper at an MLA session. There may be no necessary reason why noting the politics which enable such an appearance in the first place necessarily means that the discontinuities will loose their distinction and be reduced to the fact that, say, someone teaches at Brown while someone else teaches at the institution where my protestor is from. But when the consequences of institutional hierarchies are proposed in this manner, a "re-ordering" is only going to seem destructive, and so yet again subordinated energies will have to be consigned to the debased, safely distant realm of "sour grapes," resentment, vulgarity, and so on. Rooney spoke at her session as if there were such a thing as an in-itself of discontinuity. On the contrary, it seems to me, some discontinuity is better than others, and some had better dare not speak its name at all.[7]

Of course one may well ask: what is its name? Is it gendered? Is it really comparable to a class? Does it draw on some racial analogy only to empty the very category of race? (For a critique that restores the category of race to these same issues, see Joyce Joyce.) What exactly *are* we discussing when institutional differences get mentioned, and is a second-rate university actually in a subordinate position to a first rate one? To consider this last question: another reason I found the protestor at my first Chicago session so compelling was that he wasn't really a protestor. I don't know what else to call him. He wanted to learn the rules. The only language available to him was that of the rules. Alas, he was able to express only what he *lacked*: not only his own occasion but some space to be, presumably, oppositional.

The man never protested the fact of this space. However he might have occupied it for himself, he merely sat down instead, as effectively "beneath" ordination, and it is in this position that he left the room. The rest left with their own imaginary relations to the session intact. The real relations had been surprisingly dramatized, and yet would most likely persist as no less mystified—the man was a stupid fool, etc.—because the very professional ideology which had brought all to the convention depends in part upon excluding someone who revealed too crudely the consequences of its institutional politics: all universities are pluralistically welcome to attend, but most are realistically excluded from the power either to determine or enunciate what goes on.

At the present time, the approved means of at least imagining inclusion continues to be through the mediation of gender, class, and race. Few practioneers of such mediations are either as adept

or as eloquent as Gayatri Spivak. In a recent essay on the vexa-
tions of marginality, she refers to how in literature "you get both
the benign or resentful conservativism of the establishment *and*
the masquerade of the privileged as the disenfranchised, or their
liberator" ("Theory," 159). Spivak purports to be politically astute
because she sees through the masquerade. But there are a number
of questions she doesn't give us. One is, can the privileged *only*
masquerade vis-a-vis the marginal? (If so, is liberation the best
guise?) Another: do the privileged get to be privileged through their
careful deployment of the marginalized?[8]

A final question is suggested to me by her statement in another essay: "I have no experience in long-term teaching in elite
institutions" ("Making," 789). Spivak is discussing correct pedagogy
for doctoral students in English. What's interesting is that she has
to resort to the category of "elite" institutions in order to make the
point about reading critical prose in the original language. What
about non-elite institutions? Should we conclude their own doctoral
programs are somehow marginal to elite ones? For that matter,
what about Spivak? Is she? Or is her mention of her experience a
rhetorical move? A final question might be phrased this way: is it
the fate of non-elite institutions either to be effaced in loftier considerations of marginality or to be caught up in rhetorical operations of critics from not-quite elite institutions?

Of course Spivak isn't—yet—canny enough more directly to
intimate how richly it can pay off to make a career out of marginality; so richly, it appears at present, that she can afford to have
a rarefied view of what an "elite" institution is, while maintaining
a properly theorized, politically correct, and downwardly mobilized
view of what a marginal status is. Or are we to assume there's no
relation between her notions of what is elite and her theories about
what is marginal? The relation I have been discussing is of course
too simple. At any rate, the easiest way to deal with the relation
is to say it's too simple if you don't want to deal with it at all. But
what if it's only representable as a relation at all if it is, well,
simple?

That is, one chooses an "interest" (or whatever the preferred
term is to advise doctoral candidates) and then gets as far as one
can with it. (See Bèrubè's variations on this theme in a number of
chapters in *Employment*.) Again, this is not an edifying question to
pose. Far better to "problematize" it, even if such an injunction has
the force of one of those effacing registers that Rooney's pluralistic
exclusionary strategy requires. Far better, in other words, even if

it works out in practice that having doctoral students at elite institutions read critical theory in the original becomes an important question for the profession in the '90s. It's a *Profession* question.

Spivak's fleeting encounter with the problem of how to represent inclusion is another, if special, version of the problem I have been discussing throughout: how to represent exclusion? My feeling is that it's too facile—even, I want to say, privileged—to maintain that exclusion can only come to be represented in the same way as inclusion. (The theoretical mandate is usually taken to be from Foucault; for a pointed criticism, see Caesar, *Writing*, 45–6.) Of course, if not, then—it must be asked—how? Somehow more personally? Once more, how to make the case that too many people feel misrepresented by too few? Another consequence of the pressure from the excluded margins of the profession has resulted in the new interest about what might be termed "autobiographical intervention" within the conventions of critical writing.

I take my phrase from Nancy Miller's Chicago paper. Few in the audience must have been surprised to learn that her own exclusion had to do with age, gender, and personal identity rather than institutional affiliation. Some exclusions are of course better than others. Those based on institutional factors are so degraded that there's simply no agenda by which it might be significant to maintain, for example, that all second-rate universities are not the same; the differences between, for example, Kalamazoo College and Clarion University may be far more interesting than their similiarities (namely, considerations of age and gender) from a first-rate point of view. If there is far more irredeemably non-elite professional experience abroad in the land than there is elite, this experience may initially have to be described in individual, concrete terms—just as experience was prior to feminism; these are in fact precisely the terms that Miller celebrates in her latest consideration (see "Public Statements, Private Lives"), if only strictly by women, within feminism.

Spivak's assumption, above, on the other hand, is that her own experience is *no good* for the particular point she wishes to make. Therefore, must institutionally excluded experience assume, as if in direct opposition, that what has been most excluded about it— absent professional opportunities; unfashionable ideas; no luck; unattainable social privilege; and all the rest—is precisely what is most valuable? Of course we will want to ask more questions. Valuable to whom? For what reasons? To demand answers immediately, though, easily functions as a strategy (where not deployed as a theory) in order to foreclose what authority the experience might already possess. The man at my first Chicago session had no authority. In professional terms, his institution remains unmentionable. My most unproblematized point is that too much experience at the MLA convention itself has been lost—to the convention, to the profession—because the relation elite institutions have to the politics of marginality is the only one, and constitutes the only way of speaking.

Of course, any more than a life is not completely reducible to its occasions, a hierarchical structure is not utterly comprehended by the annual convention of its leading professional organization. What about the relations between the *MLA* and the American Council of Learned Societies or the Woodrow Wilson International Center for Scholars? Are there none? Are there symmetries? Is it harder to get a paper proposal for an MLA session approved than a fellowship proposal to a major foundation or institute? If one couldn't very well expect to have a special session approved by the MLA that proposed to study such a question, could one instead hope to get a year at the National Humanities Center in order to conduct some sort of study? Not very likely, and certainly not if you're institutionally incorrect. To present my professional experience at the summits of grantdom rather than conferenceland is to fashion at once a more loveless and less accountable narrative of exclusion.

CHAPTER FOUR

෴

Taking Nothing for Granted

"To vary an old proposition, cafe society gives rise to the aphorism and essay; the college campus yields the monograph and lecture—and the grant application."

—Russell Jacoby, *The Last Intellectuals*

James Agee applied for a Guggenheim fellowship in order to begin writing *Let Us Now Praise Famous Men*. In his memoir to the most recent edition, John Hersey quotes from Agee's unsuccessful application: "It involves therefore as total a suspicion of 'creative' and 'artistic' as of 'reportorial' attitudes and methods, and it is likely therefore to involve the development of some more or less new forms of writing and observation" (xxviii).[1]

Is this the sort of statement that insures one won't get a Guggenheim, in the early '90s no less than the late '30s? How is an applicant to know? Today's brief description of the fellowship just mentions "research." Could one get a Guggenheim today on the basis of an application that proposes to write a history of successful applications to the program?

It would help to know someone who has had one (if not someone who is responsible for awarding one). By now such intelligence appears regularly in handbooks and professional critiques. Ms. Mentor is blunt: "the major purpose of academic conferences is to network, gossip, and conspire with one's peers. . . . Out of conference meetings come jobs, recommendations, knowledge, and (yes!) more conferences" (Tate, 46). Elsewhere, she advises her young charge "to improve your S.Q.—your Schmooze Quotient. . . . Schmoozing will net you friends and allies to make you feel less isolated. You schmoozers may also turn out to be the powerful people you need to know" (Tate, 190). Compare Donald Morton, making a case for multiple submissions of manuscripts, and concluding that the "ethics" for a single submission policy (articulated most centrally by *PMLA*) works "for those interested mainly in *networking*, learning to master and manipulate the professional codes and conventions that preserve the prevailing power arrangements, whose heirs they someday hope to be" (500).

But does the route to a grant lead out of conferences? How does one schmooze with a member of the Board of the Guggenheim Foundation? If networking is decisive for getting a publication accepted, what is decisive for securing a major grant? If you want to apply for one, knowing someone (even if just the right person to recommend you) probably matters even more than if you want to submit to a major journal—and therefore your institutional position probably matters still more. Elite institutions *are* elite because they have offices to facilitate grant applications—involving everything from staff to explain correct procedures or provide successful examples to secretaries to prepare error-free proposals. Of course you're far more likely to have colleagues who know the ropes or, best of all, the judges. I've never met anyone in my life who's had a Guggenheim.

If I did manage to receive a fellowship, no other applicant would see the successful application. If I didn't receive one, same difference: at Clarion there is no interest (administrative or otherwise) in making applications available; hence, nobody would ever know a proposal had been made. From the point of view of the applicant, the most important initial factor about grants is that actual examples of applications be available. The whole issue of models makes writing applications profoundly different from writing articles; no matter what factors go into a magazine's evaluation of any one submission, at least ones that get published can be read and studied. Grant applications, on the other hand, never get published. One of mine will follow in the next section. But I must hope it's clear I offer the application as less a personal document than as a datum having to do with institutional hierarchy.

No other writing an academic can do, especially someone not institutionally "empowered" (as grant applications like to say) to do so, takes place in such utter ignorance of its prospects. There may well be novels in which grant applications are given. (Could compiling which ones be the basis for yet another Guggenheim application?) But a successful application is never only a formal thing. Furthermore, you seldom, if ever, learn anything specifically about the reception of your own application if you're unsuccessful. Indeed, if you're unsuccessful, you usually get less of an idea why than you do on the most standardized of rejection notices from magazines.

No wonder that in an essay on patronage, Paul Theroux doesn't resist stating at the outset: "The idea of patronage has always fascinated me, perhaps the more because I have never received a grant or won a fellowship" (259). He's rather proud not to have been in the craven position of the applicant—or supplicant. But even if it's good to know that somebody can affect disdain, we might think twice about the assumption that he would necessarily have to be a novelist, or some sort of "creative" person. Theroux himself records the fact that the post-World War II rise of Creative Writing in departments of English has led to arguably the most systematic installation of patronage of any disciplinary practice in academic life. Although patronage is not an exclusively academic enterprise, it's as hard for anyone who writes to avoid being embedded in it as it is for anyone who writes to avoid becoming an academic. I have a friend, a poet (to himself) before he's a professor, who tells me that winning an award now constitutes the main way a first book of poetry is published in the United States. He's always trying to figure out the best contests in terms of which to position his continually-assembled and fine-tuned volume.

Of course a submission to a poetry contest is not the same as a grant application. Nonetheless, this seems to me a distinction without a difference. In fact, grants themselves perpetuate it. Grant programs constitute one of the major discursive spaces in which the venerable distinction between the creative and the scholarly continues to be honored—with all the institutional favor, once more, devolving to the latter category. As it presently is, research of some genuinely empirical kind into the matter of when this distinction in fact broke down would provide, come to think of it, still another possible Guggenheim occasion. Why not propose to start with Agee? Did he appear to care about the distinction? Theroux doesn't mention him but he does note that Nathanael West was turned down for a Guggenheim, and that Henry Miller listed some successful scholarly absurdities in a note to what he proposed, unsuccessfully,

to Guggenheim as *The Air-Conditioned Nightmare*. Are novelists
and poets to this day any less ignorant than scholars when they
make their fateful grant applications? One clear difference might
be that artists can have (if not propose) more fun with the prospect
of failure.

The question of what to say about grants must always return
to what to consider about the ignorance out of which individual
applications are written. This ignorance amounts not only to the
missing question of institutional status. It includes the missing
public dimension of the whole grant procedure. (See the fascinating
ruminations by the academic entreprenur-sociologist quoted by
Aronowitz and DiFazio, 243–45.) How do programs customarily
deal with this dimension? The answer is simple: by expecting the
candidate to do so. Program instructions regularly request that the
entire private dimension of each application be resonant with all
sorts of public rhetoric about how professionally or culturally
significant a proposal is. Such a responsibility, in turn, means that
an academic proposing a grant is situated quite differently as a
writer than for any other textual occasion.

For an academic, virtually any writing takes place within a
broad continuum of self promotion that includes submitting papers
for publication; abstracts for conferences; outlines to publishers; or
just making inquiries concerning one or all of these. In contrast, any
grant application writing is different insofar as it must address the
question of your *motive*. No matter how vain or ambitious some
other textual aspiration is, no one who strives to realize it will be
troubled by having to include some personal reason for having written in the first place. Anyone who writes a grant application, however, will have to inscribe something more personal. It had better
not be too personal. Indeed, perhaps one of the main reasons so
many applications come to grief—whether institutionally foreclosed
or not—is that applicants have not sufficiently insinuated themselves into the evacuated public realm of the granting process itself.

Of course one never knows. Let me begin to relate something
of my own experience. I applied for my first grant, an National
Endowment for the Humanities Summer Seminar, in 1974. I got it.
Astonished because I had said so little about why I had applied at
all, and still uncertain how significant teaching results were deemed
to be to the program, I subsequently became frantic to compare
what I had written with what everybody else had. As I recall,
nobody else cared much. As far as pedagogical consequence was
concerned, the seminar proved to be a holiday from it. In 1977, I

was successful with another Summer Seminar application. I felt I had taken a risk by presenting less motive and more research. Flush with a bold payoff, I merrily drove across the country to the seminar, there soon to learn that my proposal had coincided with one of the major research interests of the director.

What to conclude? Pure coincidence? In part, yes. What successful enterprise is wholly free of luck? Yet is there nothing more here suggested about the discipline to which luck is nonetheless bound? Part of the hapless lack of conviction by which grant applications come to be written, I believe, stems from the following fact: the harder you try to cement all the criteria spelled out in the application form, the more you come to feel that misplaced attention or sheer inconsequence is everywhere leaking through the cracks. For example, you ought at least to shore up your textual edifice on the firm foundation of your strongest categories. Being a white male isn't one of mine. Yet in 1988, I had become interested enough in feminist literary theory to try for a third Summer Seminar in the subject, my own gender be damned. In fact, what the hell, since the director seemed (on paper) to be distinguished both by her canny wit and sexy pose, I decided to mediate my gender problem through that of age. I began my proposal with the following epigraph from Mae West: "I like younger men. They have shorter stories."

I didn't get the seminar. Of course it might well have mattered if a record of distinguished publication had been blinking on and off behind my words. Perhaps just stating the fact that I taught literary theory wasn't larger enough justification for the subject in the first place. Maybe Jane Gallop is actually one of those luminaries who reserves her humor for the page, and doesn't like competition in this vein off of it. Or perhaps my proposal simply wasn't set out well enough. I believe I weighed my personal story about right. What I proposed to study, however, was split into two possibilities. This never a seems to be a happy choice for the grant application text, which favors a stern unity of purpose, remorselessly governed with direction, all of it redolent of humanistic goals and social significance. Of course, the director may have scorned, privately, these very things. Yet at least with the NEH Summer Seminar program, you get to have some conviction, if you're successful in your application, about the inescapably human logic as to why you were successful.

I drift. Ignorance, just to be ignorance, probably has to *flail*. Back writing another application—   in lieu of knowing much of anything else or having somebody to call in the adminstration building or down the hall—all you can normally have is the consolation of form. Again, however, grant applications are quite different from virtually all other forms of academic writing in another respect: they are even more formally shapeless, not to say vacant, than abstracts for conference papers or reports of teaching observations. How long a personal story? How much to emphasize scholarship? How little to stress teaching? Application materials usually try to address each of these questions, but not the sequence in which each should be organized. Indeed, rather than anything very precise about organization, one is likely to be told instead only about the maximum number of pages. Instead of form, in other words, there is vouchsafed intelligence concerning length.

There may be those programs for whom any epigraph at all would constitute an affront—purely on a formal basis. The longest epigraph I ever gave, from a story by a Chinese writer, was to the best grant application I feel I've ever written. It's also the most foolish one. I wonder now if there isn't some vital connection in all these things. So *heedless*, I don't recall now if I applied to the National Humanities Center or the Woodrow Wilson International Center. Back from a year teaching in China; anxious not to have so much precious experience ground up in familiar routines; and still more desperate not to have their scholarly meaning used up by the inexorable classroom, I wrote a proposal to study the idea of miniaturization in China.

Would that I had had a colleague to tell me of my folly. I doubt if even another more "creatively" located academic would have mentioned in the application such reasons as I had. There was neither time nor facilities to permit me checking previous research on my subject, though at least I did possess sufficient presence of mind about crossing over into another discipline. So I sent a copy of my pages to the leading sinologist in the country, asking for his support. A brief, bemused reply from him indicated that he really couldn't see what my question was. Come again? I reread my words once more today and they still seemed to me too overwrought with questionableness itself. Another question now: is it better for a grant application to contain a question or to be contained by one?

Perhaps, I can conclude now, this proposal—doubly misconceived with respect to discipline and institutional location—was just too much of an essay. If there is a form to a proposal, it may ultimately lie along the lines of an essay. However, this in turn shifts the question to the form of the essay—a notoriously, gloriously impossible question to answer because, in part, the form of an essay proves too inseparable from the temperament or sensibility of the writer. (For more on this point, see Atkins.) In contrast, what can someone intent upon writing for a grant assume but that it is exactly idiosyncrasy, waywardness, and personal phrasing of any kind that all must be ideally effaced? Before the vast lack of any examples to the contrary, what else to assume? Again the problem of a grant application is the problem of ignorance, absent public dimension, and just plain lack.

Only a few programs, such as that of the John Simon Guggenheim Memorial Foundation, explicitly mention the criterion of reputation. It is almost as if there is either so little or so much to know about the site where the application is made (it depends upon the institution) that a number of factors can come into play which have nothing strictly to do with the *text* of application. Foremost among them is whether *you* are known. During the one time in my life when I was a member of a committee judging grant applications at a national level, I especially recall the moment when we were urged by those from the best schools (and therefore with the most authority on the committee) to approve the application of an eminent scholar, even though its focus was wobbly and its organization blurred. We did. I did.

The text may be materially all there is, but it doesn't delimit all there is to consider for an award. Indeed, one might speculate that the text is all there is only when there *is* nothing else, and most particularly a complete absence of institutional clout. Therefore, if an applicant's ignorance can finally be seen as a deliberate result of the prestige-saturated context in which patronage functions (Theroux protests about how little literature has), the following equation would appear to follow: the more prestigious the grant, the lesser the chances for someone who commands no prestige—personal or institutional. At the top level of patronage, if you lack a reputation, it won't matter how your application is written or what it proposes.

At this point we need before us an example. In the next section I want to provide the one I promised at the outset. An analysis follows in a final section. I must hasten to emphasize once more that the proposal wasn't successful. Perhaps—analogous to the fate of a certain sort of unsolicited article submitted to a magazine—it was actually judged to merit one of those how-dare-you-bother-us-with-this rejections. Or maybe it was in fact judged to merit only one of the more common we're-sorry-but-we-receive-too-much-rich-material-for-our-poor-pages replies. As always, nobody will ever know. (And those in a position to know have surely forgotten.) I've tried to emphasize what decisively distinguishes writing a grant application from other kinds of academic writing. What all of it has in common, though, is one additional thing: someone—an individual, a committee, a system—is going to judge it, and the grounds for an unfavorable judgment will never be fully stipulated. (For an analysis of rejection in publication, see Caesar, *Writing*.) The grounds never have to be. Moreover, it may be the essence of an unfavorable reception that these grounds can never be stipulated.

1.

> "Well, I *have* seen the Coliseum by moonlight! That's one good thing."
>
> —Daisy Miller in James's "Daisy Miller"

Let me put the central question of my proposal as succinctly as I can: how is the plot in the text of women's travel writing different than that of men? This question, in turn, provokes a number of other questions: do women travel for different reasons than men, or is their subjectivity as travel writers constructed differently? Furthermore, why does a woman choose to write a travel book rather than a novel? Joanne Frye notes the following: "Women's plots are nearly always 'familial' or 'erotic' because our cultural notions of womanhood require a personal context. Female characters lack autonomy because an autonomous woman is an apparent contradiction in cultural terms." How explictly do women travel writers travel in order either to exacerbate or overcome fundamental cultural contradictions? How exactly do they write in order to recontextualize themselves or otherwise enunciate more fugitive, vagrant narratives?

That such questions are both significant in a broad humanistic setting and in a narrower literary one I take for granted. Much of feminist theory has come to take an overt concern with its narrative definition, as a function of more emancipatory ones that may be counterpoised to those venerable patriarchal stories in which women have been embedded. But virtually no attention has been given to travel writing, and I believe a large part of the reason is because, in turn, this writing has been understood as careless of formal shape, unworthy of literary value, and altogether marginal as any sort of enabling cultural practice. Of course I don't agree. Much of my recent work has argued, in a variety of ways, that travel writing is capable of enormous discursive potential. I would hope that a consequence of the essay I want to write is that travel writing itself comes to be more searchingly and urgently recognized, not to say understood.

Here I'd like to gesture at a narrative of my own about how I've come to make this proposal. I trust my vitae will reveal that I've been engaged for a number of years both in travel writing and in scholarly research about it. I've seen the subject attain a measure of professional recognition in very recent years—at last year's American Studies Association conference, for example, I gave a paper for the session devoted to travel writing. I've just finished a book-length manuscript on American travel writing. One fundamental thing that dissatisfied me about the ASA session vexed me all over again as I finished the book: women were hardly mentioned. This is the basic reason I want to write something now, or that I'm chairing a session on Women and Travel at the next Popular Cultural Association convention. However, the papers I've chosen for this session mark, I think, a fundamental absence all over again. They are all on Victorian women's texts. I want to take up in some detail the sort of conceptual pressure these texts put on my proposal.

Isabella Bird and Mary Kingsley are not canonical writers. Yet, they are virtually the only women travel writers that even academics have ever heard of, and in this rather precious sense they do function in the space of the canonical. This space needs to be considerably expanded and updated. Even more, I would maintain, this space needs to be re-nationalized: Bird and Kingsley are British. The effacement of American women travel writers repeats that of American men in such texts as Paul Fussell's *The Norton Book of Travel*, where only three of fifty-five writers anthologized are women; none of those three is American; and virtually all of the men are British. Of course, the British enjoy a longer tradition of travel writing. Bird and Kingsley can appropriate it. It appears that American women at the same period produced nothing to compare to them. (I'm not absolutely certain, though, that extended research would only confirm the poverty of American texts. How well-forgotten can, say, Kate Field's *Ten Days in Spain* [1875] be?)

Consequently, travel writing by American women is devalued to this day on the basis of conventions, as well as examples, modeled on British practice; Louise Erdrich's recent *The Solace of Open Spaces* is a superb travel book in part because it is a superbly *American* text.

My larger point is that there is absence, effacement, or repression everywhere in anything to do with women and travel, whether another national tradition or the mere fact of a woman's presence. On this last instance: the astonishing single mention of his wife in Levi-Strauss's *Tristes Tropiques* has been remarked upon; the two or three times John Gunther mentions his wife in *Inside Africa* have not been; but feminist critics are by now familiar enough with how women have been written in texts of all sorts under the sign of *lack*. Whether English or American, women obviously come somewhat late to be empowered to write of their travels—and then it is no surprise that much of what they do write expresses how much they lack: mobility, security, authority of all sorts. I believe anyone who would study the practice of women's travel writing ought to be especially sensitive to the cultural license under which any specific writing takes place (the British is more social and comic). The same is true of the historical evolution of the form (Edith Wharton's *In Morocco* [1920] is, for example, far more influenced by the guidebook model than Harriet Beecher Stowe's *Sunny Memories of Foreign Lands* [1854]) but, perhaps even more fundamentally, of the very fact that women's relation to travel has never been free of the presence of men. A woman traveling alone is comprehended in part as lacking the presence of a man to accompany her. What is a woman? The lack of a man. Perhaps no other species of writing presents the issue with such crude force.

The strategies by which more contemporary women travel writers try to blunt, displace, or transfigure this force constitute the fundamental plot of their texts—and this plot is different in important ways from that of Bird or Kingsley, neither of whom traveled alone but both of whom were able to present themselves under the guise of the solitary (male) traveler. This guise has its own ruses, its own duplicities. Nonetheless, older women travelers were able to assume it, even when they traveled with (usually feminine) companions. A study of women's travel writing might well become a study of how this guise has been lost to modern women travelers so that by the time we read Mary Morris's explicitly entitled registration of the problem, *Nothing to Declare. Memoirs of a Woman Traveling Alone* (1988), we discover that Morris simply can't travel alone, no matter how much she desires to. Her text can be profitably aligned with any number by women who do travel with men, or who disclose what has to be termed their complicity with men less anxiously than Morris does. The text of a woman's travel is, whatever else, a text of *relation*, and the basic way to emplot this relation is by traveling with a man who, in turn, carries with him the very definition of "relation" itself, in terms of what sort of experiences a woman feels the need to have or just how far she can safely go. As they write themselves, men travel alone. Women travel with men.

The imperative to emplot relation differently than this is behind such a recent handbook-guide-anthology as that edited by three British women, *Half the Earth: Women's Experiences of Travel Worldwide*. Few of the editors's respondents record travel with men. Most either travel alone or with another woman. Reading this text, one can be reminded of the moment in Elaine Showalter's much-anthologized, "Feminist Criticism in the Wilderness," when, after citing Gerda Lerner's diagram of the relationship of the muted to the dominant group, she contends that all is "wildness" outside the dominant "sphere" and that "men do not know what is in the wild." Is this in fact true, if we consider the actual travel of women? How, precisely, "wild" are the sites or experiences they seek out? Or, if not as programmatically correct as Showalter allows, does woman's travel writing reveal ways in which "wildness"—loss; deviancy; power; multiplicity—is either appropriated from men nonetheless or otherwise recreated from the "zone" of the dominant? Finally, can such ways be plotted, or must they resist plot? "How do you know you are a traveler?" asks Morris at one point. She appears to travel in order to ask the question, yet the travel she describes can be read as a series of routes to a confident ignorance about the answer. How can such a logic be explained?

I must of course defer my own explanation, especially if I can be more confident about my own question(s). I certainly can't emphasize enough here how much I want to insist, explore, write up. This proposal fascinates me. Enough so that I might do it in any case. For once, however, I'd like the best possible case. My vitae indicates that I've had three Summer Seminars and one Institute. I got most written (and eventually published) during the last two of these. It's no accident that in both cases the subject was travel writing, although in neither case was this the subject of the respective seminar and institute. Stimulating as the fellowship was, for just once I'd like the financial support to do my research on my own, as one ultimately has to anyway. To me, the research is a kind of vitalizing travel of its own; it's always a thing of life; and I'd love the funded opportunity to do it at last on a Summer Stipend.

2.

Word came from the Associate Dean of the College of Arts and Sciences at Clarion University some years ago that nominations would be in order for the Summer Stipend program of the National Endowment for the Humanities. I wrote the above application for the program because I was tired of spending money keeping two homes while a member of faraway summer seminars and fed up with the cross-purpose of having the mutuality of the seminar occasion usurp interest and time from my own special research. For once, I reasoned, I'd just collect the money, stay home, and go about my business. I further presumed that the Stipend would be fairly easy to get. It was certainly not difficult to get nominated. Nobody else applied.

Do I swerve dangerously close to my real motives in the last sentence of the proposal? I felt I had to make some gesture at the curiosity of studying, in one spot, the very subject that had up-rooted me twice before, each time expressing both my most professional and personal reason: I wanted to get away from home, to relocate, to travel. The two Fulbright awards that I've had have been more obvious and thorough instances of this same desire. Perhaps I never would have known it existed in me so acutely had I not chanced to take my first sabbatical abroad. Research as travel, travel as research: is there a more unexceptionable equation in applying for a grant? Perhaps I was suspected to have assumed it too idly. This NEH Summer Stipend is the only grant for which I've ever applied that did not require me either to go or live somewhere else.

Is the fact that these Stipends are highly competitive in itself some indication of how unusual the formerly unexceptionable equation has come to be? (A friend—also unsuccessful—from another institution later assured me of this. How I wished he'd had an office down the hall.) I'm not the only one to feel the expense of the Summer Seminars, much less Fulbrights. There are of course any number of other reasons to feel that what might be called the romantic days of research have probably in the 90s come to an end; scholars are getting older; more likely to be pursuing separate careers while married to each other, and so on. At such a moment, to refer to one's proposal as a "funded opportunity" sounds at once too casual, too transparent, and too domestic.

Did I presume the overriding significance of a Fashionable Subject at even greater cost? What else is a grant proposal if not an inward exercise to push against a discipline's parameters? A study of women's travel writing seemed to me to fuse two impeccable conceptual credentials: gender and marginality. Had someone asked, which matters more? I would have replied, why choose? I suppose if someone had grown insistent, I would have argued that it's more important to textualize gender than genderize texts, for the latter hardly represents a provocative strategy anymore. Perhaps, having no one down the hall, I should have imagined someone growing more insistent. Or maybe I just smudged my fashionable fusion in the middle of its presentation by the talk of national identity. The study of American women's travel writing had intrigued me for a number of years. I had never found the right scholarly occasion, nor had one found me. A grant application is undoubtedly one in which to resist as many opportunities as it is to exploit them.

Does the proposal have too much justification or not enough? My third paragraph gestures at the extratextual fact of reputation. Based on a contradiction—how can something that abides apart from textuality be made manifest in textual terms—this gesture could have been banished as a possibility; I didn't feel comfortable writing the paragraph. Would it have made any difference if I had deferred it to the end? As much difference as it might have made if I'd already had published the book-length manuscript on American travel writing I'd finished some six months before I wrote this proposal? If you're going to deal with reputation, it seems to me imperative never to forget that the process of recognition is something that embraces you, not vice versa. Trouble is, never forgetting this can make you stumble just when you fancy you want to run, no matter how far or who organized the race.

More formally still, what about focus? When the words I write cease to feel buoyant, what I usually do is to contract them. If there's too much of this dynamic, I eventually grow unsure of the consequence. My first paragraph seems to me too sure, excessively pointed. Concerned that I wouldn't fix on one central question, I may have overloaded the focus right away with too many others— and then proceeded to get too intricate about all of them. Or perhaps by the time I mention Levi-Strauss and Gunther, the questions have just swung out too far from the first paragraph, and indicated a kind of scope unlikely to be realized during a mere summer. Ambition is of course a great good in all kinds of writing, but not if it clogs the writing itself, or pulls it in too many directions.

Development? Again, I believe there's too much. Indeed, this proposal fairly bristles with it, especially in the last few paragraphs. They've lost vital, specific, clear contact with the first. I can't quite explain why. Was I straining? Extensive study of grant proposals could well reveal that many of more than a couple of pages tend to grow into a more essayistic mode, thereby losing the crisp, systematic governance by which proposals of any kind are significantly differentiated from essays. Instead of musing on Showalter's point, I believe I should have returned to the "humanistic setting" saluted in the second paragraph. Do judges who read these applications actually love talk about anything "humanistic" as much as the forms suggest that they will? The word needs to be stirred around more here, even at the risk of thinning the conceptual soup.

Stylistically it may be hopelessly thick. I may as well confess: I don't like writing grant applications. It shows in the one I'm examining. The writing ought to be flatter. It's too busy, energetic, edgy. Something on this order appeared to be the objection of my Associate Dean when we went over the proposal, although his reservations weren't clear to me. No matter. I refused to change anything anyway. Who was he to say what the NEH wanted for this occasion? (It was his first semester on the job.) Who is anybody? There are many different kinds of academic discourse. One which employs such words as "recontextualize," "emancipatory," and "embedded" by the first two paragraphs is undeniably some one kind. The problem is that I don't "signpost" enough, as if I can't be bothered. Or as if some fundamental lack of conviction is surging throughout the whole articulation.

Another confession: I don't seem to be entirely at ease with any academic textual occasion unless I can be formally secure within its conventions and assumptions. (See the chapter on letters of application in Caesar, *Conspiring*.) Since those of a grant application are not only too subtly specific to each program but too insubstantial overall, each writing feels deeply unsatisfactory to me. This dissatisfaction, in turn, has no formal dispensation in which to operate. One doesn't so much write on certain academic occasions as *impersonate* someone writing. The best example for me has to do with reports of teaching observations. (See the following chapter.) The fact that I have taken them almost exclusively, each time, for over twenty years, as provocations for various sorts of parody only certifies that in a certain unregenerate sense I'm at ease with writing these reports.

This is equivalent to claiming, I think, that I can't write grant applications because they can't be parodied.[2] O, for the missing colleague who has the experience (as supplicant or judge or both) to prove me wrong! As it is, how to see around the text of the grant? How to get some firm ironic purchase on it? Grant applications appear to me to be so utterly embedded in the overmastering structure of patronage as to be ungraspable. One of Stanley Fish's nicer statements about this sort of thing is the following one: "The hope that you can play a particular game in a way that affects the entire matrix in which it is embedded depends on there being a style of playing that exceeds the game's constitutive rules . . . depends, that is, on there being a form of destabilization that is not specific to particular practices, but is simply DESTABILIZATION writ large" (254).

Writing grant proposals, I would say, takes place at a position which can only point directly to the core of the "matrix" itself. There's no marginal space if you want to proceed. Furthermore, the "game" is all rules. The essence of all of them is that *they* "destabilize" you. (This is one reason Henry Miller was moved, as if in disbelief, to list a selection of successful Guggenheim applications.) Such is the inevitable consequence of having to play in so much ignorance: you can't play, so to speak, "with" it. And such of course is the equally inevitable consequence of having to play within academic hierarchy: at some point—maybe beginning with whether or not you write a word such as "emancipatory" (or have a secretary available to check the spelling)—either you have the right institutional affiliation or you don't.

Of course I err in referring so breezily to a "matrix." Each program is to some extent its own special world. That represented by the American Council of Learned Societies or by the Rockefeller Foundation is of undoubted, absorbing interest to each of them, and it had better be of at least some concern to anybody who would be applying. Neither organization has ever been of interest to me. I've never applied. Instead I've supposed that their interconnection is what matters because there is a common game that ultimately excludes me. It's played for stakes I only distantly understand, defined by elusive, interiorized rules, and enunciated with vocabularies whose nuances are difficult to master. That is, in effect, I've assumed that the most "constitutive" rule in these programs has ultimately nothing to do with what I could propose but everything to do with the institutional site from which I propose it. Clarion— by which I mean, "a" Clarion—is neither designed nor expected to be a player. Clarion faculty—to a man and woman, teachers all— won't be able to disturb any of the rules in the least.

Who says this is true? Nobody has to. This is another feature of the "matrix." If called upon, of course there would issue forth from it assurances that play is open to all, humanistic setting, and so on. It is only in handbooks that one reads harsher truths, such as the following one by Paula Kaplan on the "myth of meritocracy": "The academic meritocracy is truly a myth, since many factors other than merit play substantial roles in deciding who receives the rewards. But if you believe that merit is the only criterion, then when one of these rewards is denied to you, you will certainly believe that it is your own fault" (48). Agreed. But what about those other factors?

The best thing about the National Endowment for the Humanities, on the other hand (so I've again supposed) is that, no matter the interconnection with other programs such as the above ones, its rule is more forgiving of institutional status. This isn't true of all NEH grant-making divisions and operations; for all I know, the Summer Stipend may partake of as much exclusivity as the National Humanities Center. It's true enough of most, though, in my experience, especially the Summer Seminar program, no matter how cynically this particular one is understood as a means through which faculty at first-rate institutions re-educate or fine-tune the faculty at second-rate ones.

To put the matter a bit differently: while as much of the action at the NEH probably takes place away from the proposal page as in any other grant program, a mere applicant can nonetheless assume there exists a more discernable, plausible, even defensible line of decision traceable back to the application itself, apart from the prestige that emanates off its institutional site. You may not be able to destabilize very much of anything with your proposal but you'll have a decent chance of getting accepted on the basis of it. Of course lack of success with an application will seem no less arbitrary. You'll have to be very fortunate to be able to learn anything more about why you were not successful.

Once I was. A few years ago I taught briefly with a man, on temporary contract in the department, who was interested, as I was, in American Studies. Spring brought us both an announcement of a two-week NEH Institute on the subject in Boston. Neither of us knew the other had applied until after the deadline, and then learned that we each had done so quite by chance. I tried to keep my composure when my temporary colleague received a letter informing him that his application was successful, while I received a letter informing me that my application was not. How to explain the results? We agreed to exchange copies of our respective applications.

The only thing either of us could figure out was that this was a grant where teaching mattered more than the application materials seemed to mandate. My colleague mentioned in a sentence that he hoped to devise an American Studies course in which to teach the specific subject of the institute. I'd made no such mention. Both of us knew that no American Studies course of any kind had ever been taught in the university. Perhaps only I knew that none was ever likely to be. But why had I not at least mentioned teaching? Because, with some irony, I had presumed that in this particular instance research rather than teaching is what ultimately mattered? Or is it just that I had hoped it would? My untenured (not to say untenurable) colleague, by contrast, enjoyed no luxury to imagine such freedom—nor did the National Endowment expect him to.

It makes a nice story. It might even be true. Kaplan gives as another "myth" the idea all teaching and scholarly work will be regarded as equally important and valuable, commenting thus: "[W]ithin every discipline there is a 'pecking order,' so that some areas of research and some research methods are regarded as more prestigious and intellectual valuable than others" (54–5). In actual fact, though, some areas and methods are marked off for classroom use only, while the same ones are free to peck away in most unpedogogical ways. It depends on where you are, that is, where you are designated to be, and what you are designated to do with your research. Nothing so much as a grant application presumes that you had better do something.

My colleague eventually returned from afar with the intelligence that the institute had been too interdisciplinary for his taste. By then both of us had ceased to care about the real reasons why he had been selected to go rather than me. Would it have been choked with interdisciplinarity for me as well? Impossible to say. And how to know without actually having gone there whether or not all that I ever really wanted was a couple of paid weeks early in a Boston summer? I don't even know if this is all my colleague wanted, although he told me that he loved Boston. By the end of the next year he left, having taught nothing else at Clarion but composition.

In anything to do with writing, how much do you have to take for granted? Grant writing poses the question so acutely because it's so fraught with circumstances exterior to the writing, that the interior of the writing can't address. The story I would tell about grants features institutional privilege as the very name of those circumstances, if not of exteriority itself. It seems to me very telling that grants normally speak directly to some other condition (often a destination elsewhere), from within familiar circumstances. That is, grants often have to do with travel. Did someone propose to study emancipatory narratives? The seductive thing about grants for me is how they promise freedom from the infirmities of academic location, if not the imperatives of academic hierarchy.

And yet to get a grant you first have to apply. And to apply you have to demonstrate how you can be included on some professional or institutional map. Of course you will try to take nothing for granted, not even the knowledge that you may be more ignorant than you realize about how far inside your life you have been consigned to belong. How far inside? Well, as usual, you can always write teacher observation reports if you don't want to risk writing grant applications. As I must trust my next chapter makes abundantly clear, these reports exist for me to be parodied, partly because, since so much is taken for granted about the circumstances in which they are produced, the reports ask to be manufactured, not written. If you don't know what to write because you're not sure what to take for granted, you can always produce a species of writing where everything is taken for granted. The sole governing myth is that there is only a department, in which we are all teachers, and that everybody is equal to everybody else.

CHAPTER FIVE

ᥱᔓ

Filing Away Teaching Observation Reports

I evoked Edgar on Lear at the end of my first observation report: "We that are young/Shall never see so much, nor live so long." It was just a brief paragraph. I wrote it some twenty years ago, and I wrote it as a parody, praising, among other things, my colleague's "pedagogical punctilliousness" because his brilliance had shone for exactly fifty minutes, and not a second longer. In fact I hadn't seen him teach at all. He didn't care. The class was in the evening. Why should I be troubled to make a special trip? Because the system that mandated untenured faculty to be observed each semester was so new to both of us, did we assume that my mock report would just be interred somewhere without any particular consequence, like so many other examples of textual transience in academic life?

Part of my understanding of these teaching observation reports of faculty is that their history can never be written, not in terms of any single institution or even any department within an institution. Clarion University seems to me typical of those universities that require them. Simply by the fact of requiring them, Clarion maintains its teaching "mission" (not to say its subordinate institutional position) over against that of major research universities, which don't. Liberal arts schools, in their way, stress teaching just as much. But the best ones don't require these reports either.

A reader of this chapter mentions that right away I should make more of the fact that the reports only exist at second-rate institutions. "Last night," he continues, "I had dinner with the assistant provost of Johns Hopkins. I asked him whether faculty were observed there. 'They wouldn't put up with it,' was all he said." Enough said, I think. I can only read incredulously at how casually P.F. Kluge passes over the system apparently in place at Kenyon College (to take a different sort of counter example), whereby colleagues (senior ones only?) cordially request permission to visit each other's classes. The context is the tenure review of one. It's not even clear if, or how, these visitations will be written up.[1]

At Clarion it's so clear as to be uninteresting. Officials of both the administration and the union seemed surprised and puzzled when I expressed interest in finding out exactly how long the observation process has been going on. It turns out that non-tenured faculty were required to be observed by colleagues as well as students according to the very first bargaining agreement in 1971. A colleague fondly recalls how fearsomely the infamous Article 12, authorizing the whole observation process, was once fought out, or with what disdain a now-dead colleague agreed to serve on the first departmental evaluation committee. I'd completely forgotten about all this. Who cares?

Our late colleague, I remember now, disdained the process because to him the classroom space was a sacred one. It would only be violated by the entrance of one's prepossessing peers, or vulgarized by the opinions of one's self-interested students. Could the fact that I stayed away from the classroom in order to write my first observation report have itself been some sort of mark of this same idea of the classroom? Perhaps, though it just may have been that my colleague encouraged me. Certainly little else about today's academic practices certifies how the very conception of the classroom as space has changed. People are now regularly allowed in who are not part of the class. Or, in institutions where observation reports have been routine for decades, would it be more accurate to say that part of what a "class" is includes the periodic entry of people—colleagues, chairpersons, administrators, even visiting "experts"—who do not participate in its day-to-day business? Only *students* ask anymore if a friend or relative can sit in for a session.

Who now is authorized to ask about previous observation reports? In a sense, the formerly sacralized aura of the classroom has been transferred to its texts; these reports are the only ones in academic life that purport to describe what actually takes place in any given class on any given day. (Student evaluation forms may have about them equally the air of the inviolably private, but, even when there is some provision for signed comments, these forms are not *written*, and therefore have a quite different, and less important, place in the institutional archive.) I'm simply not sure where my first report could be found, or whether I could make some valid claim to see it. Is the report lodged somewhere in the file of that observed colleague (now retired)? Is this file still retained in the president's office? If so, could I just walk in and ask to read the report right there for old time's sake?

Even if I managed to get myself appointed head of the Evaluation Committee, or, more thanklessly, head of the whole department, I'm still not sure I could get a legal look at my first observation report. Maybe it no longer exists. But who could have destroyed it? A dean from tenure past? If not, who preserved it? An even more idle question. This report, like all subsequent reports ever mandated, came into existence to be kept "on file." No phrase in bureaucratic life suggests more realms of textual luminosity than this one. Who keeps the file? In a sense, the burden of the file is not to be thought of in this way. The file is the file because it is that archive that exists to be, precisely, kept—accumulated, nurtured, *maintained*. "Disciplinary power," writes Foucault, "is exercised through its invisibility; at the same time it imposes on those whom it subjects a principle of compulsory visibility" (187). The nice thing about a file is how it contains a compulsory visibility while remaining itself unseen.

Most likely my first filed observation report still exists, access to it at once having grown in restrictiveness and diminished in rationale. The files of younger, non-tenured colleagues, on the other hand, are rich in reasoned access. All sorts of people can enjoy an official perusal: members of departmental evaluation, tenure, or even promotion committees; members of college-wide promotion committees; and, as always, deans, just to name the most obviously empowered. It is not the job of any of these people to ask why any single item is in a file, much less why files themselves must abide in the institutional body. Suppose one wants to ask, why, for example, observation reports of teaching should be continued? The question appears to flaunt logic itself. Teachers teach. Their teaching should be evaluated. Who better to do so than other teachers? One may as well ask why each faculty member should have a file.

Certainly it's no satisfactory argument against files to explain that their justification is at root tautological: a faculty member *is* a faculty member because he or she is a subject about whom files are kept. Similarly, it would be no satisfactory argument against observation reports to contend that they now function as one indispensible element in the structural "implementation" of a teacher as one about whom teaching reports are written; the purpose of the report, in other words, is ultimately to be filed, or rather, to be "on file." What I want to examine, nonetheless, are the conditions of how the observation report is received insofar as these conditions define how it is produced. The fact that observation reports are fraught with the self-perpetuating energies inherent in any bureaucratic system means that any single report is the product of a certain sort of attention and a certain sort of writing on the individual level. What sort? The question can be answered very simply: the individual is a member of a *committee*.

1.

A committee comes about as the result of impeccable, inexorable logic. As if to reproduce the wondrous tautological coils in which it is embedded, the purpose of the observation report of teaching is to *get the report done before the deadline*. Indeed, the importance of getting it done on time takes up all the space in which some critique could function concerning either how it should be done or whether it should be done at all. In any given year, my department presently comprises something over twenty–five souls, including half a dozen part-time people. More than half of all these must be evaluated in any one semester, specifically all non-tenured ones and tenured ones only every five years. The evaluation process has swelled to such proportions that no one not to be observed can be excluded from the duty to observe someone who is to be. Consequently, the evaluation committee is now merely a nominal entity, chaired by savvy seniors who can be entrusted with the tricky task of assigning who observes whom. My own fiction about the watershed moment in the departmental history of observation reports would focus on the meeting a few years ago, when our chair gave voice to the grim truth: if no one volunteered for the evalation committee, membership would have to be enlisted from *outside the department*.

My motion that no one volunteer so that the observation process could truly suffer its collapse fell on deaf ears. Fatigued hands were eventually raised. The man who thanklessly chaired the evaluation committee wearily agreed to do so again for a final year. After this particular meeting, we all came, I believe, to an unarticulated awareness that the year-by-year constitution of the committee didn't matter anyway. What did was the imperative to conduct the evaluations. This imperative superceded any departmental structure that could be devised to accommodate it—unless one understood the fundamental constituent element of the department to now be its dedication to conducting teaching observations of itself. Certainly, each semester nothing absorbs us so faithfully. Have we even ceased to resent it? Of course, new members are now present to add fresh vigor to the task. Is the truth finally that we can only retain our own collective authority (not to say self-respect) if we permit not so much as one member of any other department into our classrooms?[2]

This authority comes at considerable cost: it must be seamlessly unified. So seamlessly, in fact, that there must continue to be virtually no discussion about what we are doing—only assurances that we are doing it. We've never met to consider or stipulate criteria for observations or the form they should take. Many deans ago, there was a sudden flurry of talk about whether we should enjoin a committee to draw up a form, resembling the one presented to students for their semester's end evaluations, so that an individual observer could simply check off opinions from a numbered list of desiderata. Eventually a checklist was adopted, albeit for temporary faculty only, over the objections of some who argued that the teaching of these individuals would only be further demeaned and unacknowledged.

I've read a good number of observation reports of other colleagues, as well as some from other departments. Generally, the configuration of unspoken assumptions assumes the form of a three-paragraph scheme: the first states the facts (date, course, lesson for the day); the second describes what transpired; and the third judges what can be concluded about both the class and the instructor's performance. Most of the interest in the report is in the middle, which can be rather severely attenuated or expanded into several more paragraphs, depending upon the attitude of the observer. Ones who are confident of their position quickly dispense with the facts and cut to the chase. After a mere sentence about name, course, and date, the most recent one I have on me proceeds to a second paragraph as follows:

> Terry began the class by laying out the groundwork for their reading assignment, *Ceremony*. I find it interesting and refreshing that he is coming to the book for the first time, reading it simultaneously with his students—a sharing of the text that marked his approach to the subject of

> this day's class, Kate Chopin's *The Awakening*, 'an extremely
> interesting book because of its conclusion.'

This might sound too casual. It's not. My colleague has written so many reports he can sketch in an example of one great value, organization, without using the word, and he can deftly gesture at another—rapport—without filling it out.

Reports can often appear to be quite individual productions. Compare another on me, written ten years ago, again with a factual, one-sentence initial paragraph, after which proceeds the following: "Dr. Caesar's Diogenean humor established a relaxed pre-class atmosphere as he discussed the variety of excuses given him by students to explain their absences. 'The only one I haven't heard yet is Herpes [sic],' Caesar quipped as the burst of laughter ended the discussion and served as a transition into the period's close examination of Book IX of *War and Peace*." There is more of this sort of thing. All of it is not there for any formal reason but because my colleague was another friend. Just so, the reason that the schema of the observation report is so minimal, not to say shapeless, is because it must give way at virtually every point to the relationship the observer actually has to the one being observed. Let me state very bluntly what I've only implied: these reports are finally not about teaching but departmental unity.

The departments I know into which outside observers had to be summoned are those (usually very small) broken into hopeless factions or utterly shattered by bickering. Only departments that can conduct themselves with the belief that all is basically well can observe themselves—and of course, by another tautology, the process of observation is one way that departments can maintain this belief. (We might recall Kluge's reluctant man at Kenyon, who challenges departmental belief in its unity simply by being reluctant.) Hence, it doesn't matter in any one, such as mine, that we haven't discussed how crucial it is for good teaching to have "rapport," or how much it matters in the observation report that some neutral description ought to be given before the requisite praise. Far more crucial is the matter of the right people being in position to praise the right people. It's just as crucial that the right people be in position to criticize the wrong people. The wrong people are easier to determine: those who either have no power, i.e. all temporaries or part-timers, or those who won't, e.g. dim, untenured sorts or else tenured others content for some unilluminated reason to work off by themselves.

In my first instance above, the wrong person might have judged that I was unprepared to teach the next novel or that I was haughty rather than "sharing" with my students by mentioning I hadn't read it. Similarly, had I been the wrong person it might have been noted, in the second instance, that I was either too cute or overbearing in saying anything at all about excuses, and perhaps too timid as well before the stern demands of Book IX. As it is, affective bonds were ratified in each case, and each was of a piece with our respective representations of the department's various ceremonies of solidarity, from the corridors to the coffee pot. What has continued to matter is that we respect each other, value what we do in terms of each other, and be willing to declare our professional implication with each other when formal occasion calls. These classroom observations may constitute our foremost occasions. We write what we do not so much to the person whom we have observed (who signs the report before it is submitted to the chair) as to the whole departmental body.

People who are criticized just aren't part of it—or rather aren't part of it because they are criticized. I think especially of a woman who taught part-time for a year a few years ago. She incurred the wrath of a departmental god. This woman criticized her on an observation report. So did a friend of this woman's during the next semester. The part-timer's protest each time only exacerbated her tenuous status. She's no longer with us. I was struck during a more recent semester by how differently even seemingly factual things are dealt with on observations after another part-timer—this time a friend—told me how our chair had disapprovingly noted in his report that only a third of the man's students had participated in the discussion. Less than a sixth had spoken in my own observed class, and yet my report during this same semester had criticized them, not me. "Their loss," my well-disposed observer wrote. "Terry is a fine teacher; he deserves a better class."

I'll agree that I deserved a better class. I'll also admit that the class felt they deserved a better teacher. Furthermore, I'll wager that, all impossible things considered, my part-time colleague of the meager one-third participation was more the teacher for his students than I was for mine. Alas, however, he had no power in the department. Worse, the chair (contractually mandated to observe everybody who must be observed) didn't like him, and eventually he wasn't rehired. As observational subjects, the above two part-time people may have their place in any department. But it's a negative one, the better to enable the rituals of positivity the rest of the department negotiates for itself each semester. The observation report is such a fundamental ritual not because it involves everyone. So do department meetings. The reports are so important because they are better *texts* than department minutes, which don't so much have to be read as seconded. The chair or various committees can nod over observation reports, as they recreate them in summarized form, and pass the summaries only to higher disciplinary authorities, who nod in their turn, before filing all away.

And yet I must hope I've made clear the reports are only texts at all to the extent their instrumental function can be taken for granted, and used in order to shape the report. However, what if one doesn't do this? Or to put the question another way: what if one plays up the textual dimension in excess of its instrumental function? Will the system itself continue to be able to process it? Will such textualizing have a subversive effect? How could such a thing be determined? I wish I at least had copies of all the observations I've written. It took me years to realize why I hated writing them from the beginning: I wasn't being asked to "write" them at all.

I was merely being asked to certify the truth that a classroom "visit" (as I seem to recall an earlier idiom) had been made and some sort of "record" had issued from it, presumably favorable. How can I have lost, especially, the copy of the report on a composition class I wrote up by impersonating the style of one of the freshman students? It must have been at least fifteen years ago. My subject laughed, but worried about the integrity of her file. She asked me to do the report straight and, since she didn't have tenure, I complied. So much for subversion. To me, I thereby falsified what had been her bland teaching performance by "objectifying" it.

It took me too long to start writing, without either apology or revision, the following sort of thing:

> That's good thinking there, Msprofessorblackmaria m.j. Ms. J. is an English teacher who might wear mail order suits standing up there as the snow . . . *whistles*, outside . . . in the cavernous Carlson classroom teaching the last hundred pages of—Hmmmmmmmmmmm—Tom Wolfe's *The Electric Kool-Aid Acid Test*. Relaxed. Smiling. Fluent. Authoritative. Syncted into the *whole thing*. In 1985! And this is a special topics course on *the sixties*, for God's sake!!!!!!! Out front. Sez "ya know," "right," and "okay" a lot—TOO MUCH! Slippin' and Slidin'—and it goes on for *seventy-five minutes*. Orgggggg! Whose movie is this? Is this ken Keseyed?

The next six paragraphs were more straightforward, although I never entirely ceased to appropriate something of Wolfe's style. (The question of whose movie was the whole show remained unanswered. I concluded that the spiritless students were "on the bus" only because their teacher had led them to the door, pushed them on, and then revved up.) My relations with this particular colleague were amicable enough to enable me to feel comfortable about an experimental presentation of her teaching. But she never told me if she liked the result. What did the evaluation committee think? The dean?

Using Wolfe was a way of displacing a protest against the authority of an impersonal bureaucratic mode. It was also an attempt to impersonate my own voice, for I had managed to insinuate a number of things that seemed to me to break with convention: the weather, the dress of the instructor, and her mannerisms. Most significant, however, was the fact that I had more confidently dealt, as if for the first time, with the insecurity of my very presence in the room. I didn't want to be there. I didn't care what my colleague did in her classroom. What business of mine to have to judge what she did? Let her feel free to do what she wanted, same as me.

In short, nothing had changed in me from the previous decade when I had compared another colleague to King Lear. What had changed, nonetheless, was that the making of these observations had become so routine—a modality for the disciplinary exercise of power—that it was plain silly for anybody to worry about them. Perhaps a final consequence about my use of Wolfe is that I was at last able to take possession of some of the silliness. So in the next decade my reports got sillier. If I couldn't be subversive, I reasoned, I could at least be silly. But it took time, and always depended upon both the official status of who I was observing and my personal relationship with him or her.

A few years later, I began the following report thus:

'Oh, are you substituting today?' popped a perky freshman to me a minute or so before 9:30 outside the carpeted confines of Stevens 202. How to tell him, no, I was a mere observer? How to know if his heart leaped with joy at the moment when, a few minutes later, Ms. N.L. wheeled in a hefty pile of student notebooks on a luggage rack? An observation occasions many mysteries, even, or perhaps especially, if it's Composition 111. I only know that all was in temporal and pedagogical—not to say metaphysical—order this day for me, and I left the room happy that Ms. L. had taught the class, not me. It was a most soggy, autumnal Thursday, October 19.

My cordial relations with this colleague lacked substance. Far worse, she was teaching freshman composition, a course I hate to observe possibly more than I do to teach. Worst of all, she appeared with *those notebooks*, the very emblem of the mountain of work that entombs every comp teacher.[3] I was groaning before I beheld these notebooks. The only consolation was that by then a quizzical student sitting in the back next to me had provided the basis for an out.

There was seldom need for a better one. I duly described the class. I duly tried to praise it, and so concluded: "Confident that my colleague has all the ideas she needs—including the generous assumption that her students can never have enough—I hope I can be forgiven for jumping off here, in a sense having substituted after all." I had just quoted her having bid her students to "jump in" to what she was saying, an example of a folksy phrasing that I thought was corny but wrote as "offhand." Did she suspect my displeasure anyway? What did she think of the report? She just signed it, cheerfully. Since she was already intimate with one departmental god, could it be that she didn't much care, as long as the whole drift of the thing was favorable? Did anybody care? Once again, of course, the report had been signed by both of us on time. It could now be filed. All I cared about was that I'd gotten out.

2.

I must hope it's clear that by this time my desire was the product of nearly two decades of enduring observations. Recently, I happened to ask a woman in the field of Education how extensive is the literature on faculty observation reports by other faculty. Soon she was describing the elaborate research merely on the minute question of how the role of the critical observer can be played when the fateful moment comes to meet with the observee after the report has been read. My eyes glazed over. Who can deny that this moment is important? But it does not take place in a vacuum. What research into *that*? I simply don't believe in observations by "experts." I don't believe in routine observations by peers. I don't believe in any observations by me.

All my experience has taught me is that observations are fictions. Some are good, some not. The problem is that all of them make their way into their proper files under two assumptions: 1. they are not fictions, and 2. it makes no significant difference why some might be better in some formal way than others. It's easy to stipulate the script to which all reports must adhere. The narrative is always one of progress. Students must be instructed from ignorance to knowledge (whether on periods or the periodic table, it makes no difference). Whatever is being done is being done well— or else it can be adjusted or improved. Any observation report that departs from this narrative (or makes fun of it) does so at great peril to the script.

A few times I may have succeeded in writing such a report. I've never read one. Ten years ago with Tolstoy, for example, my colleague concluded thus: "Despite the seeming impossibility of his Herculean task . . . the students seemed responsive and perhaps even somewhat aware that one great work like *War and Peace* could offer as many valuable perceptions of the human condition as would an anthology full of stories and poems." What I concluded myself was that trying to teach *War and Peace* in such a course was one of the great disasters of my pedagogical life. We all tried (that is, the half who remained after the first class). We all failed. My colleague, however, believed his narrative, and we both knew how much my "task" fit into its subplots of challenge and innovation, each so beloved by us both.

Do I mean that it would have been more accurate to state that I should not have chosen to teach *War and Peace* in intro. to lit? No. However, something of the folly should probably have been noted. It was too easy to affirm instead my ambition. Some fusion of my stupidity and idealism could well have been articulated at the very least, for the very heart of the teaching not to have continued past its report. But so it always goes in these reports. The narrative of progress exercises such exclusive sway over all other developments that no other license is allowed to any, particularly if shadows darken deep into the instructional hour.

Furthermore, the imperative of departmental accord is so great that few in any department are going to have the power to engage in some different—inevitably counter—writing after they leave a colleague's classroom. Finally, the honorific space of the observation report is so institutionalized that nothing any one individual can do will dialogize, much less subvert it. (Refusal to write one is in violation of the bargaining agreement and is grounds for being fired.) It is to be understood that no college administration is in the business of putting fictions into the file, even as of course it must be admitted that some reports are better written or more enjoyable to read than others.

Let me give a portion of one from a couple of years ago that it gave me great pleasure to write:

> Mr. M's 'feminist intervention' (his term) was perhaps the highlight of the hour for me. Typical of Mr. M's sophistica-tion—he emerges as yet again a shining exemplar of the axiom that few things are more dreadful than a teacher who knows only what he teaches. All this granted, however, I still couldn't help but wonder if the poor kid's account of his sexual initiation of a Punxsutawney prostitute wasn't made up. Perhaps not; the girl who spoke about her "inher-ent right to masturbation" certainly had a nice argument, if somewhat elusive. In any case, I came away fully in possession of Mr. M's point that words *matter*, and that how they genderize is part of how they matter.

The last sentence here is true. My colleague has been a friend for many years. The first sentence is equally true insofar as it speaks of the play of his mind or his interest in critical theory. But he never uttered such a phrase on the day in question, nor was I in attendance to hear whatever he did. The whole observation, like the rest of the report, is made up. The only thing I didn't enjoy while writing it is the rather coy suggestion that it might be.

You can only do this sort of thing if you know your man well— and if he knows the risks. But what are the risks? That you either won't get tenure or will lose it if somebody finds out you allowed a teaching observation that was pure fiction to be written about you? Who could find out? In any case, an evaluation commitee will have plenty of other serious textuality to consider, while a chair will most likely just smile indulgently, and a dean merely worry that there is no precedent to do anything at all. My friend, how-ever, wasn't even tenure track. He didn't care whether I showed up or not, though, because all that really matters is that the teacher does—and that the right observer can so attest.

Invoking the vocabularly of James Scott with respect to power and the kinds of resistance that can be brought to it, Richard Miller has lately considered the applicability to the classroom of the public transcript and the hidden transcript. "At some point,"

Miller writes, "every teacher must enforce the boundary between the concerns of the hidden transcript, where students regularly rehearse their misgivings about the education they're receiving, and the public transcript, where the virtues of the educational system are taken for granted" ("Arts of Complicity," 21). But when faculty, as opposed to students, have misgivings, enforcement grows more troubling. It seems to me now that my writing of teaching observations has gradually strived to blur the boundary between hidden and public, or else to erode it, by demonstrating how the public transcript can be mocked by another script that scarcely remains hidden.

During the last few years, I've openly made criticism of both my own report and the uses to which it would be put a feature of every observation report I've written. For example, on the occasion of another friend's labor off the tenure track, I began with a quotation from Bakhtin: "The word in language is half someone else's." At the end I wrote as follows: "Who reads this observation anyway? What authority am I presumed to have in order to write it, and what does anyone else to read it? To what precise purpose(s) will it be put? My conviction is that far too much more than half any observation such as this is Someone Else's."

I'm especially content with the exit I managed from still another report. "Another thing I want to express here," I wrote, "is how I believe the text of observation has reached a stage of disabling formalism: either so predictable and formulaic that everybody's teaching practice is processed as a version of everybody else's or so marginal and wayward that pretty much anything can be said as long as it praises the person who constitutes its ostensible subject." My subject was in fact the department's queen of composition. "Her own profession of writing," I continued, "revealed to me so agreeably this very day, would of course countenance no less than the necessity of any writing practice to explore its construction and examine the conditions of its reception."

Only the last of the above two reports was the product of actual observation—and then the observation had just been a few minutes. It was long enough to see that the class was in a very real sense spurious. (Designed to train tutors for the writing lab, it met in the lab, this day as part of a meeting of all the tutors, including those whom the course was "training," but now with the course rationale suspiciously like a shell game.) But teaching reports are presumed to perceive merely a pedagogical surface. The report itself is simply not granted the mandate for some consideration of how limited its remorseless, empirical claim to truth can be. The report itself—well, when comprehended from the point of view of its ultimate destination, the subject's file, there is every reason to question whether there *is* any formal integrity to it, beyond the brute material fact of its evidentiary being.

How can this fact be resisted? On the one hand, I find myself having come full circle as the author of these reports, after having worked through a long middle period trying to enact my faithless duty as a classroom observer. I'm now making them up once more, if I can. (Public thanks to another colleague, a full professor like me now, who just let me go ahead and imagine what I wanted.) I still don't think anybody cares. I thrashed around in one of my last efforts as follows:

> 'Have sex before writing.' No, wait, I thought. Even well into a Composition 111 section late on a Thursday after- noon, October 10, Mr. R.S. could not have advised his stu- dents (even if they looked in need of *something*) to do this. He had been reading from a composition. I had begun to drift. Wasn't the subject of the composition something about cats? Could Mr. S. have read, rather than said, 'the cat sucks before biting?' But do cats do this? Perhaps Mr. S. said rather than read after all, and gave forth the intelli- gence that a catalyst, mayhap, 'must be inciting.' I don't know. The high occasion of an observation is not without its low confusions.

Another friend. Another comp class. More silliness. "The room was flush with excitement," I had begun an earlier one on him. "Or maybe excited with flush." I ended this new one by inscribing it as "but a part of the larger Evaluation Process by which we all now so routinely monitor each other that we hardly have to enter the classroom."

Maybe in the next report I'll cite Foucault. If you have occasion to think about them, observation reports are transparently clear as one means by which supervisory power is at once contained and released in academic life. Faculty at "comprehensive" universities such as Clarion are required by their own union, in league with the college administration, to create themselves as visible subjects by means of an observation process that cedes the disciplinary author- ity for them to do so among their various departments. I'm still striving to opt out of the spectatorial regime by making up my own reports. Yet I continue to write them, both as a condition of remaining a member of my department as well as having a job.

David Bromwich has lately contended "that we are living in a period of academic conformity as inexplicable as any the world has seen." What else do the sorts of things I've been trying to do with my reports express but the "compound of piety and cynicism" about which Bromwich goes on to speak? He also notes how "community" is the new watchword.[4] Even as I with a wink mock some of my colleagues in composition classes for fashionably deeming their dull charges to be members of "writing communities," I remain complicit with these colleagues. For all I know, I may have secret bonds with others who read these reports, mine included, outside as well as inside the department. Could the dean chuckle? The president? Even if we all never get structurally consolidated, we may abide as a wonderfully inconsequential community of sorts.

So, on the other hand, as the author of observation reports I may not have come full circle after all. Indeed, I may have remained basically at the same place. The institutional site has grown, become more interrelated with other "technologized" discourses, and been subject to a number of different historical pressures since 1971. Aronowitz writes that academic unionism (which has arisen partly in response to these discourses) "has, in general, not yet addressed the core of the crisis: the restructuring of universities and colleges along the lines of global capitalism" ("The Last Good," 107). (For more on this critique, see Rhoades and Slaughter.) My own special province in this book, however, has been in the persistence of structures almost beneath history. Rather than an announcement some time soon that next semester's observation schedule will be sponsored by Sony, I expect the reports to continue so elusive of political address as to appear immune from it.

The writing of observation reports hasn't changed. So much writing academics have to do, such as letters of recommendation or minutes of meetings small and large, abides in this same formal vacuum. (On these letters, see Caesar, *Conspiring*.) Everybody knows the observational text is so conventional as to be pretty much fictional. No one wants to know. Few like to write it. Everybody must. My own reports strive to resist the imperative, but cannot subvert it. Subversion depends upon more factors than an individual's intentions, especially if the textual disposition is designed to ignore them anyway. Subversion depends upon being able to destabilize and resist its own containment, whereas my reports have only the muffled discursive fate of the file; they are simply not designed either to be produced or received in any other way.[5]

What is the logic of the file? It abides in every institution; academic hierarchy has nothing to do with it. The logic is simple: file everything. Of course everything isn't important. But it *might be*. You can't be sure. If you think you can be now, what about the future? Such logic matters because of how the very idea of subversion is resituated within it. The impossibility of disputing future developments means that it's even conceivable today's subversion could become tomorrow's affirmation. Certainly academic life really gets interesting when it either appears less easy (or less crucial) to determine the difference between what's subversive and what isn't. A couple of people on departmental evaluation committees have remarked to me that my reports are "fun to read" or "a relief" from the usual ones. That's all. No big deal. Into the file they go along with the rest.

In Northrop Frye's second phase of comedy, he gives at one point a "more complex irony," whereby, since society isn't strong enough to impose itself, the situation of the hero becomes "quixotic." Either there is a clash of two illusions or a superior social reality thwarts the hero, who is "at least partly a comic humor or mental runaway" (180). It may be that the "superiority" of The File in academic life continually makes for this kind of comedy. Files, after all, constitute a fairly weak principle of discipline. Files are to be "kept," usually by individuals, and are only "activated" by circumstances that have nothing strictly to do with the conditions of their keeping, which are in themselves as constant as department meetings or job interviews. It's even theoretically possible for a certain kind of individual to elude files, at least insofar as they promise some particular discursive fate.

In the next section, I examine the more public subject of hiring (rather than retention), in which no one at any point is officially obliged to write up a truthful account—to candidates, to anybody else. Therefore, I believe, in no single academic area other than recruitment is the fissure between the actual and the textual more marked. On the other hand, in no other single academic area other than teaching is the fissure between the real and the textual less marked. After stating the case, like Aronowitz, for the devisive influence upon American universities of the corporate model, Jeffrey Williams continues as follows: "The unversity is not by any means an ivory tower isolated from economic determinations of the world, but functions as a critical institution reflecting and abetting the present reconstitition of the public sphere" ("Renegotiating," 300). To the degree that the public sphere depends upon files, though, my experience writing teaching observation reports reveals, I think, that it's possible to perform as an erstwhile member of an organization in a manner that remains in almost equal parts absolutely essential and completely empty. Finally, if these reports mean anything—apart from their bureaucratic occasion—they disclose how little the life of any organization really has to do with the public sphere, and how much it is determined by the timeless stories it tells itself, undisturbed.

CHAPTER SIX

ᙓ

Getting Hired

In order to have a job, you've got to be hired. If you've got a recent academic position, however, the process by which you were hired is likely to have been one of the most inward, prolonged, politically fraught, and severely rationalized it is possible to undergo in any field. Has it actually taken place within a proper legal narrative? So you must hope. But it's hard to be sure of anything anymore. In the 90s, even the venerable narrative of academic hierarchy is becoming confounded and exhausted. Jobs are tight and getting tighter. My department's last national searches—and part of the legal narrative is that virtually all searchs must be national now—came up with top candidates from Duke and Chicago. The first time the position was only a one-year, temporary one.

During his year at Kenyon College, P.F. Kluge cites the chair of the search committee as follows, concerning a position in Philosophy: "The people who apply to Princeton, Harvard, and Stanford will not apply to Kenyon. . . . We make clear it's not a research position. . . . It's a teaching institution. You must do research, but it's known you don't have to do six articles and a book to survive at Kenyon" (91). Like Kenyon, Clarion is a teaching institution. Unlike Kenyon, nothing is known about it—at least not by people from Duke and Chicago. What, we wondered, could these candidates possibly think about us? Could they know, for example, how secretly we would have loved to hear stories about their famous professors? Could they have guessed that some of us might have wished to begin their respective interviews by apologizing to them?

About precisely what might we have apologized? Perhaps just the meagerness of our circumstances. Even today, candidates from

107

Duke and Chicago must surely expect, if not more research opportunities, at least better interviews, or something more than break-
fast and lunch with a few people from the search committee; a chat
with the dean; and a hour with some members of the department,
who ask a lot of questions about teaching composition. ("Why don't
we just give the job to the one who teaches composition best?"
grumbled a colleague after our last round of interviews.) Getting
hired for an academic position, after all, has never been like business where the interview is at the clear, decisive center of the
process. Indeed, one of the curiosities of academic hiring is that it
is consequent upon a decision whose center is everywhere and whose
circumference is nowhere. Granted, in the boondocks, where the
central position of the interview is more akin to business, you might
at first be more relieved afterward not to have had to prepare a
lecture, or teach a class, or be grilled about your research agenda.

And yet it's easy to imagine a candidate from a first-rate institution who misses a fuller play of the circumference, including the
meeting with graduate students so you can ask them if they have
to share office space with the faculty, or the informal moment somewhere during the second day on campus when you get a jolly chuckle
from everybody by expressing relief at not having been asked to
pee into a bottle. Even if getting hired is now either mixing up or
thinning out the absolute structure of who applies where, and why,
I want to set out an account of the process that employs as broad
a context as possible. (See Boufis and Olsen for some consequences,
and Nelson for some solutions.) It both will and will not be an
account of this structure. It must be a definition of an academic
career, even if the definition now includes people who have to strive
for knowledge and success at levels that would until very recently
have been beneath them, according to terms that nobody understands well anymore.

Historical perspective ought to help. Yet I'm not sure it would
be possible to determine exactly how many times getting hired has
changed over the last forty years. Henry Wilbur begins his entry in
The Academic's Handbook, "On Getting a Job," with the following
statement: "The first task of the new Ph.D. is to obtain an academic position." Then he refers to his own experience. His first
paragraph concludes as follows: "On the basis of that experience, I
immediately qualify my opening sentence: before you set out to
obtain a job in a college or university, you should do some frank
and honest soul-searching" (63). Forty years ago, would Wilbur
have felt the need to make his qualification? Thirty years ago?

Twenty? When did academics begin to align themselves with busi-
nessmen as wage-earners? When did the rigors of committee work
become imperative to caution "entry-level" candidates about?

When, for that matter, did it become necessary for a book to
appear with a chapter such as Wilbur's? One feels that if he turned
any more of his skepticism on the very process he aims to eluci-
date, he simply couldn't provide wise counsel about such matters
as leaving hobbies off your c.v. or being sure to appear in business
clothes if the department has asked about your marital status.
When did getting hired, one could ask, become so thoroughly rou-
tinized that it only appears idle or fatuous to be detached about it?
Certainly, if the moment could be stipulated, it would not be entirely determined by the conditions we know today, when so many
people are in search of so few jobs that we can almost give the
following result: if there is a Peter Principle in business, there is
a Paul Principle in hiring, whereby people will descend to the level
of an institution for which they are much too good to be teaching.[1]

It's almost impossible not to settle for some point in time during which everything was easier, more humane, and on a more
casual scale. Acknowledging how offering any kind of historical
perspective risks idealization, let me consider B.L. Reid's charming
memoir, *First Acts*, which concludes with him working as a milk-
man in 1946, before an employment agency in Chicago notifies him
of a position at Iowa State College. He and his wife are both offered
jobs without interviews. Although Reid mentions "an exchange of
letters," presumably none of them was a letter of recommendation.
We can further presume that Reid didn't submit either a cover
letter or a c.v., and it probably would have been as inconceivable for
his new employers to have asked him to deliver a formal lecture as
it would have been to check their offer against affirmative action
guidelines. We do not, in short, understand Reid's situation today
according to the one characterized by Kafka in *The Trial*: "The
verdict doesn't come all at once, the proceedings gradually merge
into the verdict."

Nonetheless, proceedings did obtain, which in a sense do enable Reid's initial good fortune to be understood as merely part of
a more comprehensive sentence. Four years later, while teaching at
Mount Holyoke, the intelligence was discreetly given to Reid that
he would be fired because he lacked a Ph.D. It took him until 1956
to get one—at age thirty-nine, from the University of Virginia,
while teaching as an instructor at Sweet Briar College. The age at
which Reid got his doctorate was perhaps more unusual then than

now, but I believe it's typical of how tempting it is to emphasize discontinuities when one could just as justly stress continuities in the professional narrative of getting hired.

Rather like an astutely career-minded grad student today, Reid sent off his course papers to the *Sewanee Review* and the *Kenyon Review*. Furthermore, whether he intended it or not (Reid doesn't say), Sweet Briar couldn't hold him once he was in a better bargaining position with a Ph.D. Mount Holyoke offered not only more money but tenure. Back at Mount Holyoke, Reid was secure. Eventually he published a few books; got nominated for a Pulitzer for his biography of John Quinn; and was named to an endowed chair some years before he retired in 1983. He enjoyed a career, in other words, very much in line with contemporary notions of success.

It's not at all clear that Reid would ever have benefited from advice such as Wilbur's. It's not even very clear what Reid took the profession to be, beyond one in which he was able to follow the scholarly logic of his own interests, generously conceived. Could he have realized he was all along more specialized than he imagined if he had had to subject himself to the elaborately credentialized and sequentialized process of getting hired as it exists today? Once again, hard to say. What can someone about to undergo this process today make of a Reid, who mentions that his academic career only came about in the first place because of the need for teachers created by the G.I. Bill? Not much. There's no comparable need for teachers anymore in higher education, and there are too many institutions. S.S. Hanna mentions (the time is "the early seventies") that he got a letter from "a small college in Nebraska" which gave his letter of inquiry the following response: "Sorry, we have been forced to close down the college. If we reopen and need you, we'll call you." (11)

1.

How does a profession change when one seeks entry into it with the knowledge that one is competing against hundreds? (And often competing for positions at colleges one has barely heard of?) Reid simply indicates no historical awareness—not even by 1956—about being one among many. The real clarity his experience provides us with has to do with the one phenomenon past upon whose basis a clear difference is usually declared from the present: the fabled "old boy network." This network is not a myth. I don't entirely agree with

Kluge that "the old boy network is history now, condemned as elitist, clubby, possibly discriminatory" (89). Just because it's condemned doesn't mean that it doesn't survive—indeed feminists can now be heard speaking about an "old girl network."

One thing I believe the confident condemnation of the present means is that the old boy network still hasn't been very well understood. It can easily be made available now in order to construct another myth, this time of its own demise. What gets lost is not only a career such as Reid's, which was not a product of an old boy network. Consider Reid's career alongside that of the pseudonymous Simon O'Toole, who at one point, after publishing an edition of McPherson's letters while teaching at "Baraboo University," is invited to take over the courses of a famous old editor of letters at "his famous old university." O'Toole declines the invitation until things are spelled out: if he likes it, he can stay—and thereby have a teaching load of four hours a week; a handsome salary; an assistant to help correct papers; and a certain Guggenheim. "Did I yield?" writes O'Toole. "I yielded." (67) It's a measure of how shadowy and self-serving O'Toole feels the whole careerist enterprise to be— *Confessions of an American Scholar* is possibly the strangest book ever written about academic life—that he gives no specifics about when the great moment of his career took place. (It seems to have been roughly about the time Reid got his Ph.D.) In any case, he would probably want to emphasize how problematic was his own lifelong relation to any "network" rather than how certain it proved to be in one crucial instance.

Nevertheless, O'Toole discloses enough about his own career to reveal how profoundly implicated it was in the very rhythms of elite affiliation, privilege, and mutual interest. It's apt that his account is so muffled and painfully inward, as if the better to emphasize a professional level where the significant moves are closed to outside influences. I take this to be fundamentally the same state of affairs that continues to this day when top professors change jobs or even when top institutions try to get senior faculty. For example, in James Phelan's account of his own department's senior appointment search, it comes as no surprise that Phelan knows one of the leading candidates, who also got his degree from Chicago. Dolores Burke's research study about faculty recruitment in the 80s cites one senior person who relates the following procedure: "I gave a seminar in the department and they called me a couple of weeks later and asked me if I wanted the job. I didn't even know there was a job" (72). Such agreeable astonishment

could not be further from the earnest attentiveness Wilbur en-
trusts to his young professor-to-be, who has first to be told to look
where positions are advertised. "The 'old boy network' is more alive
in some fields than others," states Wilbur (65). He can say no more.
He doesn't say this network doesn't advertise. Perhaps he doesn't
have to. You don't get hired within some fields, not even starting
out. You get chosen.

Another senior professor is quoted in Burke as follows about
then and now: "Back in the 50s it looked like an old boy network
but it really wasn't. There were just fewer of us. The American
Astronomical Society had 800 members when I was treasurer; now
there are 3600. When I became treasurer, I knew every graduate
student in the country personally. It was a totally different world
back then." (58) So all that's changed is numbers? But this ignores
both how elites perpetuate themselves and the general truth about
professions repeatedly demonstrated in Magali Sarfatti Larson's
fine study of professionalism: "*A profession is always defined by its
elites*," as she puts it at one point (227; her italics). The best way
to enforce definition is not only to maintain inner solidarity but to
avoid visibility, especially concerning more mundane procedures
(old boys just pick up the phone to get something done, or are
pleased to be so thought of) and especially concerning hiring. One
looks in vain for clear, detailed accounts of how old boys make good
on the promise of jobs. Perhaps such accounts would be too vulgar.
Or perhaps there are no accounts because there is normally little
to detail; vocabularies of shared value and intellectual intimacy
have the character of seeming inherited, and therefore, your advisor at one worthy institution passes you along as if you were a
legacy to somewhere equally worthy.

Some of the pressure for "political correctness" can undoubtedly
be explained as a displaced response to the persistence of old boy
networks. Or rather to what are understood to be their confident,
thorough prejudices. The old boy network is presumably rotten with
them. Whether having to do with age, gender, physical disability, or
sexual orientation, each category corresponds point-by-point to the
ideological front now assembled against all forms of discrimination.
In an academic context, prejudice belongs to the days when the
chairman was always a man and usually an autocrat, or when academic stratification expressed a broader, fixed social hierarchy, now
comprehended as repellent and socially retrograde.

In those days, religion represented still another basis for discrimination. I have an old Jewish friend who tells the story of when

she and her husband were invited decades ago to the campus of a small midwestern liberal arts college in order for him to be considered for the position of dean. Things went very well. They liked the atmosphere. They even liked the president. But on the last Sunday morning, while driving around town and observing all the locals spilling out of churches, the president's wife turned to my friend at one point and asked the fateful question: "And which church would you attend?" She paused. They needed this job. They were sure they already had it. Of course her husband didn't get it, once she told the president's wife that they wouldn't, in fact, attend any church.

How could she be sure religious discrimination proved to be the reason? Of course she couldn't be. In a similar sense, I suppose, any woman or African-American can't be sure even today after a job search that gender or race, respectively, provided the ultimate reason why an expected job offer was not forthcoming. (Or, conversely, why an offer *was* forthcoming.) To each hiring procedure its own vanishing point. The difference, however, is one of ideological climate, and it makes all the difference: because an older hiring process, on the model of the old boy network, functioned more informally, the exerise of prejudice was not subject to the checks and texts of official opprobrium. Professionals had no great need to distinguish themselves from bureaucrats and technocrats—a story Larson tells very well—and so could afford to be either ideologically complacent or naive. Now, whether your c.v. contains requisite professional service or one of your letters of recommendation is from an eminent scholar, each item is understood to comprise a far more objective measure of your prospects than whether you might be a lesbian or confined to a wheelchair.

Is this measure in fact the case in the present hiring process? Has offensive discrimination really ceased to function? Ideological sophistication may simply indicate a sophistication about the very category of ideology—and not about any one example of it, or even examples which are nothing more than old-time prejudices dressed-up and "empowered." One of the more uncomfortable moments of my professional life occurred some years ago while I sat watching a candidate for a departmental position smoke cigarette after cigarette during his interview. He gave a poor performance. Nobody had to mention his smoking. Yet, I'm not sure anybody would have mentioned his smoking if he'd given a brilliant performance. They just wouldn't have voted for him, either way.

And so it goes, I would argue. Today's hiring process often merely allows the moment of prejudice to seem less decisive and to become diffused amid instrumentalized criteria.[2] One result is that an individual applicant who is unsuccessful gets no knowledge at all about what the reasons were, and knows that she won't. I know a woman whose convention interview concluded with the interviewer stating quite fervently, "I hope it's you." How could she not be fairly certain it would indeed be—or at least that she'd be invited to campus? But she wasn't. Months passed before the letter came informing her that the position had been "terminated" because there were too many unfinished searches for administrators. There was also something about "reexamining institutional priorities."

So what could she conclude about why she wasn't hired? That there had been "proceedings" which were already active at the time of her interview to exclude her? That any relation she could have either to the position or the department was already by that time beside the point? But what sort of knowledge is this? How does it enable one to improve one's chances in the future? In such circumstances, it seems to me, it's almost more consoling to feel that the unexceptionable bureaucratic operations were actually a mask for blunter and more personal prejudices of some sort. Maybe she gave the wrong response when the interviewer chanced to say something about teaching observations.

In fact, this particular case got a bit more interesting: the woman chanced to know some inside gossip to the effect that the most influential man in the above department wanted a senior appointment for his old professor; he blocked any other sort of position when the old professor decided to stay where he was. I think my friend came to prefer this reason for her failure to any other. Whether or not it happened to be true in this particular case, I believe it stands for hundreds or thousands of others, each of which bears traces of some sort of indeterminate, subterranean "network," but all of which must officially proceed to the verdict according to impeccable professional standards and proper affirmative action guidelines. What gets taken for granted, however, is that because everything is written up or spelled out, the process of getting hired is far more fair, responsible, and progressive than it was in the past. I don't believe it is. The process is just more complicated, more problematic, and more mystified.

Can there be anyone active in higher education during the past twenty years who hasn't seen a routine hiring procedure play itself out faultlessly from any legalistic standpoint, and yet who knows that in fact the whole thing was devised purely for show? My second chapter presents an account of a situation I initially took to be precisely of this sort. It only wasn't just barely. Just so, how often do the very factors consigned to the bad old days instead appear to flourish the more deeply, in no small measure because all are agreed that they've been stamped out? Why *do* people get hired today? If things are so much improved, everybody ought to know, which means having that knowledge count in specific instances. Instead, it's a time for handbooks, so that something intelligent can be summoned into existence, disseminated, and propounded. "The best preparation for professorhood," states Wilbur, "is rapid intellectual growth and productive scholarship." (76) But we knew this already. We've always known it. What we don't know, still, is why scholarship so often matters so little, or not at all—even at the best places, where it ought to matter more.

It might be very tempting to argue that things have gotten worse, not better. Suppose we compare the exercise of another prejudice, this time against homosexuality, from two separate periods of time. The first example has to do with a story of a former colleague about how he lost a chance at his best job prospect once his Ph.D. was completed, just after World War II. He had asked his dissertation director to write him a letter of recommendation. The director did (to a chairman whom he personally knew). In order to cinch the case as much as he could, the director added that my colleague's mother lived near the institution in question, so her son would be especially pleased to be there; he was very close to his mother. My colleague was sure he'd get his offer. He didn't. Only much later, through a series of events far too complex to detail, did he learn why: the chair, on the basis of the director's aside about his mother, had concluded that my colleague was homosexual.

In contrast, we may compare the recent account of Ed Cohen, who went "on the market" in 1986. His hopes, he writes, were high: awards; a few publications; the full support of an elite institution. There was only one problem: he was gay and his dissertation title showed it. Of course, Cohen can't be sure this explains why he received not a single interview that year; his "deficiencies" ranged from the fact that his publications were not yet in print to the fact that he refused to waive his right to see his recommendations. All he can conclude, nonetheless, is that dropping "homo" from his dissertation title and not using the word "gay" made all the difference from one year to the next. In 1987, he got eleven MLA Convention interviews and two job offers. "I decided that what I needed to do was to represent my work in a way that was respectful of the project I had undertaken and yet accessible to people who might not necessarily be sympathetic to the undertaking." (168)

What to conclude? At least, Cohen—whose strategy was simultaneously authorized by and subversive of the conditions of getting hired—was considerably more knowing about the moment of his own hiring; my old colleague, alas, was victimized by his conditions. But there is more. He never told this story as a victim, and only delighted in it each time. I think this discrimination spoke to him of the exquisite comedy of academic life, its sheltered ignorances and its formal entanglements. Cohen, in contrast, does tell his story as a victim. About "the experience of my own self-silencing—especially on a subject that it had taken me years to learn to speak and write about publicly," he declares it to be "acutely painful" (168). Indeed, we might say that to Cohen his experience is a tragedy, because it speaks to him of essentially nothing, except how hollow its conditions are. There seems to be little pleasure even in manipulating them to one's own advantage.

On the basis of such a contrast, it is tempting to formulate some maxim to the effect that, the emptier the process, the more formal it becomes. Of course, Cohen represents a special case. However, if the process of getting hired at present cannot deal satisfactorily with special cases, how can it be claimed to be some sort of advancement, especially when the special case is an example of the "identity politics" that the rules were expected to arbitrate? We believe, I think, that each of us, in our heart of hearts, is a special case. At least we present ourselves as best we can, on paper. We hope that we will be triumphant, if we get the chance, in the flesh. Yet time after time, the contemporary process of hiring seems to produce unsuccessful candidates who emerge with the feeling of having been merely a structural feature of proceedings designed not to exclude but to ignore them.

For such people, even Cohen's despair might seem like a kind of blessing. Let me relate the story of another woman, for whom an entry-level position seemed more assured than anybody I've ever known. Many of the reasons why had to do with her best friend, the previous occupant of the position, who set it up for her. By the time she went, her on-campus visit seemed just a formality. It wasn't. She didn't get the job. What had she done? Since she'd gone through all the motions cleanly enough, she could only guess.

Had she offended one member of the department by a jaunty remark about one of her former professors, possibly an object of veneration to her colleague-to-be? Had she scandalized the men (against whom her best friend had cautioned her) by the incipient "feminism" of her presentation, especially by being flippant over a translation of the word, "castration?" Could one of the senior men have somehow associated her with bad luck because, after she met him, he discovered that he'd lost his textbook? Or was it simply that she felt such an immediate, visceral dislike of the chairman, and (she was certain) he to her? Like good academics both, though, each knew the rules, and not an incorrect, much less antipathetic, word was exchanged between them.

The woman will never learn. In a sense, it's the job of the hiring procedures under which she was considered to prevent her from learning, as well as to protect the department from whatever she might find out. Should she know? To consider what departments term "recruitment" from the candidate's point of view, as I've been doing, prompts one to ask what could be the cost to the profession when so many who apply to enter it are not so much rejected as cast aside? Being rejected at least has the virtue of preserving a personal relation, however unfortunate or inevitable, to authority. Being ignored, on the other hand, rebukes the very idea of such a relation. Of course this might seem like, well, an academic distinction; if one can't get a job because one is Jewish or gay, then one is rejected on the basis that, in another sense, everything else about oneself is being ignored. Nevertheless, for people such as the woman above, something very much like this distinction is crucially felt, because at stake is the possibility of finding the hiring process to have some meaning. Whether or not the current rigor and regulation of national searches only obfuscate or mask local examples of personal discrimination, candidates continue to will meaning into the proceedings precisely in this way.

They do this in two ways. First, by insisting that the verdict preserve the character of a *relation*, and then, second, by keeping open the notion that any one verdict has in fact come about because a relation has been abused. The trouble with such reasoning isn't that it's at best only compensatory for the fateful terminal consequences of an exquisitely formalized system. The trouble is, a more "personalized" logic really proceeds on the basis of the very traditional model of authority that the legalistic model has been installed to replace. The result? The traditional one is felt to remain, now, paradoxically, in order to redress the injustices of the new legalistic one.

Understood in this context, political correctness is actually at cross-purposes with itself, and hence its imperatives can't be neatly explained either as agreeing with a liberal social agenda or as conservatively reacting against one. And from the bottom up, those under the sway of the academic hiring process have no coherent politics about the fact. They just don't have any power, and so they insist that they have been personally, irrationally alienated from the profession itself at the very point of entry.[3] Meanwhile, elites respond, from the top down, by trying to refine the very criteria which have been responsible for the abuse. Second-rate institutions try to fall in line. But they don't share the same scholarly "mission" to refine the same criteria. (See Jones for one example of the resultant misunderstanding.) So everybody winds up agreeing about the wrong reasons to hire someone, while not knowing the right reasons.

Meanwhile, the most readily available handbooks urge candidates for the job interview, under "Do's," to "shake hands firmly and stand until offered a chair" or, under "Don't's," not to "hang around after the interview." Meanwhile, hundreds and thousands of candidates continue to get regretful letters each year about how worthy they are, if not quite adequately so considering the hundreds and thousands of other candidates. I have another friend who told me that her year's rejections were much more bearable because one place wrote her a lovely letter. She showed me the sentence that moved her most: "The profession needs many, many more persons of your skills, dedication, and love for our discipline." What to say? That it's a formula nevertheless? I didn't. Yet my conviction is that hiring abides now in a time of formulas.

What should a candidate think after reading several of these letters? That they are all designed to conceal how total is the evacuation of any personal connection? Or should a candidate wonder if she sat down too soon? Or if he should have shown up at all? The rigor and regulation designed to replace the old boy network seems to have instead bred a vast ignorance, by means of which the occasion of the interview emerges, by default, as the most determinable moment in the hiring process, regardless of the position of an institution within academic hierarchy. The cost to the profession is a widespread cynicism about the hiring process, which by now, I believe, is essential to the continuation of the process.

2.

The clearest examples of this cynicism are textual ones. The statement that so-and-so university is "an Affirmative Action/Equal

Opportunity employer" (sometimes followed by some statement to the effect that minorities are urged to apply) is in fact a code, and a bad one, because there's no way to accurately decipher it as meaning necessarily that a position is for minorities only. Letters of recommendation are possibly even more deceitful, with even less reason. A pseudoanonymous piece on a real affirmative action search in *Lingua Franca* records the following result of the interview round at the national convention: "Virtually everybody was worse in person than on paper, which was inevitable, given the implausibility of their letters of recommendation: every applicant was the 'best in years.' (This was true, in one professor's letter, for each of three candidates he was recommending.)" (23).

Let me not linger over the curious intricacies of either of these two texts alone. One could assess them by saying that it's one thing to claim such textual practices continue because no better ones have been found. It's quite another to maintain that the practices continue because nobody much cares about them anymore, except as phases through which the verdict has to proceed. Because, furthermore, no definitive text is necessary for the verdict—administrations just inform departments that positions have been disallowed and departments are free to inform candidates or not that searches have been aborted—everybody can feel that the real action is going on off the page anyway.

Is it? What is going on? Safe, not to say shrouded, within both an opaquely traditional and luminously legalistic framework, "the real action," when it finally issues in the form of a verdict, may simply be impossible to adequately stipulate. Burke, describing the various facets of the visit to campus and noting the importance of "collegiality," makes a somewhat surprising point: "Yet the basis of choice—the clincher that gets the job—was rarely described in personal terms by the chairpersons interviewed"(64). Instead, it seems the terms—ranging from quality of research to "style"—were pretty much in place before the visit. Such things as poise or warmth were also mentioned as factors, however, and there appears to be no substitute for "personal dynamism."

A reader of Burke's own research could speculate as follows: if chairs are reluctant to mention "personal terms," it's not because they're more comfortable with standardized, objective criteria. "The clincher" may be, at root, most often the result of factors that no one fully comprehends—as in my earlier account of a department vote. Similarly, one looks in vain for the precise moment in Kluge's account of a Kenyon hiring when the tide turns in favor of the eventual winner. The clincher may well be the result of factors no one cares to comprehend, for it has been the burden of all the other factors which preceded it to make the clincher appear inevitable and logical. Could the silence with which I concluded my own account be an indication, in one instance anyway, that we all lacked the solace of an appearance?

"At the gates of the professional world," writes Larson, "the professional minorities who control a field do not receive an undifferentiated mass of entrants, but a super-filtered, super-classified, specialized, and hierarchicized cohort" (204). Exactly. So once a gate swings open, it makes no sense to think that a newly-authorized professional strides through for reasons which were accidentally formed, deeply biased, and fundamentally undifferentiated. The entire hiring process as it exists in academic life today constitutes a massive effort not so much to produce "the clincher" but to create it—as if, somehow, a group of human beings can consistently evaluate other human beings on an individual basis which is perfectly reasonable and just. No wonder, we might say, that those who are evaluated emerge just as consistently incredulous.

I believe that at the center of the hiring process, especially when it is mandated to have no center, is mystery. "The cincher" is a profoundly inexplicable thing. There are those who are in touch with the mystery, and those who are not. Those who are can at present purchase their intimacy with an affective vocabulary of victimization, while those who are not preserve their distance with a bureaucratized vocabularly of ideological rectitude. Granted, the possibilities of each vocabulary are mediated through the hierarchical position of any one institution. At bottom, though, what separates each vocabulary is not a vision of the profession, or even of the institution, but of human relations.

You don't even necessarily have to be on one side of the hiring line or the other. Let me illustrate with another example from my own experience. One of the loveliest moments I've ever witnessed during an interview occurred some years ago while my department was undergoing its annual search for someone to fill a position in linguistics; a local favorite, undissertated, waited in the wings. This particular year yielded one of the most impressive candidates I'd ever seen. On paper, it was obvious she had to be invited to campus, although it was not yet required for members of the search committee to operate according to a schematic checklist; such action would eventually come under the scrutiny of the office of "Social Equity," as is the local case today.

On the search committee that year was a member who had become rather seriously smitten by composition theory, especially one particular theorist whom she made a point of asking every candidate about at a crucial moment in the interview. None so far had heard of him; she was content. When she asked the fateful question to an unusually poised and articulate linguist, however, the woman just turned to her, smiled, and replied: "No, I haven't heard of him. Could you tell me something about him?" The member was so startled she couldn't explain very well. I tried not to laugh out loud. Another member had to intercede in order to finish what our colleague had fumbled.

The superb reply was wasted of course. Participate in a hiring process even for a year and you're likely to see—or imagine—enough waste to last a career, especially when what goes under the name of "scholarship" has gotten sorted out among the candidates and you are down to human cases. At Clarion, such cases are really all that hiring can be about. During this particular year, the faction for the local favorite held firm; eventually the department couldn't agree on anything, and had to roll the search over for another year. I never had a chance to vote for the above woman. The search had been wasted. The only thing cinched was its waste.

What I realized, once it was apparent the verdict was foreclosed, is that I'd have voted for the above woman solely on the basis of her reply. Of course to me it epitomized everything about her, on paper as well as in person. I could have made a perfectly reasonable case had I been called upon to do so. Yet what seems to me especially compelling now is that I didn't care. Her reply clinched things for me because it simply transcended the pointless occasion. Moreover, the contrast was just too garish between the shabby departmental stage and the radiant human actor. I wanted—what? Justice? Revenge? I couldn't say. I still can't. Perhaps I wanted an entirely different hiring process. Or maybe I was suddenly shocked at how cynical I'd become about it, and then longed to vote as if the position were a lost belief that could still be affirmed nonetheless. How many times in a career is one impelled to represent incoherence?

Writing over a decade later, I probably make the power of my feelings less mysterious than I believe I felt them then. Feelings are misleading, after all. So are words about them. This is why hiring has procedures and why these procedures have guidelines. Yet this is also why procedures and guidelines are continually in danger of being overcome with stray thoughts, irrelevant considerations, symbolic possibilities, and deep-seated fears. Because of tenure, academics have to make decisions about new people who could be colleagues for the rest of the lifetimes of all concerned. Aronowitz states that "typically the successful candidate must demonstrate his *lack* of independence, originality, and hubris" ("Last Good Job," 98). Because academics are able (so far) to retain the security of tenure in the downsized, cut-back 90s, there is now as never before only the condition of getting hired.

Therefore, the successive phases of a professional career are increasingly collapsed into its initial one. (This is part of what "preprofessionalism" means.) First-rate institutions may still command the scholarly criteria by which faculty should not be granted tenure. Second-rate institutions continue to suffer the lack of such criteria. It will be some years before the infusion of people from Duke or Chicago at these institutions will alter expectations, if at all. (Meanwhile, the cost-effective, revenue-driven business model traced by Rhodes and Slaughter continues apace.) For the present, each time what continues to be at stake in a departmental hiring is deciding all over again how old you want someone to be whom you hire, or how aggressive, or even how phycially attractive—and not finally having to publicly justify the factors that cinch a Number One choice, not to anybody outside, and sometimes not even anybody inside the department.

And of course, from a purely social point of view, this is just as it should be. Social equity be damned. Why shouldn't a ready smile at the departmental coffee pot be preferable to a quick excursion into the theoretical frontiers of the discipline? Just because the officials who guard the roads and issue visas decree that people shouldn't care about such things? How can even professionals be prevented from caring, or from getting the ceremonies of the coffee pot mixed up with the imperatives of the post-colonial critique? Moreover, if a candidate is black or female, the negative judgment a group of people can make is too easily understood as a prejudical one. More often than not, it's probably just a more broadly social one; in any case, race or gender doesn't explain everything. As somebody remarks during Kluge's Kenyon search, regarding a man who might not "connect" with the students: "I'm concerned about having people around who are thinking, but it's no good if there's no one around to talk to" (156).

Furthermore, if to prevent the possibility of racial or gender prejudice remains the reason why the rules continue to insist upon these very categories anyway, it's not clear what clarity this insistence offers either those who receive a verdict or those who deliver one. How to insist on the mystery of what *cinches* a choice without seeming either to defend or decry its most reactionary components? I suppose finally we have only our imaginations. Consider the familiar horror story with which Wayne Booth begins his latest collection of essays, *The Vocation of a Teacher*. A former Ph.D. student reports that in her only interview at the national convention—one response to twenty-nine letters of inquiry sent—the six people there hadn't read her dossier, repeatedly misunderstood one of the main points she emphasized about her dissertation, and got both her name and marital designation wrong. Booth is outraged. Now, some years later, he imagines a protest letter to the main offender, with the following postscript: "Your victim recovered; she now teaches and publishes—brilliantly, as you could have predicted if you had taken the trouble to see her" (4).

This seems to me an excellent example of how the routine applicability of first-rate standards acts to limit a comprehensive understanding of getting hired as much as the application of second-rate standards does. Is it conceivable that Booth's student didn't get her ideas out fast enough, or lacked the poise to deal adroitly with stupid objections? Is it not too appropriate, moreover, that Booth tells a story which has a happy ending? The *sheer* waste of the hiring process isn't really waste if it can be recuperated as success. (I did chance, though, to learn that the linguist in my own story above in fact got a job.) Its injustice isn't mysterious if it's always the result of rudeness. Getting hired in horror stories outrages too easily. On the contrary, losing a job doesn't always mean that the right people lost out for the wrong reasons.

Getting hired probably shouldn't be continually recreated as if it ought to make sense, especially if it doesn't always make sense anymore even in terms of academic hierarchy. Let me give another kind of story: Alexander Theroux has a little essay in which he maintains, to his own venerable credit, that "trying to survive by means of one's pen is a noble but precarious alternative" to teaching. So what to do? "Many an autumn I've found myself standing cap in hand in some English department or other where various poke-nosed officials and subheads—often without my experience, sometimes without my degrees, almost always without my competence—gathered together, peevishly took my measurements, and generally regarding me as an outlaw or a mongrel or both, grudgingly threw a course my way" (36).

This is wonderful stuff. Reading Theroux, one thinks that getting hired is so little written about because, like writing a dissertation, it is something to get through or get done. Theroux, however, defiantly without dissertation and proudly remote from the tenure track, can excoriate academics with rare gusto. Therefore, we wonder, since he still needs a job, how does he get one? I'd like to suggest one reason: academics like him. It makes some sense: who else could appreciate the gusto? It doesn't make enough; what about competition from people such as Booth's former student? Theroux himself might be embarrassed. He likes to snarl, and he'd rather be thought a cur than just another animal in his cage. Yet how, then, can he explain why he comes across—on the page anyway—as instead just the sort of fire-in-his-eyes being, subcategory: creative writer, who makes everybody glow?

Theroux reinstates the question: why does anybody get hired? What's the clincher? Perhaps he suggests a simple answer: the clincher may be unrecoverable, in pretty much all cases. Legal narratives don't deliver the clincher; they just set up a story line. Professional narratives don't deliver the clincher; to the degree these narratives function smoothly, they just express the stratifications of academic hierarchy. If we have to have narratives, I prefer fiction, so I want to focus on a clincher of unusual resonance and beauty contained in Bernard Malamud's academic novel, *A New Life* (1961). The first thing to say, however, is that there hardly seems any hiring process to be described; the hero, S. Levin, merely recalls at one point how relieved he is that the director of composition apparently doesn't know he, Levin, applied to over fifty other places, including the more prestigious rival of the one which accepted him.

The novel takes place in the mid-50s, when Reid, it will be recalled, got his dissertation and when O'Toole got his ascension. "We've been hearing from people from every state in the Union," muses the director. "For next year I already have a pile of applications half a foot high." (12) He could be speaking in the mid-90s. The difference is that it's clear to him this pile constitutes recognition, not work (and certainly not work for a committee.) That is, at least on the evidence of this example, the conditions of hiring are becoming national in scope by the mid-50s, yet evaluation remains local in operation. Indeed, we might think no more about exactly why Levin was chosen if he did not later ask another colleague about it, because he suddenly fears he accepted a cheaper salary than anybody else would: $3,000.

With this query, the matter of why Levin was hired comes to exert a shaping force in the novel. Much later, after learning that Levin is refusing to support his candidacy for chairman, the director exclaims: "Sometimes I curse the day I brought you here" (284). Levin asks why; the director refuses to answer him. Not until very late in the novel does Levin learn that in fact he was chosen because the director's wife—with whom he is now having an affair—was engaged by a picture of Levin that he chanced to include with his application. He knows he didn't have to. "It was an old picture. I wanted them to know what I looked like." "You looked as though you needed a friend," says the wife. "Was that the reason?" She replies, "I needed one." "Your picture reminded me of a Jewish boy I knew in college who was very kind to me during a trying time in my life." (331)

From among a number of ways to interpret this story, I would like to emphasize two: first, getting hired as a manifestation of human presence, and, second, getting hired as an amorous relation. Perhaps the second is more scandalous, but the first is bad enough. One thinks no further than how haunting the absence of a real human being is in letters of recommendation, or how grimly ironic actual presence may be in terms of these texts. (See the chapter on them in Caesar, *Conspiring*.) It seems as if by the mid-50s, the inclusion of pictures with one's application was already somewhat unusual; certainly in our own deprejudiced and undiscriminated day, a real photograph could only be quite literally seen as providing too provocative grounds for all sorts of retrograde judgments. Levin's lover-to-be makes one.

Of course his attractiveness to her has, in one sense, absolutely nothing to do with his performance as a potential member of an English department, teaching composition. In another sense, however, the qualities of sympathy, concern, and vulnerability which Pauline intuits are precisely those which Levin effectively demonstrates, even in his professional capacity. *A New Life* becomes a rich exploration of the mystery of human choice. Levin turns out to be the right man for the job. Pauline turns out to have made the correct decision, for properly compelling reasons, based on the accurate evidence.

Malamud's text constitutes a rebuke to any process of getting hired, insofar as it is predicated upon voiding all but the most abstract, impersonal registers of human presence. The more one restores this presence, the more unreasonable, subjective, and irrational one's response is likely to be—which is only an argument against such qualities if one has a conception of human relations in which much of what is human simply is not to be trusted. One thing, paradoxically, is trust itself. What is the basis for it? Does Pauline, looking at Levin's picture, trust her response? What should she have in order to do so, other than a vision of remembered love or a conviction of human need?

Of course no hiring procedure can satisfactorily answer these questions. My quarrel with the one currently in place is finally that it conducts itself as if such questions simply didn't exist. They do. Answers to them move actual human beings, because some sort of trust must be summoned up—even before a few live candidates will eventually fly in. Transcripts, letters of recommendation, and statements of interest all speak of more than facts, or of identity politics either negatively or positively considered. What else? There's no way of guaranteeing. The happily chosen few candidates always already appear in the flesh too late. Just as often, they arrive to unsettle as to cinch the logic of proceedings from which they have been constructed to emerge.

Once they appear, of course the candidates don't offer themselves to be loved. Nevertheless, Malamud's narrative is one of love—the love that, so to speak, is embedded in the "calling" of a profession, or of the profession considered as a calling. No matter that love can't express itself as such in this context and can only justify itself—if at all—in some other context. Levin initially presents himself as someone in need of love; the narrative provides someone to love him just as it provides him with a job. This may not be the state of affairs suggested by any candidate in search of a college teaching position. But it's close enough. Many things about getting hired are clarified by its correspondence to an amorous relation.

3.

One thinks, for example, about the many feelings unsuccessful candidates are left with once the fateful letter comes, thanking them for their interest; mentioning the multitude of other candidates; and wishing them luck in the future. How to comprehend the inescapable envy these candidates feel at others chosen instead—not to mention their baffled desire, lost innocence, or lingering bitterness over some felt unworthiness? An objectified hiring process has to be presumed to exist in some form, if only so that there are measures to insure against the actualization of some "personal" connection, founded on the equation between hiring and loving.

So many amorous overtones abide as constitutive features of the hiring process (from how either party "woos" the other to how certain sorts of contracts are modeled on prenuptial agreements) that it would be tedious to list them. "Nobody wants me!" I heard a desperate friend with a dissertation nearly "in hand" cry awhile ago. She's a woman. In the erotics (if not the politics) of hiring, is the candidate always in the "feminine" position? To consider in these terms the above two women, whose prospects first seemed so good, it was as if the first had been stood up (he had promised to call), and as if the second woman was abandoned at the altar (it was all a mistake). Kafka's characterization about the verdict is so acute because it can just as easily apply to falling in love as getting hired.

I want to insist upon getting hired as an amorous proceeding now that a tenurable teaching position in American higher education, at virtually any level, is fast coming to be accepted as effectively remaining in the same place for the duration of your career, (pending tenure itself). Indeed, we might well ask, how much mobility have the rest of the tenured faculty had at all levels for the past ten or twenty years? Apart from the upper echelons, I would guess not much. In comparison, Reid or O'Toole each appears to have assumed far more, and got it. They were each members of the last generation to enjoy wide and substantial job mobility in their discipline. At present, there is marriage or there is nothing, and this has been the case for some time.

Of course, I'm considering only tenured professors in this connection, not those temporary faculty who've had, by default, careers trying to get tenure, or those part-time faculty who've never been able to get on the right track. One regularly reads now that teachers on temporary contracts staff anywhere from 40% to 60% of any one institution's classes. The amorous terms of hiring are only exploitive for temporary teachers. On the other hand, those faculty fortunate enough to enjoy conjugal rights during the past two decades can be characterized in the following manner: especially at second-rate institutions, they have had marriages from which there has been little or no chance for divorce. Can it be any coincidence, therefore, that the specific amorous correspondence that developed in the hiring process during those decades was the one of a loveless marriage?

Susan Sontag has an essay on Camus that she begins in the following way: "Great writers are either husbands or lovers. Some writers supply the solid virtues of a husband: reliability, intelligibility, generosity, decency. There are other writers in whom one prizes the gifts of a lover, gifts of temperament rather than of moral goodness. Notoriously, women tolerate qualities in a lover— moodiness; selfishness; unreliability; brutality—that they would never countenance in a husband, in return for excitement, an infusion of intense feeling" (52). In precisely the same way, candidates for a job are either husbands or lovers. What has happened in recent decades is that a hiring process has evolved in order to solicit husbands, exclusively.

Why? "Things changed," writes Kluge, "everyone agrees, in the seventies and the eighties. The college made it clear it wanted faculty to do research, to stake a claim in their fields, to be known by their counterparts in other places" (164). But this only gestures at the fact of professionalization; it doesn't explain why professionalization came about, and why "research" would have some impact even at institutions in the hierarchy that, unlike Kenyon, had no means to implement or even enforce it. (For incisive surveys of future prospects, see Clark, Oakley, and Massey in the *Daedalus* volume.) Whether we link the current job crisis to inflation or the corporate ideology of "downsizing," there is one thing I would emphasize: professionalization proceeded, as usual, from the top down, and, as it proceeded, cut off further the chances of upward mobility from the bottom up, which could have taken place only by means of research.

An importance consequence follows: professionalization amounts to a systematic discrimination against lovers in favor of husbands. Sontag concludes thus: "It's a great pity when one is forced to choose between them." Nonetheless, in recruitment as well as love one is forced to choose, especially if the reasons in the first place to go looking for love dry up.[4] In addition, husbands have been consistently chosen for college teaching positions in recent decades by professors at all levels who have been getting, like the times, older and more conservative; there's simply no reason to risk the civil pleasures of the departmental coffee pot for flashy candidates who might move on or witty ones who look as if they might not want to volunteer to head the curriculum committee. "He won't stay," I heard from more than one colleague about a particular candidate during another recent departmental search. Translation: he'll be unfaithful.

Lately, we might say, things have grown more tense and vocal. Lovers have been insisting that they should have the chance to be regarded as husbands, while husbands have been lamenting that there are suddenly not enough lovers—unless there are too many, all of them either graduate students (where they can be nevertheless taken for granted for the service they provide) or part-time (where they can be ritually lamented for the service they provide). (See, for example, Boxer's account of the most recent MLA.) But the peculiar kind of official relation to an institution represented by entry-level employment has not been infused by fresh energies, much less eroticized ones. The point of the professionalized narrative of getting hired continues to be to pledge young Ph.D.'s (who have themselves been getting steadily older) to the stable, permanent virtues of the tenure track. It is as if the point of falling in love were to get married. Teaching off the tenure track has, therefore, not been quite *respectable*—like being a single person looking for sex in a room full of married couples who don't smoke, drink, or disparage each other's children.

Or to put it another way, teaching off the tenure track has not been to have a career. What has it meant to have an academic career during recent decades? In a sense, nothing more than to get tenure. (See Phelan's efforts to generate a rationale after tenure.) Fixed, not to say fixated, at the moment of entry, it is as if the very imagination of the profession has gotten very intricate about what it means to be hired, in proportion to how it has gotten very slack about what it means to have a career beyond tenure. Of course, if you're not expected to do research, there's not much reason to worry about this disproportion. (See Bèrubè and Nelson for a widely-cited proposal to revalue teaching in such instances, 14–17.) If you are, then the project of what to do after tenure can be left to itself, once the imperative of what to do before tenure is substituted for it. Such a substitution may have become inescapable with the continuing increase of so many in competition for so few jobs. What this has meant in practice, however, now ought to be clear: a transformation of an older conception of the academic profession as a "calling."

The idea of a "calling" is, I think, a charismatic one. Its very force is enshrined in academic lore by the professor whose way with learning is so vivid, or challenging, or maddening that the student, and eventual professor-to-be, is enchanted. (See Kluge, for example, on his beloved Professor Denham Sutcliffe, 8–11, or Tompkins, 61 and 79.) Furthermore, the idea is nothing if not a

religious one, as recalled most memorably to me, at one point in
Lionel Trilling's famous story, "Of That Time, Of That Place." There
the tortured student, Tertan, says the following in a letter to the
dean about his Professor Howe: "To him more than another I give
my gratitude . . . a noble man, but merely dedicated, not consecrated"
(81). To be called into a profession, that is, is something not to be
reduced to a mere *motive*. Perhaps Wilbur, in his handbook entry,
registers the venerable conception in his own way when he forebears treating the question of why anyone would want to enter
college teaching in the first place.

His own treatment, however, cannot avoid evoking a quite
different, far more disabused, realistic, and instrumental conception. In the same way, as I've already tried to narrate in an earlier
chapter, any hiring process recreates in its own image those whom
it would solicit. In Larson's remarks upon a profession as representing a "calling," she stresses that no matter how the calling
comes to constitute, as it must, "an essential dimension of the self,"
this notion remains an ideologically constructed one. Therefore, she
continues, the more instrumental its choice becomes, or the more
material, the less peer esteem matters and the more the idea of
calling is eroded (227). Of course, she is speaking of peers here in
the honorific professional sense.

Today, on the contrary, any conception of a calling in the professional narrative of college teaching is so submerged, socialized,
and domesticated that it may as well be effaced. I read somewhere
that intelligence agencies the world over measure a potential agent's
vulnerability according to an American acronym knowm as MICE:
money; ideology; compromise; and ego. Departments in American
higher education are not yet so ruthless. But I think it's widely
understood that, for hiring purposes, noble ideals are beside the
point, unless the occasion requires some judgment about how well
a candidate can manipulate a rhetorical vocabulary.

Indeed, the discursive idiom these days in higher education
appears to emphasize what one's job has in common with those in
other professions, or even those that are not professions at all. At
a crucial concluding moment in his study of English departments,
Evan Watkins invokes the experience of an old junior-high friend,
a baker, and his previous pages are filled with comparisons of
English departments to advertising agencies (or of *Hamlet* to a
Wheaties commercial). Contra Larson, it's as if to Watkins what
matters most in his profession is what it has in common with the
larger labor market. At one point, he states: "English is not a

workplace in the same way as a GM plant, but it governs the designation of work just as surely" (12).

Such hedging seems to me to disclose not only the consequences of candidates from Duke having to apply to Clarion. The fact is, college teachers are no longer certain about what professional story to tell themselves—especially when each passing year discloses that, if an academic workplace is not an auto plant, it is being run by the administration according to the same principles.[5] Have the old narratives simply been exhausted? Whether what you need is not ideals but a job, or not the same old job but some other one, to profess the sheer wonder by which you were once called may simply be embarrassing anymore. (Compare Jane Tompkins, whose efforts to reinvigorate her teaching are unashamed.) Watkins, for one, would find such testimony appallingly naive, even if he appears to have none better—or even any at all—with which to replace it.

This is why hiring is so important. Through the process we are initiated not only into the "ideological solidarity" of a profession, but into the profession as the basis for a life plan. How ought departmental sociality fit into the plan? It depends upon too many factors; it needn't even fit at all. What about institutional legalism? It's ultimately beside the point, because it proposes no plan at all, being only concerned that minority or disadvantaged groups get the opportunity to have a career in the first place. No matter how ineffable the constituent elements or how laudable the goal, getting hired is vitiated by unacknowledged tensions and misplaced consequences. Prejudices have not been eliminated. They have not even been understood. It may be debatable who understands them less— those who support the ideological rectitude of the legalistic agenda, or those who oppose this agenda either because it's mystified or politicized. (See Williams, *PC Wars*.) But there seems to me little to debate about one thing: no one understands prejudice who refuses to recognize the sheer oppression of legality itself. If it hasn't transformed the whole notion of a career in college teaching, it's more or less already banished an older conception of such a career.

The traditional model of authority, when it reigned unchallenged, may have countenanced wayward, eccentric, or deviant energies no better. All that might be claimed for it is this: the model was more intimate with charismatic license—the very license which today's legalistic model has to repress in order to enjoy any authority at all. Of the multitude of reasons why one person gets hired, how many, even today, are in fact so wide of the mark

as to amount to a mockery of the rules? We'll never know. We only
know the rules. We just don't know their relation to the Therouxs
who somehow manage to get their bones each semester, or to the
Reids who just manage to go their own ways, even at places where
there's more social or institutional pressure to keep everybody in
line. And what reasons can we tell about the rules to people who
don't get jobs, who would probably reply, in turn, that they themselves are better than the reasons, if not the rules?

In any case, nobody's telling. Getting hired means not entering
into a dialogue with anybody about it, but instead listening to what
you need to know—from eminent critics of the profession, from
handbooks, from the MLA, from the peers who have secured jobs
and from those who have not. I've been claiming that ultimately
there may be very little to know that will prove decisive, especially
if the return of older, repressed energies is reinstated at the very
inception of the employment process, where, I believe, getting hired
is always very difficult to separate from getting chosen. How to you
get chosen? Because you're exceptional. But how can you be sure?
On what basis? You really only know when you're chosen—and
then, if you're adequate to the realization, you receive it as something to celebrate, but not necessarily as something to understand.[6]

The moment is therefore nothing if not a fictional one, and I
want to resort to a last fiction in order to illustrate something of
how it works. There's a lovely passage early in E.L. Doctorow's
Billy Bathgate after Billy has been rewarded a ten-dollar bill for
his juggling prowess, along with the judgment that he's a "capable
boy," by Dutch Schultz. Dutch and entourage proceed to leave. Billy
is suddenly surrounded by a gang of jealous boys. But he slips
away, and delivers the following exultation:

> Oh you miserable fucking louts, that I ever needed to at-
> tach my orphan self to your wretched company . . . you dumb-
> bells, that you could aspire to a genius life of crime, with
> your dead witless eyes, your slack chins, and the simian
> slouch of your spines—fuck you forever, I consign you to
> tenement rooms and bawling infants, and sluggish wives
> and a slow death of incredible subjugation, I condemn you
> to petty crimes and mean rewards and vistas of cell block
> to the end of your days. (41)

Is it conceivable that a professor of English—Ed Cohen, say—
could direct such words at the hundreds above whom he is about

to ascend, now that he rather than they has been hired? Probably not. It's hard to feel exceptional against a background of hundreds; the point about getting hired today is that you're simply not entitled to feel that you've been, in some profound sense, chosen. Why was it you? You'll probably never learn, any more than you'll ever learn why it wasn't. And what if you've only landed a temporary job? In this last instance, the burden may be merely to feel lucky rather than exceptional, especially if you've had an education at a fast-track, exceptional institution, whose terms could never have prepared you for winding up somewhere below where things feel slow and subjugated.

Among many other reasons why Billy's exultation would not be appropriate at present, let me mention a final one: Billy himself would most likely have long ago been excluded from consideration. His notion of a career, after all, is that it sponsors a "genius" life. This represents, in turn, another profession entirely. Or at most it embraces teaching only at its most elite level, where the theory is heavy and the travel is light. These subjects, respectively, comprise my final two chapters. Meanwhile, for the profession as it actually determines itself at the point of entry, particularly at all institutional levels below, the life to which Billy condemns his fellows is precisely the same slow life with which everyone is presented.

CHAPTER SEVEN

Theory in the Boondocks

"Apparently he wasn't prepared to be a metaphor."

—Paul Simon on Joe DiMaggio's initial dislike of the
lyric, "Where have you gone, Joe DiMaggio?"

1.

In the fall of 1991, three things converged my life. Two were textual: reading an article in that summer's *Critical Inquiry*, "Masterpiece Theatre: An Academic Melodrama," by the eminent feminist critics, Sandra Gilbert and Susan Gubar, while receiving both the local and national reading of an article of my own in that summer's *South Atlantic Quarterly*, "On Teaching at A Second-Rate University." (See my first chapter.) The third thing was pedagogical: teaching a graduate course in literary theory. What these three things have in common is a certain space in which the central experience of *naming* comes about. The space is institutional. The space for academic life is always institutional. Gilbert and Gubar's spoof about academicized ideology gives it a generic name, Boondock State University, whereas at an actual institution I simultaneously gave it an actual name and studied it from a specific site. One purpose of this chapter will be to raise the question whether my course could have given this institutional space another name.

First I must separately unravel the course I taught with respect to its institutional setting. Not everything is said by stating
that the subject of literary theory is simply impossible to teach at
a university such as Clarion. But much is. Most of the students are
mediocre at best. They read, innocently. They have absolutely no
background in literary criticism and no knowledge of literary theory;
although the department's modest graduate program was recently
redesigned in order to emphasize the importance of these things,
only English 509 is installed to address them. Nobody has any
authority to oversee how theory might have some implication in
the rest of the curriculum.

At the end of the semester, I asked my students to write what
they felt had been at stake in the course. One said, "In many cases,
the central question is whether or not I have even understood what
the authors wrote." "What is at stake in this course is my ability
of perception," another put down. For students such as these the
matter of what textbook to require is crucial. The material is hard.[1]
That fall I chose *Literature in the Modern World*, edited by Dennis
Walder. As the title suggests, it's really not a theory collection at
all. Most of the writings have a more practical aim, and what
especially commended me to Walder is his introductory apology
that one will not find "very many examples of the higher reaches
of theoretical debate, the 'post-structuralist' work of Lacan and
Derrida. . . . But you should find those higher reaches more accessible once you have worked through what is here" (3).

In Gilbert and Gubar's narrative, the heroine, Jane, needs help
after a poor, confused Text is found abandoned by the fast track of
the railroad crossing. A junior professor who doesn't know much
about theory, she decides to fax a memo to all the important critics.
She is so naive as to term them "humanists!" Jane would not have
faxed Dennis Walder. But, above, is he speaking like a humanist?
I didn't care. His strictures were fine with me. For once, I would be
content to work in the clear, lucid regions below. Soon we were
peering and squinting among such of Walder's categories as "Ques-
tioning the Canon" and "Literature and Commitment."

It was slow going. "Did we seem too please-Teacher-tell-me-
what-this-story-means?" another student reflected at the end about
her education prior to the course. My own answer: yes, alas, we
had been. In fact, we hadn't been sure from the very start how else
to seem, particularly when "meaning" was presented as a "problematic" affair and the very teacher's authority arguably a "hegemonic discourse." During our second meeting one woman said she

saw no reason for all this "jargon." I tried to persuade her that much of our own cherished critical vocabulary was once so reviled. Who mentioned the example of "irony?" I think it wasn't until the fourth meeting that the woman dropped the course.

Back at Gilbert's and Gubar's timeless Boondock, of course, the students have never been violated by such idioms. Jane has, presumably, during a few theory courses taken in grad school, and the only result is that she's just all mixed up now. But the aims of her teaching are remorselessly practical and faultlessly undergraduate anyway. She doesn't know what to say to the Text, when it is brought to her by campus security. At one point during the first few weeks of my own graduate theory course at Clarion, on the other hand, I had made the fateful decision to require everybody to read Louis Althusser's, "Ideology and Ideological State Apparatuses."

A mistake. Indeed, midway through, a disaster. Must the narrative of teaching always be a success? Sometimes it's not because of apparently trivial things; I didn't know until well into our first session on it that the full text is not included in the most widely available anthology. (See Adams and Searle.) But then, would the students have understood better the long portion they had read? Who can say? "Ideology," in Althusser's celebrated claim, "represents the imaginary relationship of individuals to the real conditions of their existence" (Althusser, 159, 162).

That is, what if Althusser, or ideology, or theory itself simply can't be taught in the actual conditions of many institutions? Indeed, if Boondock State isn't one, then why is Boondock the boondocks? By the time we got to Althusser, there was a more significant development: several students had become almost openly hostile. It may have been that the one Hungarian student's antipathy to anything "Communistic" (I was never sure how she'd found her way into the country, much less the program) had focused their insecurities. Such things in the classroom are always enormously elusive. It's just as likely my eventual impatience with only one student may have made others at once more protective of her and more aggressive toward me. But then such dynamics seldom include everyone, and in this case they don't explain at all my impression of an implacable hostility to the very occasion just *there* as soon as our first session began.

What line would you need to sell theory to anyone at Boondock? Jane hasn't a clue. Gilbert and Gubar provide her with a faultlessly theoretical situation—nobody can make sense out of an abandoned text about which absolutely nothing is known, and the students who find it are scared of it—and then flood it with a comedy of ideological competition. What about Jane? At the end, when she resolves to try to read, she declares: "And I'm going to ask some students to help me" (Gilbert and Gubar, 712). Would that it were that easy! Instead, in my experience, you've got to appeal to their idealism. One of my favorite solicitations of theory is a passage where Elizabeth Bruss speaks of "a special quality to theoretical solutions, the peculiar allure of intelligibility in a highly concentrated form—a pattern so refined, so intense, so generally or even infinitely deployable, that it seems to verge on intellectual apotheosis" (129). I had passed out a xerox.

Of course such words are not guaranteed to have students screaming for Althusser, much less panting with indeployable joy after having read him. Yet in every theory course I've ever taught before or since but this one, the room was at least usually alive with something of the allure Bruss evokes. Previous students may have held back from it. But they felt it, and I felt it. After citing Jameson, Adorno, Weber, and Blanchot, Bruss goes on to speak of "the romance of transcendental intelligibility." Although this is not, in my experience, a prospect at which everyone swoons, at Boondock most students will at least get unsettled and provoked. A teacher of literary theory is best advised to look no closer into how long the romance will last, or whether it should have come about at all.

At Clarion during this fall semester, there was an inevitable hostile bright student. When she came to me after the second Althusser class to express how depressed she was ("it seems like there's no literature anymore, just ideology"), I chanced to give her "Masterpiece Theatre" after we talked for awhile. By then, I suppose, I just felt sunk in a differently-named Boondock once more. The anthology I had chosen was too conceptually thin. (This is one reason I had decided to supplement it with Althusser.) The students were too hapless. The course was obviously not going to go anywhere. Did I want, as if in apology, to disclose to the student something about the larger discursive conditions of a hopelessly small, isolated course in a woefully unhegemonic institution?

If so, such a real condition wasn't funny—to her or to me. Perhaps I hoped that reading about Boondock might apprise the student of the sheer comedy of ideological contention, and not merely its inescapable nature. Next week she returned my copy of the magazine. "Amusing," she allowed, still looking troubled. It was the last human word that passed between us. By semester's end she appeared to despise everything—all we'd read; theory itself; and, of course, me. If I had been able to ask her, what *name* would she have given for all that had gone wrong? My name? And what name would I have given? Boondock? By semester's end the class could be understood as a systematic failure of naming, and it seemed the essence of the conflict that none of possible names could be spoken.

There was one exception: Clarion. I have not tried to indicate the marked, yet elusive and withdrawn presence of my article on campus during the whole duration of this particular semester. Although I was very conscious that, for a time, everybody on campus was talking about me ("You're famous!" exclaimed a friend one day) nobody cursed, criticized, or even commented to my face. What had I done? In one sense, very simply: I had *named Clarion*. Not criticized it, necessarily; just named it. Had the theory course been somehow foreclosed before it had even begun by my awareness that it lacked a *name*? But what name could it have had? Clarion? "Clarion" as the name of a fatal second-ratedness? How many of the graduate students had read my article?

I believe now that during these months too much transpired in the seminar room about which names either couldn't be given or else just couldn't be expressed. Of course I could limit the nominative hollowness to the room. If I hadn't come to dislike a few of the students, I might have come to hate myself: in the face of so much intellectual timidity, my teaching of theory had lost what I took to be its customary poise and instead been subtly transformed into a species of advocacy. Yet what if the problem ultimately lay outside the room, far above campus, in the very sovereign conditions of institutional hierarchy, professional politics, and discursive power that Gilbert and Gubar had all so ingloriously staged at Boondock? Or rather, at Boondock's expense?

2.

The thing which riveted my attention immediately once I turned on Gilbert and Guber's "Masterpiece Theatre" was the setting. I was puzzled. In the boondocks, television is the closest one gets to the stars. Some places don't even have a railroad, much less a fast track. So why Boondock State University? Just so that there can be *somewhere* for a text to be discovered whose origin, meaning, and ideological profile are not known?

Certainly Boondock wouldn't be Boondock if, unlike Harvard or Duke, it either knew these things or knew how to know them.

Nor would Jane Marple be at Boondock if she knew; she knows something, to be sure, but it seems she has to teach too much (e.g. those handouts for the nine o'clock class) and so she must call Phyllis Franklin, the first of many others who know more, and, more important, have the institutional authority to make what they know count.

Boondock, in other words, is a blank space in which to write ignorance, drudgery, and stupidity.[2] Of course such horrors only have to be suggested, because the real point about BSU is that it exists for the imperious gaze of all the non-BSU institutions, each so empowered by sophistication and privilege that to hear of a Boondock is an occasion for wonder. So off everybody goes to re-write Boondock. Boondock is suddenly, as Frank Lentricchia says, "where it's at," because enormous political and theoretical energies have used up everywhere else (706).

Understood this way, the setting of "Masterpiece Theatre" has a more subtle rationale: what Harold Bloom terms "the text in Boondock" is in fact a displacement for the text of Boondock. BSU has, like Gilbert and Gubar's text, no history. When interrogated, it can hardly tell a trace from a glyph and it doesn't understand about all the fuss over thematizing, much less hegemonic hetero-sexuality. The difference is that the text, unlike the institution, has been invested by elites with interest and provocation. There is little known about BSU, on the other hand, because a little suffices.

And yet a little doesn't really suffice. It's been an idea of mine for some time that such key *topi* of contemporary theory as margin-ality and materiality function as they do because the institutional politics of the profession are so top-heavy. The discourse about canonicity, in fact, registers how few universities are actively in-cluded, at the price of excluding so many others.[3] The same names, from the same universities, continue to speak to each other about the same questions; what "Masterpiece Theatre" does is circulate everything once again, this time as farce, but now staged at Boondock. Could it be that BSU was all along a repressed textual domain of its own?

But why? On nobody's map, its job has presumably been to provide a commonplace, stable setting against which could be waged exciting bouts over such issues as canonicity by critics at major research institutions. (Or, more lately, excited considerations over graduate job prospects; see, for example, Bèrubè's contemplation about such places as the College of Lake County or even "Central High" in *Employment*, 84–5.) What Gilbert and Gubar disclose is that these bouts, in turn, can be comprehended as efforts to make sure that Boondock stays in "the hinterlands," as Johnathan Culler locates it at one point, while announcing, bravely, that he's on his way there (707). That a heretofore unclassified, untheorized text has been found at *Boondock* is as grave a crisis as could be imagined by the profession. The margin cannot hold!

The fact is that in order for there to be Brown or Cornell, it is vital that there be BSU. Arguably, it is even more vital that institutional hierarchy be understood as something so obvious as to be not worth remarking upon, much less investigating. However, the sheer blankness of Boondock remains perpetually available—for comedy, usually, but suddenly for charm, seduction, and even fear when the centers discover themselves grown so infatuated by decenteredness that they are almost bored. Gilbert and Gubar are very funny at demonstrating the mood; the attendant result, when there are only so many theoretical claims articulable before the very idea of centrality itself becomes evacuated, is that it falls upon Boondock to take up the slack. Another consequence may be less intended by them: BSU, a marginal site because it had no cultural authority to participate in some discourse about centers, is now disclosed more overtly as the name by which centers write themselves, this time shifting excitedly to the very locations they have heretofore marginalized.

Of course, essentially, the same show has been playing for years. People at Harvard and Duke, or even the University of California and Indiana, respectively, have been interested in margins insofar as these could be used either to consolidate or produce centers, each situated in her or his own institution. Blank pages? We have been shown—most recently in postcolonial critiques—how masters love them.[4] Boondocks? We haven't been shown that a good part of the reason they love the pages is because they disdain the institutions which so naively presume to read them as if they were full of meaning and significance that can be agreed upon. Some such agreement seems to be what Jane has in mind at "Masterpiece's" end, when she proposes (to the Text's delight) to read, just read, maybe off the fast track, and with a couple of students, no less.

At the moment of this proposition, BSU is emptied once more of its specificity. How is what Jane proposes different than what she has been doing in her "Intro to Lit" class? Boondock, presumably, has plenty of sections. None of them is a happy place for fancy or fashionable theoretical moves. Plenty of sections probably have students such as the culturally illiterate basketball player E.H. Hirsch tries to speak to on a plane. What to do with such students? What sort of reading practice to hope for, or settle for, at BSU? "Masterpiece Theatre" signs off just at the moment when Boondock, that is, threatens to become too *real*. By the end, once again, BSU can be left to itself, basically mute, because ultimately it exists to be produced—just like a text—elsewhere.

I am thinking of Clement Rosset's formulation, where the real "is the negation of the here to the benefit of the elsewhere."[5] My point is almost too simple: Boondock exists to be negated. Or, to put it another way, just enough of some putatively "real" Boondock needs to be characterized (normally for comedy) so that Elsewhere can (re)produce itself after reading it. "Masterpiece Theatre" deals with a sample of Elsewheres so powerful that it appears they may be effectively nowhere themselves; and so they are continually, ravenously (is this why there is so much eating?) in need of migration, relocation, reconfiguration. If this sounds like a description of job mobility at elite institutions, it's not at all apart from my point. "The highest reward of the profession," concludes James Phelan, "is defined as getting paid a lot for relocating to a prestigious school and not having to teach" (215)

Where *is* Boondock, finally? What goes on there? Just the felt need, before or after class, for superior authorities from elsewhere to explain what goes on there? Or could it be really possible there is in some hard-to-define terms a sort of subversion, heretofore under the sign of retrogression? But how? Could such a thing be possibly free of the fast track? Yet what would this mean? Who can say? Who speaks for Boondock? What would Boondock say if it itself could speak? Or is it merely the fact that Boondock, to *be* Boondock, can't "speak for itself?" The situation is as theoretically provocative as it is politically or culturally static. Rather, it is so provocative because it is so static, which is why institution has to be converted into text.

Especially in conjunction with "Masterpiece Theatre," I think of the following passage in a symposium on "The Changing Culture of the University" reprinted in *Partisan Review*. Catherine Stimpson emboldens herself at one point to remind her fellows "what the average English department is like." She instances the University of Texas at Arlington or Southern Illinois and then continues as follows: "It is a middle-of-the-road place, pluralistic, using the *Norton Anthology*, using it seriously, using it conscientiously, spending most of its time teaching writing and composition, and feeling within the university as a whole marginalized because of the place of the humanities in general in American life." Robert Alter, however, isn't so sure. He opines that by "the so-called academy" we in fact mean "maybe twenty, perhaps thirty institutions in the country. And I think that if you go, not only to the kinds of institutions you mentioned but let's say to small, excellent liberal arts colleges like Carlton College in Minnesota or wherever, the picture is more variegated and sometimes looks very different" ("Revolt," 308–09).

From a number of comments that could be made about this moment, let me choose two. First, Alter, after having correctly, in my opinion, noted how institutionally constricted professional discourse about higher education really is, expands the base by moving up the hierarchy rather than down. Is this because he isn't comfortable about places less distinguished than Southern Illinois? Or just because such places are unimaginable to him? In any case, a Boondock State University is written off. Stimpson, in some contrast, doesn't write it off. Her characterization, if we compare the BSU of Gilbert and Gubar, is simply way off. If BSU's department were "pluralistic," Jane wouldn't be concerned about the Norton-anthologized views of her chair; and if Jane were crucially marginalized by the Place of the Humanities, I don't think she would be so fretful about her theoretical vocabulary or so eager to call in the elites.

In "Masterpiece Theatre," what marginalizes Jane is the very theoretical discourse which talks about marginalization. From her point of view, there's really nothing wrong with this discourse. It's all she has in any case. What's the matter is that she quickly gets very confused by it because she doesn't enjoy an institutional situation which would make her dialogue with the text productive for her. Instead, she has to be worried about classes, xeroxes, and students. Graduate school, it seems, hasn't prepared her for the material conditions of her job, which are what they are, in one sense, because they are utterly careless of the theoretical parameters generated by the discipline's fast track, which originates, of necessity, elsewhere.

Gilbert and Gubar have inscribed, I would claim, an accurate enough portrait of Boondock, at least in terms of its junior faculty. (An Associate Professor of English would have been impossible, irredeemable, perhaps indistinguishable from Officer Friendly.) What they have not given is any idea how Boondock could ever exist in any way different than for the edification of far loftier and more prepossessing institutions, where more-politically-correct-than-thou

critics can war agreeably among themselves. Of course Gilbert and
Gubar aren't obligated to write everything in (or out). It would
probably have only spoiled the fun to have tried to bring onstage
BSU graduates, for example, who have never heard of most of the
eminences in "Masterpiece Theatre." Without such people, though,
it's a precious kind of fun, public television with the barest trace of
a public, and literary theory in name only.

3.

For my fall, 1991 theory course at Clarion, I thought I was
sure what theoretical space I wanted: "transcendental intelligibility." For just one time, I secretly, devoutly, ardently prayed for no
more undergraduate prattle. So, two-thirds of the way through,
when it was apparent that I was only going to get the most predictable kinds of all-too-intelligible criticism, and when even the prattle
had largely dried up, I wrote a statement of instructions about the
final paper that contained the following two central paragraphs:

> The single most important consideration will be the follow-
> ing: the depth, range, and sophistication of the theoretical
> presentation. When in doubt, theorize, don't just 'read.' Even
> if there is no doubt, theorize, rather than 'interpret.' The
> point of a paper is to saturate a text with theory, and not
> 'read' it, or at least to read it solely for its theoretical provo-
> cations. You don't have to engage in what Paul de Man once
> memorably called 'vertiginous possibilities of referential
> aberration,' but you can try.
>
> In order to facilitate this ignoble aim, theoretical treat-
> ments of anything else [I had earlier allowed consideration
> of the other required text, *Let Us Now Praise Famous Men*]
> must be of mute, naive, marginal, or otherwise tradition-
> ally 'non-literary' material. No literature, much less can-
> ons, please! Instead, for example, comic books, army training
> manuals, travel handbooks, brochures of various sorts, and
> even, God help us, phone books.

The bright student of the ideological crisis of literary value
mentioned above (who had once objected that by no stretch of the
theoretical imagination could a phone book be considered a "text,"

much less "literature") wrote a fine paper on three "Outland" cartoons, mocking the inscription of the Other in each, and throughout caricaturing a lofty, imperious creature known as The Theorist. There were other papers on cartoons: Bugs Bunny and *The Far Side*. The remainder of the subjects chosen included *T.V. Guide*; the biker magazine, *Easyriders*; an official publication of the Hungarian Ministry of Foreign Affairs, *Democracy Reborn*; the Pennsylvania Driver's Manual; food stamps; and a box of rat poison. Every paper featured an ideological analysis. Few cited Althusser in their pages, but he represented the headiest theory we had had. One who did so wrote as follows: "Examining ideology is somewhat like the interpretation of dreams. Since ideology exists in a kind of meta-textual state, we can see its role as the unconscious of a text. Representations can then be extracted from the text and interpellated much as the symbols with in [sic] dreams can be interpreted." But this gets it all wrong. One simply cannot stand apart from ideology in this manner and Althusser's point is that you *are* "interpellated," not the reverse!

So it went. What I learned myself is that it's easier than I anticipated to determine the difference between an expression of ideology and an examination of it, as in the following example: "By anyone's standards, *Easyriders* must be hailed as a monument to individual rights in the face of crushing bureaucracy, as a triumph of freedom of speech over censorship, and as American as Harley-Davidson." This sounds like an editorial from the magazine. Of course there were compelling analytic moments: how naively the state driver's manual employs the masculine pronoun; how tellingly an X-Man comic characterizes a gang as Mexican; or just how massively ideology is affixed to a food stamp coupon when it reads NON-TRANSFERABLE EXCEPT UNDER CONDITIONS PRESCRIBED BY THE SECRETARY OF AGRICULTURE.

But one could argue that a theory course is not strictly necessary to produce such moments. Let me cite a passage from the best student in the class (by far): "Bugs Bunny gives himself up [to Elmer Fudd, a member of the Royal Canadian Mounted Police in the cartoon], not because of any moral or compassionate impulse, but through a kind of Nietzschean generosity made possible through a superfluity of power." *That*'s the overdetermined, saturated, vertiginous note I called for. It was made possible, I knew, because the student had been led to Nietzsche through Foucault.

It seemed to me most of the rest had just been led away. One of the few who lingered, or seemed to, produced the giddiest paper of all, e.g. on the "demise" of carousel and wire-jawed rat traps linked to "the Derridean notion that we can never know exactly what we are doing" and "the post-structural notion that every coding is merely another encoding." There was lots more of this. I especially liked the following: "We instead let the rat come to us; ideological passivity, an off-hand validation of a slackened work ethic, has become a way of life." (And so on, to the charge that we are "hegemonically subverting ourselves.") Is this what you get when you let someone without any background loose in primers on critical theory?[6]

The student's insistent point about us and the rat is the same point agitated freshmen make about us and anything: hypocrisy. That is, his theoretical vocabulary is utter gobbledygook. How long does one have to study before exposure to this vocabulary becomes something like possession? Meanwhile, only a conservative ideologue—and one who never tried to teach anything—would think that my radically ideologized course politicized this student or anyone else dangerously leftward. Granted, my syllabus served up as much of the deep-dish "leftist" menu as I felt my customers could digest. But most refused to chew anything and the rest suffered from indigestion. As it happened, the day before our last meeting I read a column by Peter Shaw from the previous week's *Chronicle of Higher Education*. To the surprise of no one, he protests against a recent MLA press release that all is traditionally well in the teaching of literature, upon which "new trends in criticism" have had little effect. I only wished Shaw could have met with my class.

At one point, he makes a particularly astounding statement: "As everyone in the profession understands, 'theory' of any kind is at present a code word for the politicization of literature" (B3). On the contrary, this is not what "everyone" understands. At "small" universities there are undoubtedly those who do. But such universities do not constitute a unitary phenomenon, except in the discourse of "large" universities. "Small" universities include Boondocks, where the English chair has barely heard of "theory," or Clarions, where, at mine anyway, "politicization" best describes only the occasion of our last departmental election of a chair. And students at such places, in any case, will not be politicized just because they are theorized.

What they will be instead is much harder to name. I don't believe the examples from their papers suggest anything coherent, not even about why so many of them react negatively to theory. Did most even have political views? Once one of the few lively students mentioned to me outside class that a couple of others objected to something she said because it "sounded Marxist." The student herself was no more a Marxist, or interested in "Marxism," than Peter Shaw. I think the reaction to whatever she said, and to much of the agenda of the entire course, is explicable because the students had discovered that there *were* such things as political views. It's as if before this they effectively had none. Come to intellectual maturity in the Reagan '80s, what of a reasoned politics beyond impressions and convictions could they have been expected to have? Indeed, if they had, the course could well have been more profitable to everyone because there might have been something at stake beyond its difficulty.

Instead, in a course which was a very literal textbook definition of how to politicize literature, there emerged only incomprehension and even ignorance about precisely this fact. I'm not sure I should have known this. Can I now claim, in any case, that ignorance is what the example of my course (if not my institution) could contribute to some more comprehensive theoretical space? One student wrote that Althusser was valuable if you wanted to keep people away from you. Another, who couldn't get a copy of *Of Grammatology*, had scrawled on a note to me: "What a waste to drive to Grove City [forty–five minutes from Clarion] for Derrida." The more comprehensive understanding of theory urged by my course is that not all objections to it are "political." Many are, as always, merely the product of fear, provinciality, and stupidity.

Or are there other names? Better names? What vocabularies would be employed if Boondock spoke for itself? I must trust that my account of one theory course makes another thing abundantly clear: in the boondocks there are *names* for things different than the names produced elsewhere for them. These names have an almost wholly reactionary function, they possess very little conceptual power, and they are unaware of their resonance in larger cultural discourses. My strictures about the final paper to my class were in a sense designed to prevent any sort of enunciation about how the students could denounce theory, affirm the beauty of literature, and embrace other humanistic pieties involving the usual suspects. I didn't believe they could produce much else.

Do Gilbert and Gubar believe Boondock could? I don't know when it became clear to me that their alignment with respect to Boondock is too uncomfortably close to my own with respect to my students (and, through them, to Clarion). Teaching the course represented for me an effort to keep the realization away. (Just as writing my article had represented an effort to confront the same realization.) "Transcendental intelligibility" blocked it and, curiously, permitted me to try to keep faith with an unarticulated possibility that the boondocks could produce some other sort of discourse, or some other names, or *something*. Gilbert and Gubar, by contrast, are only interested by default in such a difference. There's no personal, professional, or political urgency in how they would imagine it into existence. They don't have to recreate either difference or its consequences under the sign of a *lack*.

How not to protest against the Gilbert and Gubar in myself? I can only do so by reimagining a relation with my students in which I acknowledge the status of a common subordination, both to theory and to the institutional structure that empowers it. In the chapter, "The Hegemony of 'Hegemony,'" from his mordant critique of theory, *Academic Capitalism & Literary Value*, Harold Fromm makes an incisive observation at one point while considering a mightily theory-crossed author whom he wants to like more than he does: "That he is not a slavish reader of these sources does not alter the force they have exerted over both his mental life and his prose" (150). Here might be posed the real question of any theory course: how can you read theory *without* being, well, slavish? There's too much force in too many texts. Once you feel it, your prose will never be the same again, not to say your life, either inside or outside the classroom.

However, since much depends upon the institution in which the course is given, what my students did was essentially to refuse to read the texts, no matter how "slavishly" they tried. In the name of what? Freedom? If so, not just freedom from theory. In addition, and with all due irony to say so, I believe they refused to read in the name of freedom to read. It didn't especially matter what. Call all of it "Literature," read not merely according to the old questions and the old answers but in terms of its intelligibility, its aesthetic value, and, most of all, its exemption from ideology. In other words, it is exactly the kind of reading Gilbert and Gubar's Jane hurries off to perform at the end of "Masterpiece Theatre," with a couple of willing students in tow. It's the sort of reading so theoretically scandalous that it can only be located in the boondocks. It's the sort of reading in whose name any theoretical sort can only be mocked.

Only one of my students did. For this I admired her only a little less than I disliked her. Mockery seems to me the only *genuine* voice from off the fast track of the discipline. The theory course

I taught was, in this sense, a mockery. It included me, and embraced my own impulse to mock Gilbert and Gubar in turn. But I can't say it spoke for me. Instead, the voices staged in "Masterpiece Theatre" proclaim themselves in my own program. I don't have any decisive authority apart from them, just as I can't think about ideology apart from Althusser and I can't write about power without Foucault. How much does it matter that I don't teach at an institution where very much is said about such people? I don't know how to *name* how much it matters.

This situation can be put another way: I had no name. Theory—not to say the whole profession—is about names. Gilbert and Gubar, for example, unfurl many of the Great Ones, including themselves in the bargain. How can others so much as speak unless they employ the language of those who have already articulated the terms by which any conversation can be conducted? We hear a lot about "subject positions." Everything has to do with power and authority; what if you don't have any? Fromm ends his above chapter most memorably: when all is said and done, he writes, and all the texts have proliferated themselves as well as everything else away, "the hidden script of these high-minded fights only boils down to: 'It's you or me, you bastard' " (165). Could my students have sensed some of this high brutality in what we'd read? (And we didn't read Stanley Fish!) The only way to get power is to wrest it from somebody else, and students, alas, just don't have enough to bring off a classroom coup.

Furthermore, if you're in the boondocks, you hardly have enough power to manage vaster and more circumscribed political maneuvers. Jane, for example, is *all* Elsewhere. Would she be any less so if she taught a theory course? It must be granted, I think, that there are some courses where it's simply not possible to avoid the knowledge that you're only Here at the pleasure of Elsewhere.[7] It might be better, say, not to read *Critical Inquiry* in the boondocks. But is it still the boondocks if you do read *Critical Inquiry*? (Or if you embolden yourself to submit something to it?) If you teach a graduate course in literary theory, and no matter that it winds up acting out how it's scarcely worth the name? How are you presumed to be situated?

Moreover, if not precisely mocked yourself in teaching such a course, in the name of precisely *what* do you aim to prevent the students from mocking the subject? Graduate education? Ideology? There's no name. Perhaps no map as well. Indeed, once you give your whole professional way with the course the auspices of a name—"responsibility," say, on your part, or "liberation" for the part of your students—and you are simultaneously on the map and in the boondocks. If, on the contrary, you withold a name, you'll only be attempting to substitute your own act of negation for that already performed Elsewhere.

Another favorite statement of mine in contemporary theory is the following one from Geoffrey Hartman's chapter on "Words and Wounds" in *Saving the Text*: "The very production of speech may depend upon a disentangling of blessing and curse, on the outwitting of that eternal complex" (133). I want to put it this way: during one fall semester Clarion, Boondock, and Theory had gotten all tangled up for me. I'd already written an article, I had to teach a course, and then I read Gilbert and Gubar. It seems to me now that I never ceased to be involved in a continuous process of cursing both the boondocks and theory under one name: Clarion; Boondock was just Clarion at once effaced and renamed, and the students in the theory course were pretty much Jane's.

However, it wasn't quite this simple. It could just as justly be said that I tried to bless the very same things with the same blessed name. The trouble was, I couldn't get past the fact of mockery. No matter how unremitting you appear to be, cursing is not going to be so unequivocally disentangled from blessing. You're never going to know fully whether you're using the name you have in order to curse or bless. What would all the performers in "Masterpiece Theatre" say? Of course this particular knot may only be a theoretical one, and it may have already been confidently disentangled on another level, somewhere else.

Somewhere else: where would this be? After such theory, what practice? Or better: after such a class, what sabbatical? I confess that it always feels like some sort of betrayal for me to think of a sabbatical. But what could be betrayed? The department? The profession? Home? Does one require a sabbatical in order to determine this? Such questions merely displace a more fundamental one: in order to consider the question of somewhere else, the significance of travel to the construction of an academic career must be assessed.

cↄ

Sabbaticals, Travel, Frames

"I myself find safety in locating myself completely within
my workplace."

—Gayatri Spivak, *The Post-Colonial Critic*

On the night before my last sabbatical officially ended, I sat
down and wrote (and subsequently published) the following article
on sabbaticals. Over the course of the previous six months, I'd
become convinced I'd write something. What I couldn't have known
is that it would be an interview. One reason I wrote one is because
on a sabbatical you wind up talking to yourself a lot. Another
reason is because I felt loose—relaxed somewhere in between talking and writing, free to partake equally of the difference between
talking to myself and talking to others. Why go on sabbatical if it
isn't to loosen up?

Yet why go on sabbatical if you're only going to think about
what a sabbatical is? I thought about it anyway. I wanted a sabbatical in order to have access to thoughts I don't normally have.
One was simply the following: what a strange thing a sabbatical is!
Why (for example) is a sabbatical something that you "go" on? Once
you "have" it, why go "on" it? It's as if, once upon it, it becomes a
foundation for something else? Or by means of it, does it become a
vehicle, such as a plane, to somewhere else? Is there a constitutive
relationship between sabbaticals and travel? I couldn't stop thinking about these questions.

The last one came to seem a version of a larger question: what's the relationship between academic life itself and travel? Academic life, to be academic in the first place, is typically described with a vocabulary of enclosure, if not imprisonment. A professor venerably abides even in the postmodern world as one of the great *rooted* figures—teaching regular classes at the same department at one university, year after year. On this basis, P.F. Kluge compares a professor who teaches well but doesn't do research to a "lifer," and then he concludes: "you can't move. You haven't got the publications. You've surrendered your passport" (164).[1]

Of course, if you do have publications you can travel widely and often, such as Stephen Greenblatt, who fulsomely acknowledges colleagues and occasions in five countries (other than the United States) in his book, *Marvelous Possessions*. What is the relationship between such travel and that afforded by a sabbatical? Is there none? Must those of us who don't have publications be content with expressing either our occasional or our permanent need to get out only through sabbaticals? Or, if not content, then how are we to regard the spectacle of those high flyers who take off as a virtual condition of being on the ground?[2]

What sort of passport is it that to most teachers will only be given on condition—apart from a sabbatical—that it never be used? Richard Miller has lately reminded us that "all academic work actually occurs under conditions the circumscribe what statements may be made as well as how and where those statements may be made." He instances the processes of peer review, tenure, and promotion. Then he continues: "There is no escaping this array of constraints, no argument that will allow one to elude their grasp, no way of speaking or writing that can fully succeed at suppressing their contradictory force or their contaminating presence" (*As If*, 42–3). I do not disagree. A sabbatical is not a way of escaping or eluding constraints. But if there *were* such a way, it could only be represented for most of us by a sabbatical.

That is, escape from constraints is best represented by the travel. If that of such celebrated high flyers as Spivak and Greenblatt cannot be ours, we nevertheless take what we can. What we are given is sabbaticals. Their potential for escape or subversion explains why they are monitored very carefully. For example, while discussing the importance of valuing "the different phases of our academic life," David Damrosch decries the characteristic suspicion of administrators that faculty may stray. He instances the letter he received from the Secretary of the University upon being awarded tenure. The letter includes a precise definition of the "residence" entailed by the period of any teaching assignment and the importance of proper excuses for absences (or leaves) during this period. The tenured professor, he comments, "is also a kind of truant schoolchild, who must be sternly admonished not to wander off to the playground before recess begins" (203).

Damrosch wants to argue that there need be no conflict. "If we can achieve a more integrated and collaborative sense of scholarly life," he maintains, "we can dismantle the false oppositions between on-campus ward heeling and off-campus work (or is it play), between our teaching and our 'own' work, thereby reducing the structural schizophrenia of our professional lives" (202). My own view could not be more contrary. Such "schizophrenia" is woven into the fabric of academic life, and built upon the foundation of institutional hierarchy. Because of this hierarchy, we cannot dismantle the oppositions between here and there or in and out. If what we ought to do instead is to recognize them, the best possible place to begin would be with sabbaticals, even if we have to begin by talking to ourselves.

1.

On Sabbatical: The Interview

"The classical sabbatical is a year abroad fortified with support from a foundation or the government. Faculty members go to great trouble and endure almost any hardship to experience the sabbatical.

— Hazard Adams, *The Academic Tribes*

——What did you do on your sabbatical?
——Nothing.
——Nothing?
——Nothing.
——But you must have done something.
——All right. I wrote five articles, and revised four more. I finished the preface as well as three other new essays for a book-length collection of essays. I gave papers at three conferences; chaired a session at another; and attended two more. I worked up

a new professional interest for myself. I expired into the revision of another book-length manuscript during the last month, and managed to walk away from it completed.

——I thought you said you did nothing!

——Well, it's something, I admit. But I didn't do anything as I'd planned. The last book, for example, was the basic reason why I wanted the sabbatical and I couldn't face it until I thought there was no more time to do it. Worse, whatever I did seems to me nothing to what I could have done. I think of myself during the precious months gazing dumbly at yet another college basketball game on television rather than working my way diligently down still another blank page on the typewriter. You have a lot of time on a sabbatical. Henri Lefebve once defined everyday life as "whatever remains after one has eliminated all specialized activities." You have only everyday life, you could say, which is I think what we mean when we say that we have nothing to do. My sabbatical had its moments of specialization. But all embraced by the everyday, and so this is part of what I mean when I say nonetheless that I didn't do anything.

——I'm not sure I follow.

——Me neither. So it can go on sabbatical. You're on your own and you can get off by yourself. I was. I didn't have to explain my meaning to anyone for a whole semester. This can all by itself be a wonderous experience for a teacher, whom someone once defined as a person who must speak for fifty minutes and who is obligated to repeat everything at least once.

——It sounds like you didn't miss teaching.

——Anyone who misses teaching while on sabbatical shouldn't be teaching.

——What's the reason for sabbaticals?

——Once I believe I read that it was the name the ancient Hebrews gave for the seventh day when the fields were granted a rest after being plowed the other six. My dictionary doesn't mention this. But I like it anyway. If I could have had a longer sabbatical, maybe I'd have gotten round to an article on fanciful etymology. There's an intimate relation between productive work and relaxation from it. To me, a "sabbatical" is the academic name for this relation.

——You sound defensive. Wouldn't everyone agree?

——Probably not. Over the course of at least the last decade the function of a sabbatical has changed significantly. One change: people only take a sabbatical for one semester. In 1981 at Clarion, for example, there were six faculty members granted a sabbatical for a full year. In 1989 there were three. The second change is even more significant: people opt for a sabbatical strung out over either two or four summers. In 1981 four faculty chose to do this. In 1989 ten did.

——Why? Your man Adams says above that what we want, passionately, is a "full" sabbatical. And taking one during the summer seems to defeat the whole purpose of a sabbatical in the first place.

——Not if professors are getting older—which is the first of many reasons which come to mind for the change. Adams wrote his book well over a decade ago. Moreover, he wrote of academic life on the model of large research institutions. Clarion is not such a place; in a sense, I just wrote a book about this myself. As far as summer sabbaticals are concerned, they make sense if you're looking toward retirement and therefore interested in building up your yearly income during your last three years, which are the ones upon which your retirement benefits are based.

——So a sabbatical isn't a sabbatical anymore, in your "Hebraic" sense anyway?

——Well, I'm not sure there was ever an "original" sabbatical, from which the aging professoriate of the postmodern pendulum has sadly swerved. There certainly is what we might term a sort of demystified one now, purely functional and wholly integrated into the bureaucratic structure in ways that make everybody happy. Administrations especially like these summer sabbaticals because then nobody has to be replaced and costs can be kept down, this last desideratum arguably being what Higher Education finally continues to be all about into the '90s. But the whole subject of sabbaticals is susceptible to vast deeps of speculation. It's curious, for example, that sabbaticals shrunk at about the time the student population pool did.

——What about your own sabbatical? Now that you mention it, it seems more than partly mystified.

——You got me. Even my nothing partakes of too much something. I didn't take Adams's venerable sabbatical. Maybe nobody does anymore. Are they sabbaticalizing their summers at Harvard too? Emerson says that life consists in what a man thinks all day. What I wanted for my own sabbatical was simply to be able to think freely all day, or to explore my constraints when I had nothing to do.

——Very philosophical. I'll bet you had some heavy thoughts. Can you give an example?

——Sure. In Douglas Hofstadter's commentary on Thomas Nagel's famous essay, "What Is It Like to be a Bat?," he asks as follows: "What is it like to bat a bee? What is it like to be a bee being batted? What is it like to be a batted bee?" I was unable incidentally, to come up with satisfactory answers to these questions.

——Read any good books? You're an English professor. What was the best fiction you read?

——That's easy. Denis Johnson, *Angels*.

——What about nonfiction?

——Much harder. David Marc's *Comic Visions. Tele Culture and American Culture* was a pure joy to read. Greg Ulmer's *Teletheory* wasn't, and yet it was immensely stimulating. So it went. I didn't read many novels. I wanted to write my own books. Others lured me away to the end. Robert Weisbuch's *Atlantic Double-Cross* proved so absorbing that I almost forgot about my own blank pages. By the way, want to hear a good quote?

——I love quotations.

——E. M. Forster was once asked if he thought truth lay halfway between extremes. "No; truth, being alive, was not halfway between anything. It was only to be found by continuous excursions into either realm, and though proportion is the final secret, to espouse it at the outset is to ensure sterility." I forget where I read this.

——Anything else you want to remember? Your most consistent pleasure, for example? (Keep in mind this is a family publication.) Or your worst times?

——The taste of Mr. Donut coffee every morning. March 2 and April 11, the beginning of the winter holiday and of spring vacation, respectively; I'm happier than the students on such days, but this time round there was nothing special about them.

——Mr. Donut coffee? Every morning? Didn't you do anything exotic? Go anywhere?

——I drove to conferences as far away as Toronto or Ithaca. But basically I stayed in Clarion. It was early one morning at Mr. Donut, in fact, that I had the sabbatical's most disturbing conversation. A former student spotted me on May 10. "Finals for you too, eh," he managed. "No, I'm on sabbatical," I chirped. "You are!" he cried, outraged, "Then what are you doing here?" I couldn't reply.

——Why not? Why was this so disturbing?

——Recall Adams above: get a sabbatical and you get away. I didn't. Recall also that I admitted to being mystified; getting away—getting out—is, or, sob, was, at the center of being on sabbatical for me. I think it is to most people, as if "sabbatical" is synonomous with "vacation." It's not of course. You lose the way not doing what you normally do participates in what you normally do if you merely cease to do it, and, well, vacate it. And yet, and yet. I lost at least the scope of what I think a sabbatical ideally ought to be when I chose to stay home.

——Why did you then, especially if you knew it would bother you so much?

——I didn't say it bothered me, exactly. For one thing, I'd applied for a Fulbright to Argentina, scheduled to begin after three months into the sabbatical. This was, in turn, perhaps the basic reason why I chose to stay home, so I could do sure work here before transposing it to less rigorous occasions there. But, Argentina being Argentina, I didn't get nominated, and subsequently selected, until over a month into the time period for which I'd applied. By then I could only accept the award for the fall semester, when my sabbatical would be officially over. There were other complications. Eventually I declined the award. Finishing the last book-length revision was a kind of consolation.

——You declined a Fulbright?

——Stranger things have been done, some while not on sabbatical. (I wonder why it's something one is "on," rather than "in?") I can't easily write of what was, to me, the strangest thing of all—when, having declined Cordoba (by all accounts a lovely city), I was mad for a brief chance at Iasi. There are no accounts of Iasi. Let me be coy and not even mention in which country it's in. Its obscurity is precisely what excited me—and what revealed to me Cordoba's lack: it didn't seem either exotic or difficult enough. This might seem strange. But I've had a lot of foreign teaching experience. Enough, in fact, to use it as the basis for a book. Having declined the opportunity to teach abroad again, I enjoyed the most exquisite irony afforded by being able instead to write a book about the category of abroad in American travel writing. This must mean something.

——But what? And what does this irony have to do with being on sabbatical?

——Thoreau is central to my understanding of American attitudes about travel abroad. As you may know, his own understanding was very simple: stay home. I suppose I enacted this in order to write about how it can be explained in the American travel text. Do you have to live what you write about? Nothing I read during the sabbatical was as intricately funny to me as this statement from Thoreau's journals: "If you want to be elected town clerk, you can't go to Tierra del Fuego."

——I'm not sure I get it. Maybe it's too personal. In any case, where's the concluding profundum about sabbaticals? It can be ironic if you want it to be.

——I think it's merely cynical and it's certainly not profound. Consider how one "gets" a sabbatical these days. It's not automatic. You apply. Each year a certain percentage are chosen from the supplicants, I mean applicants, by a college-wide committee who are given quite specific criteria, such as how a proposal will benefit the university.

However, no one who receives a sabbatical is in fact accountable for whether or not the proposal was actually accomplished, much less even begun. You could play golf and repair your roof for four consecutive summers and no one would care, even if you got those summers on the basis of a proposal which promised to research the possibility of a summer orientation program for incoming freshpersons that could hard-wire them with literacy. What you have to do is just get something past the college-wide committee. A sabbatical, in other words, is loftily rationalized at one level, while mundanely played out on another. Some might find this state of affairs to be an expedient game devised by town clerks.

What's pretty certain, I think, is that the days of the "classical" sabbatical narrative are over. One's sabbatical is rarely "fortified" by outside support. It may be that each narrative now is a highly private one. Moreover, one's sabbatical is now much more unusually vivified by travel. Each one is at least going to be powerfully tempted instead into domesticity.

There's a third thing that's harder to stipulate. A sabbatical has traditionally been defined in terms of its relation to one's professional work. Now it seems to me increasingly, if not already fundamentally, defined by its relation to the conditions that, in turn, define the work, especially years toward retirement. A sabbatical is, from a narrowly economic point of view, a paid "leave." What I mean is that it's very hard now to sustain any other but this point of view. What is a "leave" if in some fundamental sense you don't leave? Or, worse, don't even have it in you to leave in some vital sense having to do with your work or career? These are the sorts of questions one asks about sabbaticals today, and I don't see much logic available in order to oppose that of bureaucratic implementation, whereby sabbaticals are only paid vacations.

Sometime during six blissful months, I came across the following statement from Emerson: "The experience of poetic creativeness . . . is not found in staying at home, nor yet in traveling, but in transitions from one to the other, which must therefore be adroitly managed to present as much transitional surface as possible." There's what we want: transitional surface. To lose the transition is to lose the thing itself—by which I would mean here the movement from work to sabbatical and back again. The transition may well be lost already. I'm not sure my own sabbatical demonstrates convincingly enough that it can still be found. Indeed, I'm not precisely sure what my own sabbatical demonstrates, beyond the fact that I wish I could have another one in order to figure it all out and I wish even more that what one is could still be officially rationalized as ideally possessing more Emersonian surface.

2.

In her recent collection of autobiographical considerations and occasions, Nancy Miller has an essay with a lovely footnote. A version of her essay, she notes, was given as a paper in Dubrovnik. She goes on to mention how, in effect, the comfort of her room was unsettled by the view of a beautiful island. After several days of contemplation of the island and an eventual boatride there, Miller comments: "I realized I had not sufficiently figured in the ambivalence of perspective that double siting creates: the politics of oscillation. (This could also point to another fable about feminism; the referent; and movements of political liberation, but I will leave that for another time.) I thank Myriam Diaz-Diacoretz and Nada Popovich for including me in this event" (120).

The event ostensibly takes place in Dubrovnik. But it can also be understood as the oscillating one that takes place in Miller's mind. This is the first thing to say about the relationship of academic life to travel. Travel participates in the great Outside of the life of the mind, the Real World under the sign of the World Elsewhere. Typically, however, it only finds its place *in* the life of the mind. Miller has traveled. Perhaps she only gave the paper at the conference in order to be able to go to Yugoslavia. What happens, though, is that she looks out as a way of looking in: there are more perspectives to be accounted for; more oscillations; and, these days, of course more politics.

Of course it matters where the institution is that you call home. Did Miller have to submit a proposal or an abstract before her paper was accepted? Did she have to pay for her trip? If, instead, she just got invited and funded either by her institution or an organization, how are those presumed to read her footnote who have never been invited to give a paper and who pay themselves if they ever travel anywhere? This question is not answered by replying that Miller doesn't have to think of such people and that such people can only think of her with envy.

Another unsatisfactory reply: these others can always have sabbaticals. Not only has the function of sabbaticals changed. There are a good number of people in academic life, such as Miller herself, who can go pretty much wherever they want to without having a sabbatical. Among the occasions, friends, and reprints noted in essay after essay of *Getting Personal*, there are consistent mentions of travel—a London research seminar formally acknowledged, for example, at the conclusion of the first essay, or a trip to Brazil sponsored by the State Department more casually noted in another. Travel is a measure of Miller's distinction in the profession. Surely, one assumes, she doesn't have to apply for a sabbatical.

Her professional experience suggests something far more interesting: Miller might well be *beyond* sabbaticals. Certainly many eminences in every academic discipline are. Generous leave time is written into their contracts. In the text of the frequent flyer, the only others to be acknowledged are hosts from abroad, not colleagues back home. Indeed, those back home are likely to be implicitly rebuked. Consider Gayatri Spivak. No one in any discipline may take off farther and more regularly. Asked (in Australia) what effect travel has on her work, Spivak replies thus: "Well, you know I think for a time I will stop traveling. I became caught up in this traveling circus, and I think I've kept doing it for so long because it underminded some of the seriousness with which I was beginning to take myself. . . . If you are traveling on all of these continents, moving from university to university, the one thing that strikes you is that each place takes itself to be the center of the intellectual universe! (Laughter.)" (*Post-Colonial*, 37).

This "circus" is of course in one respect not new. Distinguished academics have always been able to get out of the circumstances that defined their distinction. What is new is explained by Morris Zapp in David Lodge's *Small World*, a novel in which the crabbed corridors of academic life are reborn as global routes: "There are three things which have revolutionized academic life in the last twenty years . . . : jet travel, direct-dialing telephones and the Xerox machine. Scholars don't have to work in the same institution to interact, nowadays: they call each other up, or they meet at international conferences. . . . I work mostly at home or on planes these days. I seldom go into the university except to teach my courses" (43–4).

Persse McGarrigle is bemused to hear Zapp. He says he's in no hurry himself to see the world, and of course his own university lacks distinction, not to say books. Subsequently he requests, and is granted, a leave anyway. Just so, *Small World* virtually converts academics and travelers into equivalent categories. The very subjects of the profession of English are renamed as stops along the professionalized Grand Tour. "Zurich is Joyce. Amsterdam is Semiotics. Vienna is Narrative," explains Zapp. "Or is it Narrative in Amsterdam and Semiotics in Vienna" (65)?[3] But what name can one give to such travel that keeps it within academic confines? Can it continue to be located inside the names we do have, in particular, sabbaticals?

In a sense, the traveling academics of Lodge's text are on permanent sabbatical. Or to put it another way, academic life in Lodge expresses such a ceaseless ambition to be on the move, out, and away that the very word "sabbatical" seems a slow, lame one, haplessly redolent of a world weighed down with teaching, departmental meetings, and daily compromises, now all gloriously transcended. Morris Zapp reflects on "the beauty of academic life," whereby, with just one good book, you could get a grant to write a second, and then, after promotion enables you to design your own courses, you would be eligible for more promotion, more grants, and still less teaching. "In theory, it was possible to wind up being full professor while doing nothing except to be permanently absent on some kind of sabbatical grant or fellowship" (152).[4]

Zapp, I believe, would want to retain the vocabulary of sabbaticals, just as surely as he would want to dismiss talk of institutional hierarchy. His travel must be located inside the names he shares with McGarrigle just as he himself must be, because even Zapp needs the customary structure of academic life, at home and abroad, in order to realize his career. No matter that Zapp is interested in travel, not ideas. He's not a tourist.[5] At least if coherent in academic terms, his travel must be understood as a rhapsodic, exterior form for intellectual activity pure and simple, content with its own exercise, catching ideas on the wing, and roving unbound.

Compare the manner in which Paul Theroux, no tourist either, states more emphatically the same sort of relation between thinking and traveling that Zapp suggests: "It is possible for a writer to think creatively only if he or she manages to inhabit a mood in which imagination can operate. My need for external stimuli inspired in me a desire to travel—and travel, which is nearly always seen as an attempt to escape from the ego, is in my opinion the opposite: nothing induces concentration or stimulates memory like an alien landscape or a foreign culture" (86). Of course, his real difference from Zapp is that Theroux is not an academic; hence, he cares more about alien landscapes than merely getting away from familiar ones.

Nonetheless, he has in common with Zapp the experience of having travel effectively represent thought to itself. One often comes across marks of this equation in scholarly books, usually in the Acknowledgements. Kathleen Woodward, for example, prefaces *Aging and Its Discontents* by acknowledging a fellowship from the Camargo Foundation: "Many of my ideas for this book took shape as I sat in the Camargo Library overlooking the glittering Mediterranean in Cassis." There must have been times, one thinks, when the sea shimmered with the very shape of thought, just as there were other times when thought was happy to lie idle and submerged. It was only necessary to travel to Italy.

The opportunity to "oscillate" in this way, however, is purchased at the expense of not having to represent to itself the hierarchy that enables the travel in the first place. Hence neither Miller nor Woodward is obliged to set out the circumstances through which each got to go, respectively, to Dubrovnik and Cassis. Indeed, it seems resentful for anyone else to ask. (See Spivak, *Post-Colonial*, 5 for the first of a number of examples when she stops just short of claiming to be an incarnation in her own example of an "alternate institution.") If, for an academic, the month's bureaucratic agendas or the week's office hours simply fail to express the sheer mobility of mental life, so be it. Moreover, if you teach at a place where special conferences or fellowships to exotic places aren't regularly posted on bulletin boards, then your burden is to accept the fact that your professional circumstances should not be understood as the function of someone else's more independent and more expansive ones.

I want to maintain, however, that at least one thing follows with respect to sabbaticals: they come to occupy an incipiently subversive space. Of course, not everyone who goes on sabbatical does so in a self-consciously or deliberately subversive way. However, everyone is in position to do so who is structurally excluded from the professional opportunities sponsored by elite travel. Another thing that Zapp's account of a career brings out is how complicitous its most personal, wayward energies can be with its most respectable and unexceptionable ones. Precisely. So it goes at all levels. If your institutional politics don't oscillate, but your ideas do, then your sabbatical will most likely be the only chance you'll have, either to indulge in deviously complicated ways the kind of complicity Zapp regularly exercises or else just more simply to dump the whole sabbatical as a professional project.

Awhile ago a friend wrote me an account of his last sabbatical. In twenty years of teaching he's had two; every other semester he's had to teach—five courses per semester at first, four in recent years. During his first sabbatical he wrote a book. During his second he didn't want to write anything, yet could only secure administrative approval of his request if he signed on with some sort of academic program, or "went back to school," an honored category. So he pledged to work under a well-known writer. Then he made a list of every place in the U.S. he'd ever wanted to visit; traveled as far as Alaska; spent lots of time in Washington and Boston; and finally wound up in San Francisco. "The sabbatical did what sabbaticals are supposed to do—it changed my life," he concluded.

What my friend meant is that the sabbatical enabled him to come out of the closet. For him, isolated at a small midwestern campus, such a result might have been only slightly less possible there than pursuing the most advanced work in Queer Studies. So it has always gone, in any case, with sabbaticals: an individual applies for one with the expectation that an institution is more interested to monitor the nature of the proposed professional activity than to shape it; favored criteria exist at the very outset, and a report to the president is common at the end. But what if, once "on," not to say away, you discover that in fact you are undertaking to conduct what Meryl Louis terms a "life audit?" Such an audit became the absorbing purpose of her own sabbatical, no less accurately entitled a "journey" for being primarily internal.

"Separating oneself from one's normally daily life—temporally, spatially, psychologically," states Louis, "is at the core of what sabbatical has always meant historically in both secular and religious settings" (452). Then is it implicit in the separation—no matter what one has had to declare to local administrators—that reconnection will invariably take place? The more an institution

attempts to monitor and restrict the separation implicit in a sabbatical, the more the separation is in place to continue even after
the sabbatical is over. At present, I believe an academic most typically begins a sabbatical on the model of taking revenge. Against
what? Against all the rules that define and circumscribe the sabbatical itself.

If we understand most present sabbaticals to be the product of
financially lean and institutionally tightened conditions, it is very
difficult to see a sabbatical in personal terms; *any* personal terms
have now effectively acquired the force of transgression, even if
they're merely a matter of something so apparently unexceptional
as those of my colleague next door, who just wants to live in London. "If you can figure out how living in London will benefit the
college," I ventured, "you're a shoo-in." Maybe he is anyway, about
to complete his fourteen consecutive year of "service": at Clarion
you accumulate points for each non-sabbatical year, in addition to
those awarded on the basis of proximity to the high priority category, Benefit to the College. Of course my colleague cares more
about the cost of flats in Chelsea than benefit to the college which,
in turn, only cares about him for the reasons stipulated by
Damrosch's Secretary.

This is why the prospect of sabbatical travel proves particularly disturbing today: no activity allows the energies of the personal to be more manifest, more vagrant. Eric Leed states as follows:
"Recognition of the special subversiveness of travel, the fluidity of
identity achieved through territorial mobility, has long been a
justification for laws against itinerancy" (276). Precisely. Especially
now that some representation of fluid delights and effectively subversive moments is no longer effaced by elite academics, my friend
in the midwest merely asks for the opportunity to experience his
own long-suffered release, while my colleague next door simply
hopes for the moment of his own hard-earned errancy.

Why don't they both just leave? For the same reason Miller
and Woodward return to their respective campuses, and that even
Zapp touches base once in awhile: all are academics; even if their
leaves are more generously apportioned or contracted than most,
high flyers can't just go take off. Unlike a sabbatical, a leave has
no oppositional or subversive potential because it has no clear or
systematic relation to business as usual. The reasons for leaves
tend to be exceptions. A leave only begs to be exempt from normal
conditions; it neither affirms nor denies them. Whether you stay at
home or go far away, a leave is unlikely to change your life.

This distinction needs to be insisted upon because sabbaticals nowadays have become very difficult to comprehend as different from leaves. This is why the presence of travel in a sabbatical is so crucial. No other activity has the power to disturb the elaborate system of regulations that has been constructed to contain what may and may not be done or proposed prior to, during, and after a sabbatical period. My colleague, for instance, could apply for a leave. (Though not for the purpose of living in London.) The fact that instead he has to work carefully through a whole sequence of deadlines and dicta just to have the opportunity to take off, on the other hand, is what lends subversive logic to his purpose. Only success in terms of this sequence will enable him to get what he wants, although the structure fears it, and the sequence cannot name it.

I'm not sure my colleague can either, though, especially insofar as what he wants in London approximates what Morris Zapp gets every time he takes off. But what is that? Excitement? Distinction? Traditionally the consummate academic occasion for the *release* of distance, exactly when was the sabbatical transformed into just another rule-governed area for the containment of distance and its discontents? When the job market began to shrink? When the discipline began to get seriously theorized? When professors were urged to think of themselves as "managed professionals?" When a few became stars? The only thing I want to maintain is that sabbaticals continue to have something vital to do with travel, even and perhaps most emphatically at the same time travel may well have ceased to have anything vital to do with the academic life that most professors lead. (See Begley, "Decline"—the decline being that the latest narratives never leave campus.) Indeed, even Zapp, who in one sense rebukes this life, only confirms it in another sense.

3.

Whether at home or on a plane, Morris Zapp *works*—planning how to transmute the next grant into the next book, or the next paper into the next conference, or vice versa. The profession is affirmed whether he gets on a plane or not. Academic life, albeit expanded now to global proportions, comprehends him utterly. Compare Arthur Fidelman, Bernard Malamud's hero in the novel, *Pictures from Fidelman*. It's not said that he's on sabbatical. I like to think he is anyway when he arrives in Italy to prepare a critical study of Giotto. Alas, the precious notes are soon stolen by one Susskind. It takes Fidelman the rest of the first chapter to find Susskind again, who then admits he's destroyed the notes. He insists he's done Fidelman a favor. "The words were there but the spirit was missing" (41). We are given to understand, in other words, that Fidelman was never a scholar. He just needed to travel to Italy to discover himself.

Zapp, on the other hand, is always a critic. Traveling around the world doesn't lead him to discover anything new about himself. Moreover, eventually Fidelman returns home, as travelers always do. Travel in *Small World*, however, has an entirely different dynamic. Its academics aspire to a condition of pure rootlessness. Consider the doyen of international theorists, Arthur Kingfisher, "the only man in academic history to have occupied two chairs simultaneously in different continents (commuting by jet twice a week to spend Mondays to Wednesdays in Switzerland and Thursdays to Sundays in New York)" (93). Distance is built into the minutest fabric of Kingfisher's career. Unlike the frenetic Zapp, Kingfisher's home is so decentered that it's not entirely clear how intelligible such a mundane thing as a sabbatical would be in terms of it.

Kingfisher therefore represents an apotheosis of the academic luminary who is truly beyond sabbaticals. Yet there is something of a paradox here: he is also to this degree beyond travel. For Kingfisher, travel no longer operates within some known structure that could be affirmed, subverted, or even transcended. Travel is no longer *disruptive*. Even Zapp has a home, no matter how much time he spends away from it. So it's not at all clear how academically intelligible could be the great prize of *Small World*: the UNESCO Chair of Literary Criticism. It is to have virtually no duties. Its $100,000 salary is to be be tax-free. Almost more wondrously, the Chair would be connected with no institution, in no particular country; there would be no obligation to use the office or secretarial staff at the Paris headquarters of UNESCO. Since the Chair is "purely conceptual," the successful candidate "would have no students to teach, no papers to grade, no committees to chair. He would be paid simply to think—to think and, if the mood took him, to write" (120–21).[6]

Such a Chair only becomes intelligible, I think, on the analogy of an impossibly permanent, paid sabbatical—now understood once more as a full *confirmation* of the intellectual life all-too-fatefully distracted by students and colleagues in its institutional context.

The only thing that fails to cinch the analogy is that the occupant of the UNESCO Chair evidently is to feel no particular conviction about traveling. Ultimately *Small World* asks us what sort of an academic refuses to travel, or just stops. The answer appears to be only someone released from being embedded in its very structure, in other words, an academic who doesn't need a sabbatical. But if to be an academic is to *be* embedded, and if being embedded includes the moment of temporary release (traditionally given by the sabbatical and sponsored by travel), then the academic who refuses to travel actually turns out to be no sort of academic at all.

We might put this another way: having no impulse to travel means that an academic life is lifeless, so saturated in pages (whether to grade or to write) that its spirit is dead. For academics, travel is not so much the name of that which is not academic as that which cannot be made good in exclusively academic terms. Travel provides the grounds for a continual testing of these terms—how much they can incorporate, and how much they have to exclude. Take the times in *Small World* when the exhibition of so much spirit appears to be staged there's hardly any interest in the pages. Everyone agrees that Zapp's own Jerusalem conference on the Future of Criticism is the best one because only one paper a day is scheduled to be delivered by its author, while the rest of the papers circulate informally as the conferees lounge at the Hilton pool, shop at the bazaar, or explore Galilee.

However, everyone does require the pretext of the conference itself, and the nominal structure of the single paper. Consequently, every hour away from it exacts some sort of negotiation with the conference; its framework continues to operate even if one abandons it completely. Precisely what *are* academic terms at such a conference? I would argue that what the Jerusalem conference reveals is the problem of framing. Normally considered, of course academic life is the antithesis of the Jerusalem conference. The academic framework is not at all exotic; its duties are drab; and its interactions are neither so exclusively lofty nor so intensely elite. The Jerusalem conference seems to be a preeminent example of what Erving Goffman calls "out of frame activity."[7] Indeed, the narrative of *Small World* is precisely the opposite of that typically given to academic life: absorbed in the complexities involved in inducing activities into a frame, rather than in inducing activities out of it.

So, if one manages to be able to go, would it be best to do so because the conference is taken to be a normative occasion in terms of its academic framework or else a holiday from this framework? That is, do academic terms contain the conference, or the conference academic terms? Of course this may seem as we say, an "academic" question. Perhaps it is. It's certainly the sort of question the worthies at the Jerusalem conference would be interested in taking up (although possibly not at the Jerusalem conference itself). But they already know the answer, which lies in the institutionalization of the question. Harold Fromm concludes an excoriation of superstar academic careerists thus: "The intellectual's planned revolution always begins tomorrow, not yesterday. Today one negotiates for a Chair in the sun at Irvine or La Jolla" (13).

Fromm's Chair in the sun is straight out of *Small World*. In fact, the Chair is a sunny, sited version of Lodge's UNESCO chair, with the difference that Fromm's Chair continues to be enshrined in order to organize further involvement with its own distinction. This difference granted, however, I believe each chair marks the same hierarchical space where academic life and travel continue to be inextricable even at the point where the latter leaves off the former, and either escapes into pure deracinated meditation or relaxes into sublime contentment on the beach. The privilege of the Chair, we might say, is precisely the privilege of enjoying this inextricability.

Let me now recall my own self-interview as the writing of a very different institutional position. There the only name of travel is a sabbatical, which I want to extricate from academic life, but can't quite, because I remain grounded. My sabbatical finally inheres in my real professional circumstances as something radically different, but not really subversive because I never bring myself to take off. There are the first three months as merely marking time until Argentina. Yet the fact that I would be off courtesy of a Fulbright complicates the nature of the sabbatical, if not fundamentally alters its oppositional thrust. When I don't go, I'm left with wanting the sabbatical to go somewhere—anywhere. Was "Argentina" just an empty signifier?

The interview format doesn't make this state of affairs entirely clear. This was deliberate. I thought I knew precisely why I wanted a sabbatical. I didn't. Interviewing myself was a strategy for making allowance for the fact, while at the same time maintaining the illusion of knowledge. It was hard to admit that I wanted to write more than to travel, much less to write so much I didn't even need to travel. To admit this would be to concede that my sabbatical conformed perfectly to my proposal to the campus-wide committee in order to be ranked at all—and no matter that my institution only valued me as a teacher rather than a scholar.

Worse, even if what I most wanted to do was writing that explored my deep and abiding antipathies to academic life, it could not be denied that I needed the frame of this life. Or at least I couldn't escape it: a sabbatical was necessary in order to do any writing at all. Impossible just to apply for a leave. Unthinkable to quit. I had to be somewhere. But the months passed. I didn't go anywhere. The Argentina Fulbright fell through. There may have been times when I felt that I had been reborn as the holder of my very own little chair in the sun. I'm sure there were times when the writing felt so happily *immanent* that I ceased to care that there wasn't even much sun.

"Power," Emerson writes in a famous definition, "ceases in the instant of repose; it resides in the moment of transition from the past to a new state." If we want to suppose that even the merest conference represents the better part of academic life, this could be granted, even at the highest professional levels, provided that academic life is the better part of the conference. But what if you lack conferences—by which I mean scope, energy, transition, and power? Then you've only got academic life, which, next semester's class schedule or next year's promotion notwithstanding, is going to be all repose, in Emersonian idiom. Transitions will be ephemeral at best. The power remains the property of a select few, whose global travel is the measure (and no small portion of the pleasure) of their authority to write the new states that the rest read about.

An exclusive vocabulary of repose permits you to aspire no further than a sabbatical. Thereupon this vocabulary circumscribes the whole notion of travel so utterly that even some "proclivity" occupies the realm of the subversive. (See Tate, *Miss Mentor's*, where even this realm is effaced in her one comment on sabbaticals, 193–95.) Regardless of how far you might have hoped to go if a sabbatical were granted you, you had first to be granted one—you couldn't just take it. Then you discover that a sabbatical has no power to dispute the terms that both authorize and define it. Only your travel does, and its possible relation to those whose own travel is so much more vast, frequent, and sovereign that it affords them, everywhere on earth, thrilling or disturbing moments of professional transcendence.

These moments don't have to be theorized. This is because for the people who enjoy them they're institutionalized. Similarly, conferences, grants, job mobility: these things abide to be experienced, as if they were as either casually possessed or exquisitely problematic. What to reply if you think they're neither, or if you can't experience either possibility in the same way? There may be no reply. At least there may be none that will not oblige you to take the high road, and consider the ideology behind or beyond institutions. At least you ought to try to avoid the low road—it might now be easier with e-mail—where you will only get mired in conditions of your exclusion as if for their own sake.

I've constructed throughout this book a reply designed to crisscross both roads. Much of being excluded involves so many preliminary considerations about the conditions that it looks as if there's nothing else but these conditions. Of course there is—especially teaching. But I've already tried to explain why I've said little about teaching in these pages. Teaching is the name of what it's left to someone who teaches at Clarion to represent, moving from classroom to classroom rather than conference to conference. Instead, I've endeavored to speak finally about sabbaticals, as something that stands for what I'm not in place to represent—and not for abstract reasons of ideology but for quite concrete and material reasons of hierarchy.

How far are we ever in academic life from a sabbatical? We are all presumably in the profession together because of our opportunities to travel, as well as our duties to our students, our service on departmental committees, and our papers in refereed journals. But these opportunities must remain scarce. It is important that travel remain in place as something rare, in addition to be unsettling, inescapably personal, and potentially transgressive. Otherwise, travel would enjoy no prestige, or rather, it would lack the basis upon which prestige can be constructed in the economy of the profession, and success be demonstrated.

Thus we are never close enough to a sabbatical, because proximity depends upon the fact that others are already so close that they may as well be up and gone. Best of all, a few are already aloft, traveling to chairs in the sun. Good luck to them. Even there, after all, the sun can't always shine and the chairs are probably more wobbly than I can imagine. Even there, names and figurations for some farther or greater outside must seduce and madden. No one gets out of academic life simply and cleanly, after all, not even the few for whom the outside is regularly booked and prepaid.

In any case, the ticket is research. Consider Kluge on how scholarship troubles Kenyon: "It's a tension everyone feels, a continuing drama in everyone's life, a drama played out in offices that are locked—are they home writing or raking leaves?—and in lights burning late—grading papers or updating resumes?—in mail that does or doesn't arrive, in phones that do or don't ring, those phone calls you move a little faster for, the double-ring phone calls coming in from the outside, not the single ring calls from the intramural PBX" (166). This book has been an account of institutional life where there is no such tension to be felt, because, were it not for sabbaticals, there would only be raking leaves and grading papers.

An examination of travel in academic life discloses that the career plans for recognition are actually very few in number, and perfectly consonant with flight plans. The classes taught and the meetings attended by the rest of us, on the other hand, will never suffice to get us off the ground, so these activities must provide for most both the only mobility we have and the only basis for whatever else we need. The inescapable fact of our professional lives is this: by the circumstances, intricacies, and limitations of our individual institutions we will be driven, as academics. By our travel away from them, however, we will be known—even if the best route we can hope for is the one represented by a sabbatical, and even if any particular one leaves you only traveling through the boondocks, while talking to yourself about its ins and outs.

Notes

Introduction

1. Lauter also speaks of his life rather self-consciously because apparently he does not feel a part of "the culture of antobiography" as David Simpson entitles it in his chapter, "Speaking Personally," from *The Academic Postmodern*. For a full range of discussion about this culture—and in particular, the theoretical provocations as well as the revived notions of professionalism behind it—see the collection edited by H. Aram Veeser (which also includes the Simpson chapter). To Lauter, compare Simpson's more canny self-efffacement in his own introduction: "But I am not going to tell you my life story in this book, and if I am everywhere in what follows, as I must be in serious as well as trivial senses, then it will be in disguise" (14).

For one result of what follows if the notion of disguise is taken not so much more seriously as systematically, see Caesar, *Writing*. In any case, Simpson's following conclusion can be given as an unexceptionable statement of truth: "[I]f you function within a literature department in an English or American university, there is a very strong likelihood that you are going to be more interested in (and better prepared to address) the problem of subject and object than that of the vangard party" (90).

2. For an academic, the easiest way to open out onto these energies: access to what Bell Hooks refers to as "the lecture circuit." How to gain access? Like most who have it, Hooks doesn't say, and just confidently inserts herself, in order to seek consolation over her fears that she might be forever trapped in the academy. She has just received tenure from Oberlin College. See Hooks, *Teaching to Transgress*, 1.

Fortunately for Hooks, as an African-American woman, not only does her experience possess an enviably issue-driven, public resonance. It also provides the basis upon which she can eventually leave Oberlin, move up

173

to a Distinguished Professor position at CCNY, and disdain writing anything in a judiciously personal book about either the wider occasions or the narrower ambition in being able to do so. What happened to the newly tenured person who once feared being trapped? A reader of Hooks can perhaps be forgiven for wondering if the "transgression" of her title doesn't ultimately function as a means of splitting the difference between being trapped and being mobile. See especially on this last point, Leatherman's cover story on Hooks in the *Chronicle of Higher Education*.

3. Compare James Phelan's lament in *Beyond the Tenure Track* about "how so many academics don't have much choice about some of the basic conditions of their lives—especially where to live" (61). In a significant sense, the subsequent exchange in *College Literature* between Jeffrey Williams ("The Life of the Mind") and Phelan ("Reply") turns on this question, with Williams arguing that the book is insulated, precisely, from such academics, among other discursive omissions, and Phelan replying that "there is no one-to-one correspondence between locations and success in attaining [the ideal of the life of the mind]" (158).

4. Jacoby's book can be recommended as offering an account of higher education in America thoroughly nuanced by the issue of hierarchy. Whether in the form of a book review, a periodical column, or an article (see, respectively, Woods, Cook & Frank, and O'Dair), the varied consequences of hierarchy as well as the very fact of it are becoming more widely known. This does not, however, mean that such accounts are becoming easier to produce. Susanne Woods, for example, ends her critique of Helen Vendler's book on Shakespeare's sonnets in the light of job cutbacks, N.E.H. funding reductions, and work load inequities between elite universities and others by allowing that her complaints are "churlish" and avowing that "privilege" need not disuade anybody from curling up in front of a fire with a copy of the sonnets.

5. Aqueous metaphors appear to come inescapably to teaching. See Kluge, on how a Kenyon dean turns his summer's adventure of whitewater rafting into a figure for four years of college, guided by professors: "A funny thing happens while this is going on, though. . . . No way, I think. We [the faculty] *are* the rapids, we are the boulders, and I, personally, am a sunken, rotting log, half in water, half out, with a sharp, infectious branch aimed right at the soft plastic underbelly of a kayak full of summer campers, a cargo of entitlement headed my way" (30)! His comparison of the campus to an island appears throughout the book. Compare Jane Tompkins, excoriating the manic academic imperative to talk, after citing a friend's experience of snorkeling in Tahiti: "Just floating there, effortlessly borne up, your body rising and falling with the water, only thus could one exist without the need for words" (65).

6. At Clarion, an unusually instructive example of the procedure is provided by the "Faculty Development" opportunities made available each

year. A special college-wide faculty committee distributes from a fund of some $45,000. Proposals are judged during two separate rounds, with a maximum of $5,000 for collaborative projects and $1,000 for individual projects.

What does "faculty development" mean? There are only two categories: Multicultural and Teaching and Learning. Although it's not completely accurate to say that "faculty development" has nothing to do with scholarship, it's close enough. There appears to be some theoretical distance from the classroom possible in the first category; there is none in the second. Development means renewed application to teaching. Writing doesn't count. Release time is impossible.

Hence, most successful proposals are in the second category and virtually all have to do with traveling to conferences or workshops that aim in some way to improve teaching. A letter to unsuccessful applicants proudly declares: "No other SSHE school has committed so substantially to empower faculty to develop." It can be fairly supposed that every other one strives in the same way to position teaching so that it answers all the questions of research, not to say of faculty who want to "develop."

7. Lentz opines: "I've seen more cutting edges come and go than—what's an assemblage of cutting edges?—a Cuisinart" (81). Kluge eventually establishes the unsettling (if unarticulated) relationship of research to teaching at Kenyon thus: "It affects the way you're regarded—by the administration and by your colleagues—after you arrive, before tenure, after tenure. It affects the way you think of yourself. And it affects your ability to leave. It's a measure of your freedom. If you're a great teacher, you probably can't leave. You're a lifer, maybe you're a local hero. But you can't leave. . . . As your scholarship dwindles, your marketplace value becomes nil" (163–64). I don't see how these pages can be bettered.

8. Again, compare Phelan who, at a national convention in 1987, meets an old friend "now at a good place" but still coming to terms with having been denied tenure at an Ivy League school. He later attends a session on part-time faculty where he hears an especially awful story from a man shamed by the full-time faculty for proposing to teach a literature course free. Phelan's conclusion: "I feel lucky to have landed between the Ivy League and the part-time world" (169).

9. Within the discipline of English see, for example, many of the essays in Richard Bullock and John Trimbur. This volume is virtually a case study in how academic life can be understood in terms of class—but only insofar as it is structured as a particular disciplinary formation. So, for example, one contributor takes administrators to be Tayloristic planners, teachers to be workers, and students raw material, while another takes the whole subject of rhetoric to constitute an "underclass," peopled largely by women and part-timers. Everybody understands composition as an "ideological site." Nobody mentions the institution itself as another

such "site," albeit an uncontested one because it is so utterly stratified according to elite standards.

On the more celebrated recent instance of the strikes by Yale teaching assistants, see Sprinker and Bartolovich. Bartolovich cites Evan Watkins on the analogy between a factory and a university, and then comments thus: "Watkins' point is that while it might not be accurate, strictly speaking, to analyze English teachers as proletarians (a view he vehmently rejects), it might be important to wonder how the structure of the university as a workplace changes as capital restructures, and what impact these changes have on English—and other—teachers" (226). Contra Bartolovich, it might now be easier to posit teachers as proletarians after the actions of the Yale graduate students, a group hitherto uncomprehended by Watkins within the category of "teachers."

10. Public notice of how seamless this state of affairs actually is is so rare that one particular example is worth citing: Russell Jacoby's strictures about Gerald Graff's *Beyond the Culture Wars* in *Dogmatic Wisdom*, 184–88. Jacoby concludes thus: "Graff proscribes hustling conferences of upscale professors fleeing their campuses as the cure, not the disease. He confuses networking with teaching, backscratching with scholarship, jargon with thinking" (184). I would only add—not in defense of Graff—that probably only those haven't been infected with "the disease" can proscribe the conditions for health so confidently. Jacoby is not an academic.

Hence, he can be taken to task by Bèrubè as "the he-man left's favorite gadfly... a wannabe who's made a career out of mocking academics (after having failed to land an academic job himself) and advocating a return to class politics (which he himself never manages to practice)" ("Pistols," 108). Bèrubè is defending himself against criticism by a journalist. The question left begging is about whether a political critique that originates outside the academy must necessarily be either defused or co-opted once it is assimilated by institutional forces—Bèrubè teaches at the University of Illinois—within the academy.

11. Especially for a man. See, for example, Joseph Allen Boone's almost comic attempts to secure theoretical sanction merely to *mention* something personal (or rather, in duly problematized quotation marks, "personal") in "Of Me(n) and Feminism: Who(se) is the Sex that Writes?" in Kauffman. The following essay, by Toril Moi, then takes him to task for being a typical academic. "It is as if the political horizon of these feminists, male and female, stretches no further than to the MLA," she writes, and continues: "Does Boone really expect outsiders—non-members of the US literary critical community—to take an interest in the seating arrangements of faculty dinners at Harvard, or the time-tabling of various sessions at the MLA? Who exactly did he have in mind as *readers* of his essay" (186)?

It's not entirely clear if Moi's objection is that Boone's experience is too personal or still not, in another sense, personal enough (because it is too lost in its occasions). Perhaps her real point is that some academic experience is simply not worth mentioning at all because it's of no interest to anyone else. But—from my own admittedly self-interested point of view—the trouble with such a contention is that it leaves the most haplessly professionalized academic experience in place as a hushed, interiorized, precious thing that has no potential for greater meaning, much less a wider audience. Boone's problem may not so much be that he lacks the politically-correct authorization to be autobiographical as that he doesn't write well enough about himself.

12. The literature on women's autobiography is by now extensive. See Miller's own review, "Public Statements, Private Lives," for some current examples of what she terms "nineties memorists." A collection with a somewhat larger base can be found in the Diane P. Freedman, Olivia Frey, and Francis Murphy Zauhar. Douglas Atkins can be recommended for a study with still broader and less exclusively feminist sympathies.

13. The persistence of these values, I believe, is precisely what severely limits the power of a recent collection, *Wild Orchids and Trotsky*, edited by Mark Edmundsen. Not only do the universities of contributors comprise all the usual suspects (Virginia, Duke, and so on). Individual discussions (with the exception of an interview with Harold Bloom) all pivot carefully on safe pieties concerning gender and familiar animandversions about the canon. Perhaps the most exciting, "intuitive" piece, by Eve Kosofsky Sedgwick, also turns out to be the most reasoned defense of the whole privilege of hierarchy. See her concluding pages particularly.

Chapter One

1. See Caesar, "On Teaching at a Second-Rate University," reprinted in *Conspiring with Forms*.

2. Compare Kenyon, which attempts to shrug off a new ranking in *U.S. News and World Report* that has it even further behind the leading twenty-five national liberal arts colleges. Kluge gives this account: "Ticked off, the college reacts, cranking out a statement that deplores the vulgarity of it all, hints that some other places may be cooking their figures, and argues that as long as a college's financial resources are taken into account, poor Kenyon will never get the respect it deserves"(55). Later, the Dean of Admissions volunteers that Kenyon has made another list of the country's thirty-five prettiest colleges (91).

3. Examples of this sort of feeling are occasionally given in Kluge's unusually candid account of Kenyon—a very different, smaller, thorough, and far more self-conscious "community"—but always by somebody else. Kluge himself is just passing through and, indeed, only arrives in the first

place in order to write a "report," as he tells everybody from the start. Compare Patricia Gumport: "The new style of academic management regards the notion of a professionally autonomous faculty, if it ever existed, as no longer affordable, let alone appropriate for state employees. In addition to the evaluation of teaching performance, there is a more comprehensive surveillance of academic work, including requests from campus administration to report office hours, consulting activities, and time spent out of town. . . . [T]his approach treats faculty as workers who need to be monitored rather than as professionals who are trusted to work according to internalized standards" (127). Gumport reveals, I think, how the internalized fears of faculty among themselves in fact intersect with the externalized concerns of administrations about faculty.

4. See the reading of a number of other similar, but differently positioned institutionally, letters to the *Chronicle* in Sosnoski, *Token Professionals and Master Critics*, xxv–xxvi.

5. Almost equally crude is the proposal by Hansen and Heath that all faculty members stop doing research and do more teaching. "A strict limit on publication," they write, "is three decades overdue . . . the best way to ensure teaching is to remove the incentive to do anything else" (238). *Who Killed Homer?* is full of this sort of thing and extremely amusing, if only because so exuberantly maintained in the teeth of so many unexamined pieties about the importance of research.

6. See the chapter in Aronowitz and DiFazio on "A Taxonomy of Teacher Work," for an unusually succinct and incisive portrait of of the occupational structure of American universities. "In general," they write, "the institutional context determines how much time the faculty member devotes to teaching, research, writing, administration and other tasks. . . . The rule is that the institutional setting is crucial in deciding the kind of work the professor tends to do and becomes a fairly accurate predictor of career trajectory. There is considerable evidence that, as in other sectors of society, the cream is more likley to sink to the bottom than to overcome institutional obstacles" (237).

7. Phelan is, to be fair, speaking critically of a profession driven by market value. Nonetheless, he consistently fails to see how his own activity within this system is structured by a fundamental blindness to contradiction. So, at the end of his account, when his hope for an endowed chair at Hartford College has not been met and instead a contract for his second book is forthcoming from the University of Chicago, Phelan winds up "shaking my head at my socialization, at the power my need for external validation seems to have (had?) over me" (216). In comparison, the quite different accounts of the same socialization by Kluge or Sosnoski are superior to Phelan, I think, because each more deeply follows out the logic of this same need.

Chapter Two

1. The most candid account of an academic hire that I know is in Kluge's memoir. The Philosophy Department has a position during his year, and Kluge sits in on things from the beginning, including the search committee's final deliberations. Of course one wonders if the important reason Kluge (only a temporary faculty member) can be so candid is because this committee—as befits a small liberal arts college—includes both members of the administration and students, as well as faculty from the Philosophy Department.

The cloak over hiring in higher education continues in marked contrast to its lifting concerning tenure. See, for example, Douglas Lederman and Carolyn Mooney, whose story concerns the decision of the Ohio Supreme Court to allow access to tenure as well as promotion documents at the state's public colleges. Several cases at Ohio State are discussed by name. For a student of academic hierarchy, the most interesting item is the disclosure that these documents have been open for years at most of the state's public institutions. None command the prestige of Ohio State, however, and this prestige (based on research expectations) constitutes, in turn, the actual basis for the *Chronicle* piece.

2. Gerald Graff awards Daniel Cott Gilman, the first president of Johns Hopkins University, the honor of having created the modern research university on the model of the German graduate schools, which included specialized departments. "The word 'department' had been in use in colleges throughout the nineteenth century," notes Graff, "but only now did it take on connotations of disciplinary specialization and administrative autonomy" (*Professing*, 58). For the best recent consideration of the costs of the specialized model, see Sosnoski, *Modern Skeletons*, although his alternative attempt to redistribute the same methods and subject matter as those he contests seems to me to set aside the important distinction of his earlier study between token and elite professionals.

Arguably the most unspoken question in the profession today is what sort of specialized department is possible anymore for a group consisting largely of either "token" professors, unrewarded with research time, or "defielded" or "Taylorized" ones, overcome with general education courses and bureaucratized timetables. Such departments may now be comprehended in terms of the larger critique of downsized practices and corporate values to which the entire spectrum of American labor is subject; see Aronowitz and DiFazio.

3. This is an extremely complicated question. Phelan just deals with it by taking the high road; of an ideal department, he writes as follows: "They make a commitment to each other, and to their institution because they know that without it the ideals won't be realized" (196). Back on the low road, can we assume that the commitment of many departments to

each other is, very much on the contrary, based on the felt fact that the institution will never realize their ideals?

Or, in a very real sense, the institution can't, just because it's too obscure and enjoys no reputation? Ohmann's discreet citation from the minutes of a "major midwestern English department" could not be more in contrast; the whole point of the meeting is that the department has suffered a loss of ranking in a national report. But what about the majority of departments whose institutions enjoy no pretense in national terms? The less claim to larger social or cultural recognition an institution has, I believe, the more inward—in my terms, incoherent—a department will inescapably be.

4. It is, however, the chair's concern. Colton's interest in the human lineaments of this figure is in striking contrast to the rest of his exposition. At one point, for example, he effuses over "the ideal chair": "mediator, negotiator, and arbitrator; budget, personnel, and recruiting officer; advisor on community housing and schooling, and on career opportunities for spouses; chief justice; pastor; parliamentarian; social director; lecture bureau director; team coach; Dutch uncle (or aunt); statistician; housekeeper; general office manager; and personal counselor and mentor" (274). As is common in many accounts of academic departments, the multiplicity and hererogeneity that could be accorded the department as a whole, as well as many other members of it, is used up in a highly interactive, process-oriented idea of the chair, as if this figure could restore in himself or herself the effaced social dimension.

5. Graff continues the assumption of his earlier *Profession* that "there is a sense in which a literature department (and curriculum) is itself a theory, though it has been largely an incoherent theory, and this incoherence strengthens the impression that the department has no theory" (2–3). Very much to the contrary, my deepest sense is that most departments do avoid being represented in theoretical terms, even the most distinguished ones. In this connection, see the attempts of certain departments at elite institutions in some initial issues of *New Literary History* early in the 1970s to tell their story in terms of theory, e.g. Jordan. Decades later, it looks as if each one was in fact attempting not only to personify theory but epitomize it. How enfeebled most other departments are now to play this sort of game can be seen in Doan and Town. They don't even identify the name of the university where they taught their theory course.

In this sense, one might speculate that many departments of English at present are theoretically unified to the degree they are hostile to theory. Nevertheless, my supposition is that the social dynamic of a department, rather than its theoretical orientation, is its decisive one. Note the slippage, for example, in the following assertion by Russell Jacoby: "Universities encourage a definite intellectual form. They do not shoot, they simply do not hire those who are unable or unwilling to fit in" (232).

6. That is, these conferences have little power to contest the logic of disciplinary specialization upon which the prestige of more venerable conferences is founded. In fact, many flounder on the basis of this same logic, raising the question of the fitness of the specialization model for their institutions in the first place, as Richard Ohmann noted long ago with his reading of an advertisement for a Renaissance specialist at Missouri Southern College: "Does the department itself even need a renaissance specialist? It is not even clear that the winner of this position was to teach a renaissance course" (210).

Fish has an interesting objection to Ohmann's point that the needs internal to the profession itself, rather than the culture or the society, dictate the choice of such a position. Ohmann "falls into the trap of reserving 'real' for choices that depend on no previously instituted circumstances whatsoever—choices that would be, in some strong sense, original. The problem is that it is hard to imagine what those choices would be like; by what noninstitutional standards they would be made" (*Doing*, 234)?

But from a more practical perspective, it's easy enough to imagine choices departments make every day about highly contexted matters that result in, if not acontextual fictions, at least fictions so heedless of institutional propriety that they seem "original." I mean my detailing of one departmental vote to constitute one such fiction; to many in my department, the local favorite defined the position's field, and not vice versa.

With respect to specialization, see Graff's *Beyond*, whose argument to heal theoretical and ideological wounds by "teaching the conflicts" may be understood as an attempt to re-tool the traditional specialization model, while at the same time to re-negotiate failed departmental sociality by having more inter-departmental (or "transcourse") meetings and conferences.

7. And friendship is likely to be more sorely tested when the vote is over tenure rather than a new hire. I must trust it is clear why my account has to do with the latter rather than the former: nothing is normally at stake at an institution such as Clarion. Instead, hiring someone is equivalent to giving the person tenure, because we relate to each other not as scholars but as teachers who share common problems and close quarters; whether or not the presumption of common intellectual interests prevents the harder, deeper labor of some more well-founded sociality, at Clarion we want to get along with each other because we have to. Therefore, social controls govern the tenure process long before a tenure vote occurs, so anyone who could have been denied tenure simply has not lasted to the point of a tenure decision; this is why no one in my department has ever been denied tenure.

It is also why the one person who for the first time was lately refused by the department was nonetheless confirmed by the administration—as a department we simply lacked experience in the tenure process as something other than a form of ritual acceptance. The episode illustrates, I think, how tenure decisions, unlike ones involving hiring, are less timeless, even at institutions such as Clarion; as Jeffrey Williams puts it (invoking Pierre Bourdieu), "The habituating mechanism of tenure ensures the reproduction of extant socio-institutional arrangements and hierarchies by its continual adjustment and revision" ("Life of the Mind," 137).

Chapter Three

1. Although *PMLA* is not without its own Forums in recent years, some bearing very directly on issues of the Forum's own constitution or rationale. See especially the Forum on "The Personal in Scholarship" in October, 1996, and most particularly the contribution by Caesar, which argues more forcefully an adjacent contention by Ruth Perry: "As academic discourse became commodified, personal criticism was used less as a political strategy to acknowledge or challenge the special interests and blind spots of particular critics and more to the service of the cult of personality, the emerging star system in university life" (1166). A subsequent Forum even prints a response from a graduate student at Clarion, Jennifer Peachey.

2. See Trainor and Godley. This practice continues in the very best critiques of the field—for instance, Slevin's superb reading (in Lindeman and Tate) of a fictionalized exchange of letters concerning a job search. Compare O'Dair's ready acknowledgement of her own institution: "My point here is not to equate the University of Alabama with West Jesus State, but to suggest that the structure of our profession is such that the hinterlands begin almost as soon as you leave one of the institutions at the very top of the prestige hierarchy" (627). Precisely, and my strongest feeling is that until the hinterlands begin to acquire *names*—for better or worse—they will not be able to contest the power of naming, which continues to reside in the fact that some few institutions can be named at the expense of the many who can't. In addition, and perhaps with more irony in the field of compostion and rhetoric, the fact that a veil that must be thrown over the whole business of naming serves the interests of these same few institutions, whose protocols of discretion reinforce the disciplinary logic through which writing programs acquired their debased status (both Slevin and O'Dair speak very directly about it) in the first place.

3. My question might be less rhetorical. Susan Horton provocatively wonders if the MLA might not be seen as a classic instance of the institution of the *fair*, considered not only as a place where social inversions and carnivalesque free play take place, but an intersection of commerce and culture. Who is ultimately to say from how far can come the "vagabond desires" she mentions? See also Ms. Mentor's list of reasons on why anyone should attend the MLA (Tate, 55–56).

Horton herself argues that we, as theorists, ought to talk to fellow teachers from kindergarten through high school as well as to ourselves. A kindergarten teacher at the MLA is perhaps, in one sense, as "transgressive," as well as ignorant, a figure as one can imagine. Perhaps kindergarten teachers attend the NCTE or CCCC conventions. But I doubt it, just as I doubt, if they did, anybody would care about the names of their schools.

4. Speaking of this particular contest for the control of American intellectual life between two opposing groups, David Bromwich finds a common agreement: "Both groups are addicted to the word *culture*, yet they use it as cross-purposes. . . . Both groups on religious grounds show an enormous deference toward institutions: they believe in the power of institutions to shape the thoughts of an individual mind; they think this power is irresistible, and the great question therefore becomes how to give it the correct bias" (xiii).

Compare Jeffrey Williams: "The broad commitments entailed by particular theoretical camps and affiliations have dispersed to provisional, localized, pragmatic interventions, rather than building or drawing from a systematic critique" ("Posttheory," 66). What he means, I think, is not only the "balkanization" of Theory but of the institutional sites from which theory can be practiced—even if in practice this only means that young Posttheorists have to teach somewhere other than where they got their degrees.

5. Or someone else, namely me, can of course get published in *South Atlantic Quarterly*, discussing this very subject. My reader will have already discerned from my first chapter, however, that the politics of neither my own department nor institution was much changed as a result, not to mention the institutional map of American higher education. Meantime, although subsequent issues of *Profession* have exhibited some self-consciousness about the matter of who gets published and why, *Profession 94* leads off with pieces by people from Cornell, Berkeley, Cornell again, and so on.

Very much in contrast is a woman from Western Oregon State College, whose subject—no one should be surprised to discover—is "How Composition Scholarship Changed the Way I Ask For and Respond to Student Writing." There is also another woman from Mississippi State. Her subject is being a temporary professor, off the tenure track.

Although in *Profession 1998* the number of pages has expanded, the institutional ratio remains approximately the same. Moreover, as usual, while contributors from Stanford and Cornell discourse on the theoretical big picture, a few from Knox College or Montana State consider such subjects as the practicalities of teaching diversity or career possibilities in administration.

6. On this point, see Kluge, 55–56, especially, and even more especially 180–81. "Williams has a high rate of predictable success," concludes one professor. "We have a high rate of *un*predictable success."

7. Understood in this way, James Sosnoski's refusal to "avoid polemics, especially those that turn *ad hominem*," by forbearing a more personal presentation of his own study of theoretical hierarchy, is a fateful concession that allows some of the most fundamental underpinnings of this hierarchy to go unchallenged. See Sosnoski, *Token Professionals*, xxvii. Compare—again—Philip Lopate: "The very act of composing [informal, familiar essays] seems to implicate the writer in humanist-individualist assumptions that have come to appear suspect under the modernist critique" (79). In the post-structuralist theoretical critique, such assumptions have simply ceased to exist.

Meanwhile, back at the MLA convention, graduate students continue to make common cause with part-time teachers; see Sarah Boxer's account in the *New York Times* of the 1998 San Francisco convention. Also, Cary Nelson continues to become more prominent in the MLA itself, although, at least from the example of the articles collected in his *Manifesto*, he has yet to link up his critique of the organization on behalf of entry-level graduate students to a possible critique of the organization's definition by the hierarchy that consigns these students, at best, to jobs at institutions where they neither want nor expected to be. See, for example, the essay by Barbara Unger of the College of Saint Rose in Boufis and Olsen, 103–07.

8. It's important, however, to distinguish Spivak from someone such as Bell Hooks, whose latest book is, I think, as good an example as can be found of how—Spivak to the contrary—it's not only in literature that you get the establishment and the disenfranchised each masquerading as the other. In addition, Hooks's use of the word "transgression" provides another instructive example of how theory uses discontinuities (among them, the pedagogical distance possible from research) that function very differently in terms of institutional levels. See the exchange between Bèrubè and Chris Lehmann in the recent *Baffler* for a blunter conflict of these same discontinuities and how they are differently registered once institutional status is restored to the equation.

Chapter Four

1. Hersey quotes from the piece, "Plans for Work: October, 1937," given in the collection edited by Robert Fitzgerald. In fact, Agee applied twice for a Guggenheim. The statement is evidently from his second application, or rather a long appendix to it, listing an astounding total of forty–seven possible projects followed by brief explanations of each one.

2. This may simply be because so many grants are so exacting in their specific requirements or occasions as to defeat generic expectations about how to apply for them. Compare, for example, the application to college. The other day a friend e-mailed me a parody, ostensibly written by

an applicant to New York University, in response to the following request: "In order for the Admissions Staff of our college to get to know you better, we ask that you answer what significant experiences you have had, or accomplishments you have realized, that have helped define you as a person?"

The parody begins as follows: "I am a dynamic figure, often seen scaling walls and crushing ice. I have been known to remodel train stations on my lunch breaks, making them more efficient in the areas of heat retention. I translate ethnic slurs for Cuban refugees. I write award-winning operas. I manage time efficiently."

So it continues for seven more paragraphs. The last concludes thus: "I have played Hamlet. I have performed open-heart surgery, and I have spoken to Elvis. But I have not yet gone to college."

Chapter Five

1. See Kluge, 168. The man in question is angered when Kluge asks him if he should just drop in or if advance notice is necessary. It seems the man has an offer "from a big place down south," where, presumably, such vulgar visitations can be dismissed. Of course, the reason they can persist so cordially at Kenyon may well be because the institution is so small; many other informal ways will invariably disclose whether or not an individual is a good teacher. The existence of these ways, in turn, forms much of the basis for the differences between teaching at liberal arts schools and small to mid-sized public institutions.

2. See Aronowitz on how tenure is "job security only in the last instance. Typically, the suceesful candidate must demonstrate his *lack* of independence, originality, and hubris. Peer review is often used as a way to weed out nonconformity." He goes on to mention the case of a younger scholar who decides to accept a book offer from a "Stuffy University Press" rather than one from "an agressive hotter house." "How much did this decision take out of his chance to become an intellectual rather than a professional clerk of the institution?" Arnonwitz concludes ("Last Good," 98). At Clarion, on the other hand, where a book contract is not an option, nothing insures the fate of becoming a professional clerk—observer or observee—like teaching observation reports.

3. Cary Nelson never seems to me more admirably honest than when he confesses: "Although I have taught composition and enjoyed it, I would now find it demoralizing and intolerable to have to grade hundreds of composition papers each semester. There is no way I could do it as carefully and thoroughly as my graduate students do. So what is to be done" (178). Compare Richard Miller: "Do we imagine ourselves as somehow

outside the very system that employs us to instruct entering students in the language arts" ("Arts of Complicity," 15). In his book, Miller specifically criticizes Nelson as "exemplify[ing] a strain of the profession that strategically represents itself as beyond the reach of instruction, remediation, retraining, reform—as, in effect, an unteachable, depleted human resource" (*As if*, 204).

4. See "Higher Education and Group Thinking," 36. The essay is reprinted as part of *Education by Other Means*. Alas, however, in his book Bromwich does not do for "community" what Bill Readings does in his book for the word, "excellence," whose consummate emptiness is, in turn, the stuff out of which academic "communities" are regularly celebrated.

5. Compare the remarkable October 1994 issue of *College Literature*, which features over a hundred pages on "The Subject of Pedagogical Politics/The Politics of Publication," specifically an article by Mas'ud Zavarzadeh, followed by four reader's reports, Zavarzadeh's response to these readers, and so on—to a long concluding Marxist reading of the issues by Zavarzadeh, all over again. (See Maguire.) The result is much heat but, I think, not so much light, although the spectacle of so many hidden transcripts (and energies) summoned into being as public transcripts once more reveals— if nothing else—how permeable is the boundary between them.

Chapter Six

1. I owe this wonderful formulation to a reader of an earlier draft who has, apparently, suffered his own descent. For the best account of how such a descent is built into the structure of the profession as it stands today, see Guillory. At one point he states thus: "The norm of productivity, according to which every professor is accountable as a research scholar, is clearly a phantasmal mode of professional desire" (98).

2. Two of Jacoby's chapters, "The Free Speech Movement, Party Two" and "Say the Right Thing," provide probably as fair-minded an account as one can expect about the effect of speech codes and political correctness on the academy, including faculty employment security. Significantly though, Jacoby says nothing about hiring. Is public attention to the political conditions under which a faculty member is fired in inverse relation to interest about the conditions under which any is typically hired—even though the conditions are the same in each case?

3. Of course there are those who, in response to the job crisis, would push the point of entry back to the moment of application to graduate school by cutting back on graduate programs and students enrolled in them. For a summary of the issues at stake in decreasing graduate admis-

sions in the humanities, see Richard Levin's reading of the exchange between Bèrubè (who proposes them) and Jim Neilson and Gregory Meyerson. Neilson and Meyerson follow with objections to Levin's reading.

4. I forebear here some extended consideration into why candidates continue to present themselves for inspection (a question that troubles everyone who writes about the job crisis) and remark merely that a sublimated amorous identity now defines their situation. Considering, for example, the sheer cost of graduate education at the present time, Stephen Watt concludes about graduate students and junior faculty as follows: "It's hard to be on the cutting edge and the edge of financial ruin at the same time" (33). Translation: it's hard to be simultaneously a lover and a husband—especially if you're not yet married but have to be willing to offer yourself to just about anybody in the country for any reason, just to demonstrate your capacity to be faithful.

5. "Intellectual labor," write Aronowitz and DiFazio, "its ideology of professional autonomy in tatters as a result of its subordination to technoscience and organization, becomes a form of human capital the components of which are specialized knowledge and differentially accumulated cultural capital determined mainly by hierarchically arranged credentials" (339). Their whole chapter, "The Jobless Future," is, I think, must reading for eager and burnt-out academics both.

6. Compare Tompkins: "To be empowering, discipline must be chosen. At some fundamental level, if you have not chosen it, the skills a discipline may give you are not yours, are not an outgrowth of who you are, but a disposable proficiency, a bit that could be dropped from your script without being missed. What my teaching has been aiming for is not the empowering discipline itself but the wisdom to know what it might be when it comes along. . . . Perhaps I should add that 'knowing' may include allowing the discipline to choose you" (160).

Chapter Seven

1. I don't remember what text I chose during the first time I taught the course at the graduate level well over a decade ago. During that initial meeting, I do remember at one point mentioning the idea of "genre." For example, I asked, what's the genre of *Paradise Lost*? "Short story?" one of the sweetest students I've ever had managed—and what else to reply, since her knowledge of Milton was derived from a selection in the Norton anthology?

2. Compare poor Jane Tompkins at Temple: "Some semesters I carried the books, Xeroxes, teaching notes, students papers, and odds and

ends of material for three different courses" (108). She writes this of course without any apparent awareness that most faculty in English teach such schedules. No wonder Nelson can state thus: "If higher education becomes like high school, or like community college teaching, so thoroughly crammed with scheduled responsibilities that it offers little time for independent intellectual pursuit, then it will lose the difference that makes it what it is" (8). It remains an open question, though, if at Boondock such difference is firmly established in the first place.

3. When did such awareness become so pervasive that it even began to appear in *PMLA*? See, for example, Jeffrey Williams's 1992 response to Bruce Robbins, especially the following passage: "The stories of the advent of narrative and of history are both limited by an exclusive focus . . . on the hegemonic story of theory as disseminated from Yaledom and by academostars. Now, don't get me wrong. I'm a fan and purveyor of this dominant story of our profession, at least of the theoretical line of it, and I happily teach it every spring. However, I've come to realize that there are alternative narratives to be told about what people do in our profession and about what is considered as work in the other ninety percent of literary departments" ("Letter," 1281). Much of the point of my own story, however, is why Williams has to say, "Now don't get me wrong." By 1999, when *PMLA* itself has published Shumway on the phenomenon of superstardom but still none of these alternative narratives, it seems to me still a matter of continuing doubt whether or not Williams would feel the public need to have to make the same qualification.

4. See, for example, the recent special issue on postcolonialism and the Third World in *Social Text*, and such a representative comment by Ella Shohat: "[T]he question is: who is mobilizing what in the articulation of the past, deploying what identities, identifications and representations, and in the name of what political vision and goals" (110). The connection between what Shohat is talking about and Williams, just above, is, I must hope, clear.

It might be added that the connection is nowhere more clear or explicit than in post-colonial criticism itself. To consider only one prominent example, see the denunciation of the implications of institutional location and affiliation on Edward Said and others everywhere registered in Ahmad's *In Theory*. It seems to me no coincidence that Andrijka Kwasny, denouncing the self-serving role of ethnicity in recent autobiographies by Marianna Torgovnick and Frank Lentricchia, should employ one of the major terms of postcolonialism by referring at one point to the practice of "post-professionalism in the form of hybridity" (231).

5. Quoted by Josue Harari, from his contribution, "Nostalgia and Critical Theory" (Kavanagh, *Limits* 192). See also Rosset's own contribution, "Reality and the Untheorizable." Finally, see Rene Girard's concluding essay, "Theory and Its Terrors," where there is another reading of

theory in the profession as theory of the profession; the deconstructionist principles of the infinity of interpretation and indispensability of all inter- pretations are both viewed in terms of tenure requirements. "I would suggest," states Girard, "that all radical theories, including Marxist theory, turn their attention on themselves and concentrate on their own mecha- nisms of production" (242).

6. Those at institutions safely distant from the boondocks may be far more familiar than I am with such papers. (There must be *somewhere* where students "don't even read literature anymore—just theory," to cite the oft-heard charge.) My sense is that you can't justify a theory course on the basis of them, although it must be allowed that you wouldn't get such papers if you didn't have a theory course. Without a theory course, in turn, you wouldn't get a Post-Theory Generation, described by Williams as one that takes theory for granted. He remarks of theory as "a function and register of the socio-institutional matrix, not a pre-defined body of texts or a discipline" ("Posttheory," 69). But how do you get it to function in the first place if you lack the matrix?

7. But see Doan and Town, who represent, I believe, one way not to be anywhere at all. Not only do the authors fudge every answer they give to all the many questions they muffle (how much their students actually understood especially and, more disappointingly still, the consequences of their colleagues's hostility); they tell a predictable story in which the small university is simply the big one writ small—the same names have to be read, the same (ideological) issues pondered. Doan and Town quote from Althussar but don't say if they had their students read him. Most significantly of all, the small university in which they taught the course is given no name.

Chapter Eight

1. Compare earlier: "There are people who have a few moves left in them, if they can manage to make them. So: there are lifers, there are candidates for parole, and there are a couple inmates digging tunnels" (27). There are also, though, people such as Tompkins: "One way of making education more holistic is to get outside the classroom and off campus" (218). So off she goes with her students, on a self-confessed "voyage," to a barrier island off the coast and then to a plantation in North Carolina. As she states in her introduction: "Sooner or later, everyone has to leave school, if not literally, then in a spiritual sense" (xix).

For a broader contextualizing of such travel in terms of cosmopolitan hybridity, see Clifford. For a critique of Clifford, see Kaplan—who takes him to task on the grounds of repressed class, gender, and geographical differences. Similarly, if more narrowly, Tompkins can be taken to task for repressing institutional differences.

2. For a consideration of these high-flyers in terms of the very different, utterly grounded travel of part-time, temporary, or adjunct faculty, see Caesar, "Phantom Narratives," in Peter Herman, *Day Late, Dollar Short: The Next Generation and the New Academy*. There is undoubtedly a wide ranger of opinion. It would include Watt, who remarks on the lamentable practice of "inducing scholars to pay expenses associated with on-campus visits, which is becoming a disturbing commonplace in the later-spring job market" (31). It would also include Marilyn Bonnell, whose paean to the life of a "gypsy scholar" is posed over against "most of my cohorts in the field, who feel trapped at institutions they hate in locations they loathe" (234).

3. Later we read that the conference circuit is "a way of converting work into play, combining professionalism with tourism, and all at someone else's expense. Write a paper and see the world! I'm Jane Austen—fly me" (231)! Shumway comments on the matter as follows: "Jet travel makes it possible for stars to appear all over the nation and even on other continents without missing—or perhaps without appearing to miss—an irresponsible number of classes" (92).

4. Contrast the way Rosovsky puts the same thing: "Faculty members love sabbaticals. Projects can be completed, sites visited, colleagues in distant places consulted. Professors tend to be enthusiastic travelers and their way of life encourages their natural proclivity" (166). What Zapp suggests, very much to the contrary, is that he is so enthusiastic about travel because his "way of life" does *not* encourage it. Compare Tompkins who, although she resolves to rededicate herself to her campus after a year away at the National Humanities Center (mentioned so casually it almost seems like a job option), reproduces the same note of ecstacy at the prospect of being gone as Zapp (182–83).

5. And yet, like Greenblatt, Miller, or Spivak, he can be compared to one, if only because his temporary presence lacks permanence and therefore becomes vulnerable to some more strict, particular political account. For an example of such an account, within the framework of travel writing by an academic, see Derrida's remarkable presentation, especially the moment when he notes the inscription of tourism in Andre Gide's earlier travel book on Russia, calls for "a systematic reflection on the relations between tourism and political analysis," and then concludes as follows: "Such an analysis would have to allow a particular place to the intellectual tourist (writer or academic) who thinks he or she can, in order to make them public, translate his or her 'travel impressions' into a political diagnostic" (215). The academic text of travel, on the other hand, is distinguished by the lack of such a diagnostic, or some awareness of the consequences of participating in a larger border-crossing global economy. On this last point, see Caesar, *Forgiving*, 169.

6. Presumably he would not, though, either write about travel or just write it, like Theroux. In Lodge's more recent novel, *Paradise News*, there

is a character who is a professor investigating the subject of the sightseeing tour as secular pilgrimage.

7. See especially Chapter 8, "The Anchoring of Activity," in Goffman, *Frame Analysis*. For example, Goffman begins this chapter by noting the "apparent paradox" attendant upon any "gearing" of a "game" to its "surround." "In general then," he states, "the assumptions that cut an activity off from the external surround also mark the ways in which this activity is inevitably bound to the surrounding world" (249).

Bibliography

Adams, Hazard. *The Academic Tribes*. New York: Liveright, 1976.

———, and Leroy Searle, eds. *Critical Theory since 1965*. Tallahassee: University Press of Florida, 1986.

Ahmad, Aijaz. *In Theory. Nations, Classes, Literature*. New York: Verso, 1994.

Althusser, Louis. "Ideology and Ideological State Apparatuses (Notes Toward an Investigation)," in *Lenin and Philosophy*. New York: Monthly Review Press, 1971.

Altieri, Charles. "What Is at Stake in Confessional Criticism," *Confessions of the Critics*. Ed. H. Aram Veeser. New York: Routledge, 1996: 55–67.

Aronowitz, Stanley, and William DiFazio. *The Jobless Future. Sci-Tech and the Dogma of Work*. Minneapolis: University of Minnesota Press, 1994.

Aronowitz, Stanley. "Higher Education: the Turn of the Screw." *Found Object*. 6, 1995: 89–99.

———. "The Last Good Job in America." *Social Text* 15.2 (Summer 1997): 93–108.

Atkins, G. Douglas. "In Other Words: Gardening for Love—the Work of the Essayist." *Kenyon Review* 13.1 (Winter 1991): 56–69.

———. *Estranging the Familiar. Toward a Revitalized Critical Critical Practice*. Athens: University of Georgia Press, 1992.

Barthelme, Donald. *Amateurs*. New York: Pocket Books, 1977.

Bartolovich, Crystal. "In this life we want nothing but facts . . ." *Journal X.* 2.2 (Spring 1998): 219–35.

Begley, Adam. "The I's Have It. Duke's *Moi* Critics Expose Themselves." *Lingua Franca.* March/April 1994: 54–9.

———. "The Decline of the Campus Novel." *Lingua Franca.* September 1997: 39–46.

Bèrubè, Michael, and Cary Nelson, eds. *Higher Education under Fire. Politics, Economics and the Crisis of the Humanities.* New York: Routledge, 1995.

———. *The Employment of English.* New York: New York University Press, 1998.

———. "The Abuses of the University." *American Literary History.* 10.1 (Spring 1998): 147–63.

———. "Pistols for Two." *The Baffler.* Number Eleven (1998): 108–11.

Boone, Joseph Allen. "Of Me(n) and Feminism: Who(se) is the Sex That Writes?" *Gender and Theory. Dialogues on Feminist Criticism.* Ed. Linda Kauffman. New York: Basil Blackwell, 1989: 11–25.

Booth, Wayne. *The Vocation of a Teacher.* Chicago: University of Chicago Press, 1988.

Boufis, Christina, and Victoria Olsen, eds. *On the Market. Surviving the Economic Job Search.* New York: Riverhead Books, 1997.

Boxer, Sarah. "Down and Out in Academia, or: Profs and Proles." *New York Times.* 16 January 1999: B7.

Bromwich, David. "Higher Education and Group Thinking." *Raritan* XI.1 (Summer 1991): 32–42.

———. *Education by Other Means.* New Haven: Yale University Press, 1992.

Bruss, Elizabeth. *Beuatiful Theories.* Baltimore: Johns Hopkins University Press, 1985.

Bullock, Richard, and John Trimbur, eds. *The Politics of Writing Instruction: Postsecondary.* Portsmouth, N.H.: Boynton/Cook, 1991.

Burke, Delores. *A New Academic Marketplace.* New York: Greenwood Press, 1988.

Butler, Judith. *The Psychic Life of Power. Theories in Subjection.* Stanford: Stanford University Press, 1997.

Caesar, Terry. "On Teaching at a Second-Rate University." *South Atlantic Quarterly.* 90.3 (Summer 1991): 449–67.

————. *Conspiring with Forms. Life in Academic Texts*. Athens: University of Georgia Press, 1992.

————. *Forgiving the Boundaries. Home as Abroad in American Travel Writing*. Athens: Unversity of Georgia Press, 1995.

————. Forum. *PMLA* 111.5 (October 1996): 1168–69.

————. *Writing in Disguise. Academic Life in Subordination*. Athens: Ohio University Press, 1998.

————. "An Ocean of Differences in Academic Conferences." *The Chronicle of Higher Education* 1 October 1999; B8.

————. "Phantom Narratives: Travel, Jobs, and the Next Generation." *Day Late, Dollar Short: The Next Generation and the New Academy*. Ed. Peter Herman. Albany: State University of New York Press, forthcoming.

Carter, Stephen. *Reflections of an Affirmative Action Baby*. New York: Basic Books, 1993.

Clark, Burton. "Small Worlds, Different Worlds: The Uniquenesses and Troubles of American Academic Professions." *Daedalus* 126.4 (Fall 1997): 21–42.

Clifford, James. "Traveling Cultures." *Cultural Studies*. Ed. Lawrence Grossberg, Cary Nelson, Paul Treicher. New York: Routledge, 1992: 98–113.

Cohen, Ed. "Are We (Not) What We Are Becoming? 'Gay Identity,' 'Gay Studies,' and the Disciplining of Knowledge." *Engendering Men*. Ed Joseph Boone and Michael Cadden. New York: Routledge, 1990: 161–75.

Colton, Joel. "The Role of the Department in the Groves of Academe." *The Academic's Handbook*. Ed. A. Leigh DeNeef, Craufurd Goodwin, and Ellen Stern McCrate. Durham: Duke University Press, 1988: 315–33.

Cook, Philip and Robert Frank. "The Economic Payoff of Attending an Ivy-League Institution." *The Chronicle of Higher Education* 5 January 1996: B3.

Damrosch, David. *We Scholars: Changing the Culture of the University*. Cambridge: Harvard University Press, 1995.

Derrida, Jacques. "Back from Moscow, in the USSR." *Politics Theory and Contemporary Culture*. Ed. Mark Poster. New York: Columbia University Press, 1993.

Doan, Laura, and Caren Town, " 'Don't Take that Class': Teaching Theory in the Small University." *ADE Bulletin* (Winter 1990): 31–6.

Doctorow, E.L. *Billy Bathgate*. New York: Harper & Row, 1989.

Dovey, Teresa. Letter. *PMLA* 110.5 (October 1995): 1049.

Dreyfus, Hubert, and Paul Rabinow, eds. *Michael Foucault: Beyond Structuralism and Hermaneutics*. Chicago: University of Chicago Press, 1982.

Edmundsen, Mark, ed. *Wild Orchids and Trotsky: Messages from American Universities*. New York: Penguin, 1993.

Finn, Chester, Jr. "Today's Academic Market Requires a New Taxonomy of Colleges." *Chronicle of Higher Education* 9 January 1998: B4–B5.

Fish, Stanley. *Doing What Comes Naturally*. Durham: Duke University Press, 1989.

———. *There is No Such Thing as Free Speech*. New York: Oxford University Press, 1994.

Fitzgerald, Robert, ed. *The Collected Short Prose of James Agee*. Boston: Houghton Mifflin, 1968.

Fletcher, Francis, Jamey Nye, and Steve O'Connell. "The Adjunct Faculty Manifesto." *College Composition and Communication* 50.1 (September 1998): A14–16.

Foucault, Michel. *Discipline and Punish. The Birth of the Clinic*. New York: Vintage Books, 1979.

———. *The History of Sexuality. Volume I: An Introduction*. New York: Vintage, 1980.

Freedman, Diane, Olivia Frey, and Francis Murphy Zauhar, eds. *The Intimate Critique: Autobiographical Literary Criticism*. Durham: Duke University Press, 1993.

Fromm, Harold. *Academic Capitalism & Literary Value*. Athens: University of Georgia Press, 1991.

Frost, Peter, and M. Susan Taylor, ed. *Rhythms of Academic Life. Personal Accounts of Careers in Academia*. Thousands Oaks: Sage Publications, 1996.

Fry, Judith. *Living Stories, Telling Lives: Women and the Novel in Contemporary Experience*. Ann Arbor: University of Michigan Press, 1986.

Frye, Northrop. *Anatomy of Criticism*. New York: Atheneum, 1966.

Gamson, Zelda. "The Stratification of the Academy." *Social Text*. 15.2 (Summer 1997): 67–73.

Gilbert, Sandra, and Susan Gubar. "Masterpiece Theatre: An Academic Melodrama. *Critical Inquiry* 17.4 (Summer 1991): 693–717.

Girard, Rene. "Theory and Its Terrors." *The Limits of Theory*. Ed Patrick Kavanagh. Stanford: Stanford University Press, 1989: 225–54.

Goffman, Erving. *Frame Analysis. An Essay on the Oranization of Experience*. Cambridge: Harvard University Press, 1974.

———. *Forms of Talk*. Philadelphia: University of Pennsylvania Press, 1981.

Gogol, Nicolai. *The Overcoat*. London: Merlin Press, 1956.

Graff, Gerald. *Professing Literature: An Institutional History*. Chicago: The University of Chicago Press, 1989.

———. "Academic Writing and the Uses of Bad Publicity." *South Atlantic Quarterly* 91.1 (1992): 5–17.

———. *Beyond the Culture Wars*. New York: Norton, 1992.

Greenblatt, Stephen. *Marvelous Possessions. The Wonder of the New World*. Chicago: University of Chicago Press, 1991.

Guillory, John. "Preprofessionalism: What Graduate Students Want." *Profession 1996*: 91–99.

Hanna, S.S. *The Gypsy Scholar*. Ames: Iowa State University Press, 1987.

Hanson, Victor Davis, and Heath, John. *Who Killed Homer? The Demise of Classical Education and the Recovery of Greek Wisdom*. New York: The Free Press, 1998.

Harari, Josuè. "Nostalgia and Critical Theory." *The Limits of Theory*. Ed Patrick Kavanagh. Stanford: Stanford University Press, 1989: 168–93.

Hartman, Geoffrey. *Saving the Text: Literature / Derrida / Philosophy*. Baltimore: Johns Hopkins University Press, 1981.

Hersey, John. "Introduction." *Let Us Now Praise Famous Men*. By James Agee and Walker Evans. Boston: Houghton Mifflin, 1988.

Hite, Molly. *Class Porn*. Freedom, CA: Crossing Press, 1987.

hooks, bell. *Teaching to Transgress*. New York: Routledge, 1994.

Horton, Susan. "The Institutionalization of Literature and the Cultural Community." *Literary Theory's Future(s)*. Ed. Joseph Natoli. Urbana: University of Illinois Press, 1989: 271–91.

Hutner, Gordon. "What We Talk About When We Talk About Hiring." *Profession 94*: 75–8.

Jacoby, Russell. *The Last Intellectuals. American Culture in the Age of Academe*. New York: Basic Books, 1987.

————. *Dogmatic Wisdom. How the Culture Wars Divert Education and Distract America.* New York: Doubleday, 1994.

Johnson, Barbara. *The Critical Difference.* Baltimore: Johns Hopkins University Press, 1985.

Jones, Danell. "Crossing the Great Divide: From Manhattan to Montana." *ADE Bulletin* 117 (Fall 1997): 42–4.

Jordan, John. "Literary History at Berkeley." *New Literary History* II.3 (Spring 1971): 533–40.

Joyce, Joyce. *Warriors, Conjurers, and Priests. Defining African-Centered Literary Criticism.* Chicago: Third World Press, 1993.

Kaplan, Caren. "Deterritorializations: The Rewriting of Home and Exile in Western Feminist Discourse." *Cultural Critique* 6 (1987): 187–98.

————. *Questions of Travel. Postmodern Discourses of Displacement.* Durham: Duke University Press, 1996.

Kaplan, Paula. *Lifting a Ton of Feathers. A Woman's Guide to Surviving in the Academic World.* Toronto: University of Toronto Press, 1994.

Kincaid, James. *Annoying the Victorians.* New York: Routledge, 1994.

Kindrow, G. "The Candidate." *Lingua Franca.* 1.4 (April 1991): 21–5.

Kluge, P.F. *Alma Mater.* New York: Addison-Wesley, 1993.

Kwasny, Andrijka. "Ethnic Occupations." *Minnesota Review* 48–9 (Spring/ Fall 1997): 227–34.

Larson, Magali Sarfatti. *The Rise of Professionalism.* Berkeley: University of California Press, 1977.

Lauter, Paul. *Canons and Context.* New York: Oxford University Press, 1994.

Leatherman, Courtney. "A Name for Herself." *Chronicle of Higher Education.* 19 May 1995: A 22,24.

Leed, Eric. *The Mind of the Traveler. From Gilgamesh to Global Tourism.* New York: Basic Books, 1991.

Lehmann, Chris. "Pistols for Two." *Baffler.* Number Eleven (1998): 111–15.

Levin, Richard. " 'Activist Politics' and/or the Job Crisis in the Humanities." *Minnesota Review* 48–9 (Spring/Fall 1997): 265–75.

Lim, Shirley Geok-lin. "The Scarlet Brewer and the Voice of the Colonized." In *The Intimate Critique*, ed. Diane Freedman, Olive Frey, and Frances Murphy Zauhar. Durham: Duke University Press, 1993: 191–96.

Lindeman, Erika, and Gary Tate. *An Introduction to Composition Studies.* New York: Oxford University Press, 1991.

Lodge, David. *Small World.* New York: Macmillan, 1984.

———. *Paradise News.* New York: Viking, 1992.

Lopate, Phillip. "What Happened to the Personal Essay?" In *Against Joie De Vivre.* New York: Poseidon Press, 1989.

Louis, Meryl Reis. "A Sabbatical Journey." *Rhythms of Academic Life.* Ed. Peter Frost and M. Susan Taylor. Thousand Oaks: Sage Publications, 1996: 443–52.

Malamud, Bernard. *A New Life.* New York: Dell, 1963.

———. *Pictures of Fidelman.* New York: Dell, 1970.

———. *Rembrandt's Hat.* New York: Pocket Books, 1974.

Malone, Michael. *Foolscap.* New York: Washington Square Press, 1993.

Massey, Walter. "Uncertainties in the Changing Academic Profession." *Daedalus* 126.4 (Fall 1997): 67–94.

McGuire, Jerry. "Introduction: Wagging the Dog." *College Literature* 21.3 (October 1994): 1–5.

Miller, Nancy. *Getting Personal. Feminist Occasions and Other Autobiographical Acts.* New York: Routledge, 1991.

———. "Public Statements, Private Lives: Academic Memoirs for the Nineties." *Signs.* 22.4 (Summer 1997): 981–1015.

Miller, Richard. *As If Learning Mattered. Reclaiming Higher Education.* Ithaca: Cornell University Press, 1998.

———. "The Arts of Complicity: Pragmatism and the Culture of Schooling." *College English* 61.1 (September 1998): 10–28.

Moi, Toril. "Men Against Patriarchy." *Gender and Theory. Dialogues on Feminist Criticism.* Ed. Linda Kauffman. New York: Basil Blackwell, 1989: 181–88.

Mooney, Carolyn. "Lifting the Cloak of Secrecy from Tenure." *Chronicle of Higher Education.* 14 April 1995: A16–22.

Morton, Donald. "Multiple Submissions and the Instititional Power/Knowledge Network." *New Literary History* 28.3 (Summer 1997): 495–500

Nelson, Cary. "Lessons from the Job Wars." *Social Text.* 13.3 (Fall/Winter 1995): 121–34.

———. *Manifesto of a Tenured Radical.* New York: New York University Press, 1997.

Newkirk, Thomas. "The Politics of Writing Research: The Conspiracy Against Experience." *The Politics of Writing Instruction: Postsecondary*. Ed. Richard Bollock and Joseph Trimmer. Portsmouth, N.H.:Boynton/Cook, 1991: 119–35.

Oakley, Francis. "The Elusive Academic Profession." *Daedalus* 126. 4 (Fall 1997): 43–66.

O'Dair, Sharon. "Stars, Tenure, and the Death of Ambition." *Michigan Quarterly Reivew* XXXVI. 4 (Fall 1997): 607–27.

Ohmann, Richard. *English in America*. New York: Oxford University Press, 1976.

O'Toole, Simon. *Confessions of an American Scholar*. Minneapolis: University of Minnesota, 1970.

Peachey, Jennifer. Letter. *PMLA* 113.5 (October 1998): 1152–53.

Perry, Ruth. Forum. *PMLA* 111.5 (October 1996): 1166–67.

Phelan, James. *Beyond the Tenure Track. Fifteen Months in the Life of an English Professor*. Columbus: Ohio State University Press, 1991.

———. "The Life of the Mind: Politics and Critical Argument. A Reply to Jeffrey Williams." *College Literature* 23.3 (October 1996): 147–61.

Phillips, Gerald. Letter. *The Chronicle of Higher Education*. 30 October 1991. B3.

Readings, Bill. *The University in Ruins*. Cambridge: Harvard University Press, 1996.

Reid, B.L. *First Acts*. Athens: University of Georgia Press, 1987.

"The Revolt Against Tradition: Readers, Writers, and Critics." *Partisan Review* LVIII. 2. (Spring 1991):

Rhoades, Gary and Shelia Slaughter. "Academic Capitalism, Managed Professionals." *Social Text* 15.2 (Summer 1997): 9–38.

Rich, Robert. "Somewhere Off the Coast of Academia." *Left Politics and the Literary Profession*. Ed. Leonard Davis and M. Bella Mirabella. Columbus: Ohio State University Press, 1990.

Rooney, Ellen. *Seductive Reasoning. Pluralism as the Problematic of Contemporary Theory*. Ithaca: Cornell University Press, 1989.

Rosovsky, Henry. *The University: an Owner's Manual*. New York: Norton, 1990.

Rosset, Clement. "Reality and the Untheorizable." *The Limits of Theory*. Ed Thomas Kavanagh. Stanford: Stanford University Press, 1989: 76–118.

Schaefer, William. *Education without Compromise*. San Francisco: Jossey-Bass Publishers, 1990.

Scott, James. *Domination and the Arts of Resistance*. New Haven: Yale University Press, 1990.

Shaw, Peter. "The Modern Language Association is Misleading the Public." *The Chronicle of Higher Education*. 27 November 1991: B3.

Shohat, Ella. "Notes on the Post-Colonial." *Social Text* 31 and 32. 10. 2 and 3 (1992): 99–113.

Showalter, Elaine. "Feminist Criticism in the Wilderness." *The New Feminist Criticism*. Ed. Elaine Showalter: 125–43. New York: Random House, 1985.

Shuman, Samuel. Letter. *PMLA* 112.3 (May 1997): 440–41.

Shumway, David. "The Star System in Literary Studies." *PMLA* 112.1 (January 1997): 85–100.

Simpson, David. *The Academic Postmodern and the Rule of Literature* Chicago: University of Chicago Press, 1995.

Sinyavsky, Andrei. *Soviet Civilization. A Cultural History*. New York: Little Brown and Company, 1988.

Slemon, Stephen. "The Scramble for Post-Colonialism." *De-Scribing Empire: Post-Colonialism and Textuality*. Eds. Chris Tiffin and Alan Lawson. London: Routledge, 1994: 15–32.

Slevin, James. "The Politics of the Profession." *An Introduction to Composition Studies*. Ed. Erika Lindemann and Gary Tate. New York: Oxford University Press, 1990: 135–59.

Sontag, Susan. *Against Interpretation*. New York: Dell, 1967.

Sosnoski, James. *Professionals and Master Critics: A Critique of Literary Studies*. Albany: State University of New York Press, 1994.

———. *Modern Skeletons in Postmodern Closets: A Cultural Studies Alternative*. Charlottesville: University Press of Virginia, 1995.

Spilka, Mark. "Parties and Funerals: An Academic Confession." *College English* 35.4 (1974): 367–80.

Spivak, Gayatri. "Theory in the Margins: Coetzee's *Foe* Reading Defoe's *Crusoe/Roxana*." In *Consequences of Theory*, ed. Jonathan Arac and Barbara Johnson. Baltimore: Johns Hopkins University Press, 1990: 154–80.

———. "The Making of Americans, the Teaching of English and the Future of Cultural Studies." *New Literary History* 21 (1990): 781–98. Reprinted in *Outside the Teaching Machine*. New York: Routledge, 1993.

———. *The Post-Colonial Critic*. New York: Routledge, 1990.

Sprinker, Michael. "Teaching to Strike: Labor Relations In and Out of the Classroom." *Journal X* 2.2 (Spring 1998): 209–17.

Theroux, Alexander. "The Detours of Art." *The Review of Contemporary Fiction*. 11.1 (Spring 1991): 36–40.

Theroux, Paul. *Sunrise with Seamonsters*. Boston: Houghton Mifflin, 1985.

———. "Memory and Creation: Reflections at Fifty." *Massachusetts Review* 32.3 (Fall 1991): 390–402.

Tompkins, Jane. *A Life in School. What the Teacher Learned*. Reading, MA: Addison-Wesley, 1996.

Torgovnik, Marianne. *Crossing Ocean Parkway. Reading by an Italian-American Daughter*. Chicago: University of Chicago Press, 1994.

Toth, Emily. *Ms. Mentor's Impeccable Advice for Women in Academia*. Philadelphia: University of Pennsylvania Press, 1997.

Trainor, Jennifer and Amanda Godley. "After Wyoming: Labor Practices in Two University Writing Programs." *College Composition and Communication* 50.2 (December 1998): 153–81.

Trilling, Lionel. "Of This Time, Of That Place." *Stories of Modern America*. Eds. Herbert Gold and David Stevenson. New York: St. Martins, 1966.

Ungar, Barbara Louise. "Introduction." *On the Market. Surviving the Academic Job Search*. Ed. Christina Boufis and Victoria Olsen. New York: Riverhead, 1997: 103–07.

Veeser, H. Aram. ed. *Confessions of the Critics*. New York: Routledge, 1996.

Walder, Dennis, ed. *Literature in the Modern World*. New York: Oxford University Press, 1990.

Wallace, M. Elizabeth Sargent. "How Composition Scholarship Changed the Way I Ask For and Respond to Student Writing." *Profession 94*: 34–40.

Watkins, Evan. *Work Time. English Departments and the Circulation of Cultural Value*. Palo Alto: Stanford University Press, 1989.

Watt, Stephen. "The Human Costs of Graduate Education; or, The Need to Get Practical." *Academe* November–December 1995: 30–5.

Wilbur, Henry. "On Getting a Job." In *The Academic's Handbook*. Eds. A. Leigh Deneef, Craufurd Goodwion, and Ellen Stern McCrate. Durham: Duke University Press, 1989: 115–27.

Williams, Jeffrey. Letter. *PMLA* 107.5 (October 1992): 1280–81.

——, ed. *PC Wars. Politics and Correctness in the Academy*. New York: Routledge, 1994.

——. "The Posttheory Generation." *Symploke* 3.1 (Winter 1995): 55–75.

——. "The Life of the Mind and the Academic Situation." *College Literature* 23.3 (1996): 128–46.

——. "Renegotiating the Pedagogical Contract." *Class Issues. Pedagogy, Cultural Studies and the Public Sphere*. Ed. Amitava Kumar. New York: New York University Press, 1997: 298–312.

Woods, Susane. "Privileged Readings." *Nation* 29 December 1997: 24–5.

Woodward, Kathleen. *Aging and Its Discontents*. Bloomington: Indiana University Press, 1991.

——. "Bureaucratic and Binding Emotions: Angry American Autobiography." *Kenyon Review* 17.1 (Winter 1995): 55–70.

Ziolkowsky, Eric. "Slouching Toward Scholardom." *College English* 58. 5 (September 1996): 568–88.